COPYRIGHT: CURRENT ISSUES AND LAWS

COPYRIGHT: CURRENT ISSUES AND LAWS

JOHN V. MARTIN (EDITOR)

Nova Science Publishers, Inc.
New York

Senior Editors: Susan Boriotti and Donna Dennis
Coordinating Editor: Tatiana Shohov
Office Manager: Annette Hellinger
Graphics: Wanda Serrano
Editorial Production: Jennifer Vogt, Matthew Kozlowski and Maya Columbus
Circulation: Ave Maria Gonzalez, Indah Becker Raymond Davis and Vladimir Klestov
Communications and Acquisitions: Serge P. Shohov
Marketing: Cathy DeGregory

Library of Congress Cataloging-in-Publication Data
Available Upon Request

ISBN: 1-59033-268-7.

400 Oser Ave, Suite 1600
Hauppauge, New York 11788-3619
Tele. 631-231-7269 Fax 631-231-8175
e-mail: Novascience@earthlink.net
Web Site: http://www.novapublishers.com

Printed in the United States of America

CONTENTS

PREFACE

In spite of its importance to so many people, copyright has long been well understood by only a few. With the widespread popularity of the Internet and related digital opportunities, it has even become more difficult to follow. This book examines the current issues and laws related to copyright, in particular copyright extension, fair use and public domain considerations.

Edward Rappaport considers the possibility of extending the duration of copyrights by 20 years and related proposals to charge a fee to the owners to receive the extension. Net proceeds from the user fee would be devoted to promoting the creative arts. An extension of current copyrights would most immediately affect works originating in the era beginning with 1922, as these are the ones next due to expire under current law.

Only rarely in American history has Congress acted to restore copyright in works that have fallen in the United States public domain. Copyright restoration for public domain works is now under serious consideration as part of the proposals to implement the trade agreements reached at the conclusion of the Uruguay Round of the General Agreement on Tariffs and Trade ("GATT 1994"). Nothing in the GATT 1994 requires the United States to restore copyright in any public domain work. If a copyright restoration provision were included in the GATT implementing legislation, its purpose would be to lay the foundation for future bilateral and regional trade-related intellectual property negotiations.

Dorothy Schrader reviews and analyzes the legal, constitutional, and practical issues relating to recapture of copyright in works residing in the United States public domain.

Robin Jeweler examines the background and significance of both the inclusion and exclusion of sound recordings as specially commissioned works for hire under the Copyright Act. While the inclusion of sound recordings in the definition was intended to signify that they *were* a permissible category, paradoxically, the subsequent exclusion of the term does not signify that they are *not* included. By returning to the pre-1999 status quo, the law remains unsettled.

Jeweler also examines the U.S. Supreme Court's Opinion in *New York Times Co. v. Tasini.* This case considers whether under the U.S. Copyright Act 17 U.S.C. §201(c), publishers are "privileged" to include the copyright articles of freelance authors in an electronic database. The authors contend that the copyright interest they conveyed to the publishers for original publication of their articles did *not* permit their subsequent reproduction and distribution in electronic databases. The Print and Electronic Publishers argued that the databases were a permissible "revision" of the original periodicals.

Interpreting the Copyright Act to emphasize the primacy of authorial rights, the Court found for the freelance authors. The Court's analysis is discussed below.

On June 25, 2001, in *New York Times Co. v. Tasini,*[1] the U.S. Supreme Court held that newspapers and magazines that publish articles written by freelance authors do not automatically have the right to include those articles in electronic databases.

Schrader also reviews recent developments in fair use doctrine, with an emphasis upon the Supreme Court's most recent decision (a commercial parody of a song may be a fair use) and the Second Circuit's important photocopying decision (corporate scientist's photocopying of entire scientific and technical journal articles for research and study not a fair use). Other cases discussed concern copying by off-campus document delivery services, uploading and downloading of video games on an electronic bulletin board, and reverse engineering of computer programs.

The history of criminal penalties for copyright infringement is briefly reviewed, summarizing the existing law, analyzing the pending legislative proposal, and noting arguments for and against the legislation.

Schrader presents the principal arguments in favor of extending the copyright term 20 years which are: 1) the need to assure fair economic benefit to authors, their heirs, and distributors of copyrighted works to encourage continued creativity; and 2) the need to conform U.S. Copyright terms to the European Union standards, in order to enjoy reciprocal protection for American works in Europe and to enhance U.S. bargaining power in trade negotiations. Opponents of term-extension deny there is any economic unfairness in the existing average U.S. term of 75 years, and argue that this term already exceeds the new European Union terms in the case of most commercially significant works (i.e., works made for hire). Opponents also emphasize the value of the public domain in encouraging the creation of new works.

The music licensing provisions of H.R. 2589 (Title II) are supported by operators of restaurants, bars, taverns, hotels, and retail stores; by small business music users in general; and by landlords and other operators of premises where music is publicly performed. Title II of H.R. 2589 is opposed by music copyright owners (composers, lyricists, and music publishers), copyright owners in general, and the music performing rights societies.

Jeweler examines the copyright issues in online music delivery. The Internet and its relation to fair use is examined by Weimer and by Schrader.

Copyright owners possess certain exclusive rights of ownership in their creative works. However, the fair use doctrine in copyright law allows, under certain circumstances, the unauthorized use of copyrighted works. Originating under common law, the fair use doctrine was codified in the Copyright Act of 1976. Under the fair use doctrine, four criteria are considered in the determination of whether it is an infringing use: 1) the amount and character of the use; 2) the nature of the copyrighted work; 3) the amount copied in relation to the whole copyrighted work; and 4) the effect of the copying on the potential market for the copyrighted work. The courts have scrutinized the factual circumstances and applied these criteria on a case-by-case basis.

The Internet is a cooperative network of networks. Millions of users are linked nationally and internationally, including: individuals, schools, libraries, governments, and corporations. No single individual or organization owns or controls the Internet. As a result of the use of

[1] 2001 U.S. LEXIS 4667.

copyrighted materials placed on the Internets, various questions concerning the control, ownership, and fair use of copyrighted materials on the Internet have arisen. Copyright owners have pursued their ownership rights against the unauthorized use of their works by service providers, corporate users, individual users, and others. Generally speaking, the American courts have treated the publication or posting on the Internet as another form of communication or publication. Hence, American courts have applied the four fair use factors to individual situations involving the unauthorized use of copyrighted materials on the Internet. The case law development is examined from the earliest cases to the most recent.

The Internet, other computer networks, and advances in digital technologies provide unparalleled opportunities for worldwide communications and economic growth. In order to reap the full potential of these new technologies, many difficult technical and legal policy issues must be confronted and resolved. One of these general policy issues concerns the scope of protection for copyrighted works and limitations on the rights of copyright owners against unauthorized copying in digital, electronic environments.

Finally Schrader examines the Digital Millennium Copyright Act and copyright term extension and music licensing.

COPYRIGHT TERM EXTENSION: ESTIMATING THE ECONOMIC VALUES

Edward Rappaport

INTRODUCTION AND SCOPE

This chapter considers the economic effects of a proposal to charge a fee to owners of copyrights in order to receive the benefit of a proposed 20-year extension of copyright duration. In addition to bills currently pending for term extension,[1] a number of Members have expressed interest in the idea of tying extension to a fee, the proceeds of which would be devoted to promotion of the creative arts. If an owner were unwilling or unable to pay the user fee at the time of its currently scheduled expiration, the work in question would revert to the public domain. The amount of the fee is yet to be determined, but presumably would more than cover the administrative cost of implementation. As most commonly formulated, the fee would be assessed only with regard to works "made for hire," i.e., where the creative personnel worked in a contractual employment relationship for the copyright claimant.

Before considering the effects of a filing fee associated with the term extension, some attention will be paid to the extension itself. As argued below, the availability of funds for paying the fee would depend ultimately on the extended stream of income resulting from the term extension. In particular, we focus on the ownership, use and value of works originating in the years beginning in 1922, as these copyrights are the most immediately scheduled to expire under current law, and would be the first to benefit from an extension.

The report proceeds as follows. First, we discuss the economics of intellectual property in general, the incentives for creation, and how utilization of a work changes when it loses its legal protection and enters the public domain. The participants in the market for older works are also described in general terms. Then we present the results of a quantitative analysis of the economic value of copyrights registered during 1922-1941 (for the principal categories of works). Finally, the effects of a user fee for extension are presented in the light of the foregoing.

---

[1] Twenty year extensions are called for in H.R. 1621 (Bono)/S. 505 (Hatch), H.R. 604 (Gallegly), and H.R. 2589 (Coble)(the last of these being passed by the House on March 25, 1998). Bills with user fees have not been introduced in the 105th Congress.

EFFECTS OF TERM EXTENSION

The Copyright System in General

Essentially, term extension continues into the future the basic effects of copyright itself. Thus, it raises anew many of the fundamental debates about the proper role of copyright and in particular the question of how long an ideal duration would be.

The economic purpose of establishing intellectual property rights (including patents as well as copyrights) is to encourage creation and utilization of new works. There are other conceptions of intellectual property, but they are not economic in the sense of being utilitarian. For example, some believe that intellectual property is a natural right, according to which the one who creates a work is entitled to full control over that creation without limit. This view has been expressed by a number of songwriters and their heirs in testimony on the issue.[2] It is a moral argument that can only be dealt with as such. It makes no reference to incentives or efficiency, implicitly rejecting the salience of the criteria of economic analysis. This chapter, however, will focus on the economic aspects of copyright: the incentives for creators and users, and how they interact in the market.

Copyright is structured as a grant of exclusive rights to reproduction or use for a temporary period. The exclusive period is temporary because the system is a compromise between two goals, creation and utilization. On the one hand, creation of works will be maximized if creators enjoy maximum possible rewards. On the other hand, exclusive ownership typically results in restricted access to the work by the public. Indeed, it can be argued that the socially optimum price for its use is zero, i.e., the public should be given free access to it. This is because intellectual property can be characterized as a *public good*, meaning that use of the knowledge or aesthetic concepts does not deplete them; use incurs no marginal cost. Clearly, though, not allowing any charge for use of a copyright would mean no compensation to the creator and would fail to achieve the purpose of providing an incentive to create. As a compromise solution, society has chosen the principle of monopoly for a limited time.

In principle, the optimal duration would be such that the monopoly-period profits of successful works equaled the cost of creation viewed prospectively (that is, including the costs of the projects that do not result in works of commercial value). To derive a single number as the *average optimal duration* would be a virtually impossible calculation involving variables that are as yet immeasurable (such as "cost of creation"), and would not be practicable. Thus setting duration remains a matter of subjective judgment, although the foregoing indicates the basics of what could be considered. Historically, there has definitely been an evolution. Copyright terms originally were very brief, with a consistent trend since then toward lengthening for various reasons, e.g., a concern about the longer life expectancies of authors. At the present time, one of the reasons offered for extension is an international dimension. That is, a number of foreign countries are offering to recognize a longer term for

---

[2] "...if I were to design and build a house, instead of a song, I could own this house and would have the right to protect it throughout my lifetime. I would be able to pass this along to my children, and it would be theirs to pass to their children and so forth." Don Henley, in "Copyright Term, Film Labeling, and Film Preservation Legislation." House Hearing, Serial No. 53, June 1 and July 13, 1995. pp. 241-242.

U.S. origin works (with concomitant revenues from their consumers) if the United States extends its terms for their works.

Users and Uses of the Public Domain

In General

When a copyright expires, its value to its owner will quickly decline to zero. This is because any publisher can take the property and use or reproduce it without limit. The owner and/or original publisher cannot charge anything for the work because they no longer own them. This does not mean that tangible expressions of the ideas (e.g., books) will be available for free, because cost must still be incurred to produce them. However, other inputs, such as printing, are presumably available at competitive markets[3] and will be priced at economic cost (which includes a "normal" rate of profits). There is no room in the public domain for excess, "economic" profits. The price of the final product will come down to the economic cost, with the result that it will be more widely distributed and consumed.

Specialized Uses of the Public Domain

Distribution of older works has largely become a specialized business. With copyright duration as long as it is – in most cases 75 years – many works enter this sub-industry even before expiration. For example, Penguin Books has not only a "Classics" line, but also "Twentieth-Century Classics" with authors such as Steinbeck, Bellow, and Neruda. With motion pictures, distribution occurs primarily in video form in tape rentals and through specialized cable and satellite channels such as American Movie Classics. Although those businesses seemingly cannot wait for expiration, other strictly limit themselves to the public domain; thus new, cheaper editions can be expected when works come out of copyright. For example, Barnes and Noble (which is primarily a retailer) prints on its own hundreds of titles from the public domain, e.g., *A Tale of Two Cities*, priced cheaply ($5.98) and placed by the cash registers to attract impulse buying.[4] Other, e.g., Easton Press, issue premium-priced editions of the classics, but the price is presumably justified by premium design and materials.

In addition to classics book publishers, there are creative communities that rely extensively on the public domain as a source of raw material for new productions. This may take the form of derivative works in new media, e.g., a movie based on a book. Or, more simply, a musical arranger for television programs or commercials will use fragments to put together background, theme and mood music.[5] Other applications are more in the nature of straightforward compilations. Certain institutions, including schools, museums and libraries, may put together older pictorial and textual materials for education and cultural purposes.

---

[3] This is a simplifying assumption. In practice, there may be other elements of market power. For example, the concentrated nature of record distribution (where five groups account for some 90% of the market) may make possible oligopolistic conduct.

[4] Knecht, G. Bruce. Book Superstores Bring Hollywood-Like Risks to Publishing Business. *Wall Street Journal,* may 29, 1997. p. A6.

[5] Reliance on the public domain appears most pronounced in the case of music, where its "timeless" quality allows themes to be recycled endlessly. See generally, Shemel, Sydney and M. William Krasilovsky. *This Business of Music*. [New York] Billboard Publishers, 1979 (4th ed.). Chap. 23 (Uses and New Versions of Public Domain Music).

There are also products (some commercially produced, some by non-profits) in the new media such as CD-ROMs and the World Wide Web, and these have a potentially enormous appetite for "content" in many formats. The Library of Congress American Memory program, for example, makes available from the Library and other institutions historical materials in many media via the Web. To date, it has focused almost exclusively on periods before 1920, one of the reasons being the ready availability of the public domain.

All of these groups are attracted to the public domain because it is free. Apparently, this is as much a matter of transaction costs as it is of actual fees. Despite application of new technology by the musical rights associations and others, and even if the owners ultimately do not require any payment, the process of seeking multiple permissions for some media (such as photographs) can be prohibitive. The elimination of transaction costs when copyrights expire is a net benefit to the economy, if all other this (such as creative incentives) is equal.

Incentives for Creation

Existing Works

It is important to distinguish between existing works and new ones, to distinguish, that is, between retrospective extension of terms ("grand fathering") and prospective extension (for new works). The effect on creation is fairly simple in the case of existing works: there is basically no effect on creation because these works already exist.

We would add one caveat, which may be important in some cases but, we believe, will more often be marginal. It has been argued that creation is continuous; that it does not end when a work is first produced and published. For a work to be commercially successful, it requires effort and investment, which, while not "creative," is still necessary to generate value. For example, authors employ literary agents, publishers advertise, etc. With musical compositions and photographs, the collection, arrangement and indexing of the works adds value. With film, preservation requires constant attention. Even the straightforward act of printing a book entails a risk on investment. Arguably, none of these activities will be pursued as vigorously on behalf of public domain works as they are for works with ownership rights. And, from an economic view, these activities "create" real value.

New Works

The additional incentive afforded by adding 20 years to the current life plus 50 appears to be small compared to the already existing incentive. This is due to two considerations: the small probability of a work surviving as long as the current term, and the effect of time discounting of future incomes.

As shown in detail *infra*, only a small percentage of works has an economically viable life even approaching 75 years. Even allowing for the optimism and self-confidence necessary in these creative and risky fields, the wildest dreams of artists and producers probably extend no farther than "smash hit" status for their works for a year or two, and healthy sales for five or ten. It is hard to imagine anyone intensifying their efforts on the expectation of their work being commercially viable beyond 75 years.[6]

Separately form the foregoing, there is the factor of *time discounting,* the tendency to attribute progressively less value to outcomes (both positive and negative), that are farther in the future. This is manifested most explicitly in the capital markets, where a dollar payable a year from now is "worth" more like 93 cents payable now. Future payments are "discounted." Over long periods, the discounting has a great effect. As J. P. Morgan reportedly said, "compound interest is the eight wonder of the world." (Interest accumulation is the mathematical inverse of discounting.) Assuming a modest rate of discount of 4% per year, a stream of income of $1 per year during years 76 through 95 would have a present value – for the whole 20-year stream—of 72 cents, adding only about 3% to the current value of $23.68 for the stream of dollars in years 1 through 75. Clearly, the *ex ante* monetary incentive would be little changed.

The creation of new works may also be affected indirectly by expansion or limitation of the public domain. Lengthening the duration of copyright will reduce the size of the public domain (compared to what it otherwise would be). It is possible that this could either facilitate or retard the creation of new works. On the one hand, postponing the wider availability of classic works may give new works a better chance of finding an audience. On the other hand, as mentioned, the public domain provides raw material for new works, so the creative community may suffer from its narrowing. It appears, though, that both of these effects would be of marginal consequence.

ESTIMATION OF MONETARY VALUES

The value (to the owner) of a copyright is the stream of royalty payments[7] expected from it. To estimate these values for the copyrights in question, i.e., those due to expire in the next 20 years, we have, first, used statistical samples to estimate the number of these that are still commercially viable, and then multiplied the number in each category by a figure representing their average value. We concentrate on three media—books, music, and movies—presuming that these represent most of the value at stake, but recognizing that others (such as still photography) will have some value. Commercial viability is indicated: for books, by being "in print," for musical compositions, by being recorded in records that are in commercial distribution, for movies, by being available on tape for broadcast or individual rental. The copyrights on works not available in these forms are presumed to have negligible commercial value. (Moreover, we make no attempt to estimate the value of derivative works, e.g., payments to the writer of *Jaws* for its movie adaptation.)

---

[6] Some may believe they are creating "for the ages," but this is not an economic motivation and would not be affected by the copyright law, whatever form it takes.

[7] The term "royalty" in this chapter is used generically to indicate the economic return to copyright owners (and related contractual beneficiaries) attributable to their intellectual property. It will not always take the legal form of royalties, and may be completely implicit. For example, if a publisher owns the rights to a book it publishes, no explicit royalty will be paid, but its equivalent is earned and implicitly included in the firm's recorded profits.

In order to estimate the number of works still commercially viable, the first step was modeled on a previous study by Economist, Inc.[8] Random samples of titles were drawn from the copyright renewal records of years 1950 to 1970 (approximately corresponding to initial registrations of 1922 to 1942). Due to the low cost of renewal ($6 through much of this period), works not renewed must have been very low value, if any (except for a few cases of negligence, bankruptcy, etc.). Moreover, it is unusual for works deemed worthless at that point to come back to life later. Thus, searching the renewal records can be used as a more efficient was of sampling works of the period than searching the original registrations. This is especially so for books, where only about 1% of the copyrights were renewed. These samples were then checked against reference works, such as *Books in Print,* to determine what percentage of the renewals are still commercially viable.

The average values of older works were estimated differently for each class. For musical compositions, we used a "top down" approach, starting with the size of the total market--$1.3 billion per year in royalties—as this is well measured by centralizing institutions such as Broadcast Music, Inc. (BMI) and the Fox Agency. We distribute this total by assuming that the value, i.e., popularity, of each song is proportional to the number of times it is recorded, this being reported by the Phonolog service.

For books, we use a "bottom up" approach, in contrast with the "top down" approach for music. Here, we assume each book has a typical "midlist" circulation of 5 thousand per year and earns a typical royalty rate (e.g., 10% of list price for paperbacks). For movies, the mostly bottom-up approach started with relative values based on certain indicia of popularity, but adjusted the scale itself to reflect value of the whole market. A few prominent transactions (such as Turner Broadcasting's acquisition of the MGM/UA library) give an indication of what the whole market for older movies is worth.

RESULTS

Books

Of the 268 titles in our sample—works originally copyrighted during 1923 to 1942 and renewed during 1951 to 1970—32 (11.9%) were found to be still in print, with 45 editions. There does not appear to be any consistent trend in survival within the sample period, so we apply the same 11.9% rate to each year's number of renewals in order to estimate the total number surviving today. There was no discernable trend in the numbers of books originally registered, but—for reasons not immediately evident—there was a definite increase in the numbers renewed, from about 2,000 per year around 1950 to more than 7,000 around 1970. Accordingly, the numbers surviving today grow from approximately 300 per year at the beginning to 900 at the end. Qualitatively, the books vary widely in subject matter and genre. The largest single categories are fiction and (especially toward the end of the period) history.

As to values, we assume that each edition (not title) has annual sales of 5,000 copies and royalties of 15% for retail for hardbacks, 10% for paperbacks. The volume assumption may

---

[8] Siwek, Stephen and Harold Furchgott-Roth. *An Economic Analysis of Copyright Extension Programs.* [Washington] Economists, Incorporated (for the National Endowment for the Arts). September 1991. 68 p. + appendices.

be on the low side of "typical," the royalty rate on the high side.[9] We assume that these older works will have a small, specialized audience but that their value to publishers will be higher than normal because there is little uncertainty or ancillary expense and the sales volume, while low, will probably continue longer than for most new books. The average list prices shown for the surviving works in our sample are $38.70 for hardbacks and $12.30 for paperbacks. Putting together all these factors, we estimate that each surviving title generates on average roughly $32,000 per year in royalties (or implicit royalties) for its owner.

Table 1 puts together the data for books by 5-year periods, showing the annual royalty revenues (by 5-year groups) as of the dates of copyright expiration under current law.[10] The revenues of books entering the public domain are expected to grow from about $9 million per year in the initial period to $15 million in the final period.[11] The table incorporates an assumed further "aging" of the catalog up to the dates of expiration but not beyond,[12] according to the following reasoning: The 11.9% survival of the renewed works over an average period of 37 years means that each year about 3.8% of the surviving titles went out of print. We assume that such a rate of decay will continue steadily ("negative exponentially") into the future. For example, for the last quinquennium, the numbers of works projected to be surviving (2,306) is less than half the number from that period now in print (4622).

Table 1. Numbers and Annual Royalties of Commercially Viable Books Projected to Enter Domain (under current law) During 5-year Periods, 1998-2017

Copyrighted	Renewed	To expire	Titles renewed	Titles surviving to expiration	Royalties (million$)
1922-1926	1950-1954	1998-2002	13,738	1,456	46
1927-1931	1955-1959	2003-2007	19,251	1,682	54
1932-1936	1960-1964	2008-2012	24,811	1,787	57
1937-1941	1965-1969	2013-2017	38,841	2,306	74

Sources: Copyright review records, *Books in Print,* calculations by CRS. See text.

Outliers: We make no allowance here for well-remembered classics, although the period in question includes major works of Faulkner, Steinbeck, Fitzgerald, Frost, Gibran, and Thurber, to name just a few of the more famous. Such works come strongly to mind precisely because they are so rare; statistically speaking they are "outliers" from the center of the distribution. To verify that our method is not missing too much in this regard, we have examined the best-seller list in *Publishers Weekly*. Its annual review[13] lists hardbacks down

[9] See Seidman, Michael. Negotiating Your Book Contract. In Writer's Digest Editors. *The Basics of Selling (and Protecting!) Your Writing.* [Cincinnati] 1991. p. 24.

[10] In this chapter, "renewal" refers to re-registration in the 28th year of a copyright (required for continued validity under the law in effect at the time); "expiration" refers to the end of the copyrights after 75 years, as currently scheduled; "extension" refers to the proposed additional 20 years.

[11] All monetary figures in our projections are in constant 1997 dollars.

[12] Aging beyond expiration is estimated below in the section summarizing results for all three media. It would not be correct to calculate the total value of affected royalties as of the last year by adding the lines, unless post-expiration aging is taken into account.

[13] *Publishers Weekly*, April 7, 1997. pp. 42-56 (covering 1996 sales).

to 100 thousand copies, trade paperbacks down to 50 thousand. Perusal of these lists shows only one title from the period under study here: *The Great Gatsby,* with 370 thousand copies in paperback. Only one other adult title (Burton Malkiel's 1973 *Random Walk Down Wall Street*) is more than a few years old. Generally, children's books are longer lived, with many from Dr. Seuss still going strong. Also, older public domain and folk stories are often reworked for children, e.g., Disney's *Hunchback of Notre Dame.* Finally, we note that the recently reissued *Joy of Cooking* is an ambiguous case. On the one hand, it has been revised so many times that only a small fraction of the original recipes are still included intact. Probably a trademark on the title would be more valuable than the original copyright.

We conclude from the foregoing that there are very few outliers from the period under study that would significantly boost our total value estimates.

Music

Popular

For musical works, we have narrowed the focus considerably, based on judgments as to where the bulk of commercial values lies. Thus, we have paid more attention to popular works than classical ones. And for the period in question, we consider only rights to the compositions rather than the recordings, as recordings were not eligible for Federal copyright before 1972 and thus are not at issue with regard to current legislation. Moreover, for the popular music from the 1920s and 1930s, current royalties flow to the owners of the songs primarily through new recordings. Recordings made in the period are of lesser interest because styles of performance have changed and, even more importantly, standards of acceptable sound quality have risen greatly.

We have basically focused on popular songs with words and music, excluding from consideration virtually all other musical copyrights, such as: choral works, purely instrumental works,[14] movie scores and incidental music, and instructional materials. In deriving our sample from the copyright renewal records, we observed that about 51% of the renewed works were in these excluded categories (including classical), and have adjusted our final estimate of viable songs accordingly.

For our sample of 266 songs, we found that 30 or 11.3% were still found on records listed in the *Phonolog* database as of 1995 (the latest available to us). Within the period, there appears to be a growth in current popularity going from beginning to end (discussed further *infra*). Our supposition that older compositions survive via new performances is borne out in the aggregate, but there are many exceptions. Thus, songs from the 1920s are often found on labels that specialize in re-issues, such as Folkways, Best of Jazz, and Arhoolie. But moving into the 1930s big band and "crooner" era, we find songs with many recordings, most from that era loosely defined, but stretching out for 10, 20, or more years. So most of the value still appears to derive from the composition rights rather than the oldest recordings.

For valuation, our key assumption is that the value of each composition from this period is proportional to the number of extant recordings of it. They come out of a tradition where popular songs were "covered" by many performing artists. In this, these older works contrast markedly with the modern era (since the advent of rock and roll). At present, new songs are

[14] Except for a few that were truly "popular," such as the tunes of Fats Waller.

closely identified with a particular performer and a particular recording, while the recordings vary extremely between hits and misses in their sales volume. The works in question here are seasoned, with a relatively small but predictable audience. We presume that each recording does roughly equally well; popularity of songs is indicated by how often they were recording. In effect, we adopt a uniform, average value per recording and multiply be the estimated number of recordings of songs written in this period. This is a "bottom-up" method that relies on the standardization of royalties for record production, but we refer to the value of the whole rights market in order to include the value of performance royalties, which are more complex.

Revenues flow to owners mainly through two channels, "mechanical" royalties for the production of records, and "performance" royalties derived predominantly from television and radio play and concerts. Both these channels are fairly well routinized and centralized, so we have reliable estimates of the "universe" of musical royalties. For music writers and publishers,[15] the larger portion of royalties derive from performances, and are collected and distributed by the rights societies—American Society of Composers Authors and Publishers (ASCAP), BMI and SESAC, Inc. The two largest reported collections of about $760 million in 1994 and we estimate that inclusion of SESAC would augment the total by about 5%. Allowing for inflation since, total performance royalties in 1998 would roughly $900 million. As will be seen presently, the key point for our method is not the absolute value of performance royalties, but their ratio to mechanical royalties.

Mechanical royalties are collected primarily by the Harry Fox Agency, a subsidiary of the National Music Publishers Association. In the vast majority of cases, the rate is just over 7 cents per song (for tracks up to five minutes in length), the rate promulgated under the compulsory licensing provision of the copyright law. The market for record albums is about 600 million units per year; if each has an average of 10 songs, the mechanical royalties at the standard rate would be $420 million. This is on the same order of magnitude as the $358 million in collections reported by the Fox Agency for 1994. We take $400 million as a mid-range estimate for mechanical royalties.

As mentioned above, we start by attributing "typical" royalties to each recording. This would be 70 cents per copy for a 10-song album, but how many copies would be typical? Clearly, most of the record market reflects a few very popular and very recent recordings; the songs of the 1920s and 1930s generally fall into the tail of the distribution, even for later recordings of them. It has been reported that the top 2.5% of album titles account 72% of sales at an average of 130 thousand copies each. For the remaining tail (some 140 thousand titles), the average sales are 1,200 copies.[16] Since not all of the older songs will fall into the tail or have the same average, we also consider more subjective rules of thumb. For example, it has been noted that the major record labels must see a certain minimum potential (apparently on the order of 25,000 copies) before re-releasing old albums, but they are often willing to license independents to do so at a lower level, e.g. with a minimum guarantee of 5,000.[17] We will take 5,000 as an average volume figure for the songs from the period in question. At the standard 7 cents per track, the mechanical rights would come to $350 per year per song.

---

[15] Performers and producers are paid by contract with record companies and concert promoters. See further below.

[16] SoundScan Inc. quoted in Standard & Poors. *Movies and Home Entertainment Industry Survey.* [New York] Standard & Poors. February 27, 1997. p. 25.

[17] Tamarkin, Jeff. Catalog Rolling. *Pulse!* October 1997. p. 5.

The data cited above indicate that for the market overall, performance rights are worth a little more than twice as much as mechanical rights, i.e., 900 million/400 million = 2.25. Applying this average ration, we figure that each song in question receives 2.25 X 350, or just under $800 in performance royalties for each recording. In total, then, each song is valued at about $1,100 per recording. Of course, there is great diversity, but this is an average that we apply to the estimated umbers of songs.

Returning the number of songs, there were 195 thousand musical copyrights renewed from 1950 through 1969 (composed 1922 through 1941), an average of 9,760 per year (with no evident trend). As noted, 51% were in classical and other categories not yet considered here, leaving 4,773 per year as our universe. In the sample, 11.3% of songs renewed then were found surviving today, implying a total of 539 per year.

For our method, which values each recording equally, the important this is the current number of "tracks," or appearances, on current albums. In the sample, each surviving song was found on an average of four to five tracks, but this was not uniform. Rather there was an irregular but definite trend toward more tracks toward the end of the period. This reached a peak with two hits from 1940-1941, "This Love of Mine" (Sinatra-Parker-Sanicola) and "Night We Called It a Day" (Adair-Dennis), which accounted for 60 tracks, far more than any other songs in the sample. We believe this to be more than coincidence, rather, a sign of a real trend continuing into the 1940s, namely the heyday of the big band era, Tin Pan Alley, and a large number of lasting songs generally known as the "standards." To examine this issue further, we compiled a list of most-recorded songs of all eras, as shown in Table 2. This shows one song already in public domain (St. Louis Blues), two from 1929 and 1930, and the rest of the top 10 dating from 1935 to 1947.

A much larger sample would be needed to delineate the "golden age" precisely, but for our purposes we fit the observed data to a trend line as follows: .A relatively low-level base period corresponds to 1922 through 1931, followed by an intermediate period (1932-1938) producing about 3 times as many current tracks per year, and then a rapidly rising finale (presumably continuing into the 1940s) yielding as of 1939-1941 more than 10 times as many tracks as the base period.

Table 2. Songs Currently Found on the Greatest Number of Albums

Body and Soul (Green, Heyman et. al.)	1930
Stardust (Carmichael-Parish)	1929
All the Things You Are (Hammerstein-Kern)	1939
Summertime (Gershwin-Heyward)	1935
St. Louis Blues (Handy)	1914
My funny Valentine (Rogers-Hart)	1937
Take the A Train (Strayhorn)	1941
Over the Rainbow (Arlen-Harburg)	1939
Autumn Leaves (Kosma-Prevert-Mercer)	1947[a]
I Can't Get Started with You (Duke-Gershwin)	1935

[a]Music and French lyrics, 1947; English lyrics, 1950.
Source: Tabulated by CRS from Phonolog database.

The results for popular music are summarized in Table 3. This includes an aging factor of 3.6% per year, very close to that found for books. Of course, there can be no certainty that past trends will be carried into the future, and there may be divergences between the works of different eras, as already evident with the standards.[18] That said, what the table shows is royalties of expiring compositions in the range of $600,000-700,000 per year in the first 10 years, then growing steadily. We project in the final year (2017) expiring royalties would be on the order of $6 million.

Outliers: Table 2 shows the very peak of popularity of the standards, ranging from more than 250 current recordings of "Body and Soul" to about 150 of "I Can't Get Started." Cursory examination of the Phonolog listing indicates that perhaps 100 or more songs from the Tin Pan Alley era each have on the order of 75 to 100 recordings. If the songs are worth our hypothesized $1,100 each, they could represent in the aggregate $10 million or more in royalties. If their expirations occurred over, say, 15 years, this could add perhaps $600 thousand per year (3$ million per 5 years) to each line in Table 2.

Classical

As the classical category accounts for 4% of record sales, we presume that total potential royalties (if all of the works had copyrights) are 0.04 x $1.3 billion = $52 million per year. Because of its small share, its generally longer survival, and data availability considerations, a different method was used for classical recordings from the Schwann catalog[19] and estimated the percentage that are of works written during 1922-41. Thus, in a sample of 231 recordings, 26 were found to date from this period, i.e., 11.3%, implying annual royalties of 0.113 x 52 = $5.9 million. As there is no evident trend during the period, we presume that an equal share (approximately $300 thousand worth) expires in each of the next 20 years, and this is included in our overall summary (Table 5 below).

Table 3. Numbers and Annual Royalties of Commercially Viable Recordings of Songs[a] Projected to Enter Public Domain (under current law) During 5-year Periods, 1998-2017

Copyrighted	Renewed	To expire	Titles renewed	Titles surviving to expiration	Royalties (million$)
1922-1926	1950-1954	1998-2002	22,592	3,130	3.4
1927-1931	1955-1959	2003-2007	22,427	7,230	2.9
1932-1937	1960-1964	2008-2012	22,427	7,230	8.0
1938-1941	1965-1969	2013-2017	24,641	13,791	15.2

[a]The table shows the projected numbers of "tracks," or recordings, or songs written in the indicated periods. These correspond to an estimated average of 539 viable songs per year with copyrights expiring during the next 20 years.

Sources: Copyright renewal records, Phonolog database, calculations by CRS. See text.

[18] The "American popular song" may now be getting renewed impetus from new permanent programs of two influential institutions, Carnegie Hall and Lincoln Center. Singer, Barry. Trying to rescue Songs Once Held Dear. *New York Times*, July 6, 1997. p. H28.

[19] *Schwann Opus*, v. 8, no. 4 (Fall 1997).

Although classical records are only 4% of the overall market, they bulk much larger proportionally in our study period: $300 thousand in royalties vs. $700 thousand for popular music in the early years. This is because these markets operate on totally different time scales. We find in our sample that there is substantial interest in works going back 300 years; the median date for the whole population is about 1895. An important economic consequence is that 64% of the classical recording repertoire is from the public domain. This is why we termed $52 million as the measure only of the potential royalty market.[20]

It should also be kept in mind that all of our figures (for both popular and classical) estimate the values only of rights to the compositions, not the recordings of them. An unestimated fraction of these compositions—a fraction that probably rises over time—is associated with still-viable recordings. The principal beneficiaries thereof include, of course, the record companies, and also the producers and performers. The latter groups are compensated according to their contracts, which typically pay 9% of retail sales to the performer, 3% to the producer. (Broadcasters do not have to pay anything to the record companies for airplay.) After a number of deductions to reach the contractual definition of "retail," the net to the creatives is perhaps a little over a dollar an album, or perhaps 50% more than is received by the owner of the composition. But again, these arrangements would not be directly affected by the proposed extension of federal copyright.

Motion Pictures

The sample used for measuring the motion picture market differed somewhat from those used for books and music. Preliminary testing showed two important differences in the market. First, for the last half of the period a high percentage of the copyrights was renewed and a high percentage of those renewed are still commercially viable. Second, the foregoing was conspicuously not true for silent films.[21] Accordingly, we used a smaller primary sample (about 50 items rather than the 250 for books and music) and started it with renewals of 1954 (original registrations of 1926). As before, certain categories of works were disregarded on the presumption that they have little commercial value. For movies, the principal exclusions (besides silents) were "shorts" (identifiable in the records as one-reel items), and industrial, advertising or instructional productions. We estimate that some 42% of the renewals were in these excluded categories. In all, for the period 1926-1941, there were 17,692 titles renewed (in 1954 to 1969), or on average 1,106 per year, with no evident trend. Considering the excluded categories, then, there was a universe under consideration of 645 films per year.

To determine the current viability of old films our primary source was the *BiB TV Programming Source Book*,[22] a fairly comprehensive compilation used by television stations

---

[20] It is interesting to note that W.A. Mozart alone accounts for 5% of the recordings, which would make his heirs eligible for some $2.5 million per year in royalties, if the works were copyrighted—more than 200 years after his passing.

[21] The precipitous demise of silent films is well known. See, for example, Eyman, Scott. *The Speed of Sound: Hollywood and the Talkie Revolution, 1926-1930.* [New York] Simon & Schuster, 1997. 413 p. The careers of virtually the whole first generation of movie actors came to an end as soon as talkies were introduced. More relevant for this study, interest in going back to see already-produced silents also ended and has not returned in any substantial way.

[22] McCarthy, Beth, ed. *BiB Television Programming Source Books, 1996-7.* Vol. 1, 2 (films). [Philadelphia] North American Publishing, 1996.

and cable channels. This showed that just under half of the films in the sample are still commercially available. However, there is a definite trend within the period toward greater survival as one moves forward. Using our primary sample as well as a test sample, we have derived a smoothed scale of current survival probabilities as follows: 1926-1928, 11%, 1929-1932, 40%, and 1933-1941, 65%.

For valuations, a particularly useful feature in the 1996 edition of the BiB guide is its classification of the films' commercial potential, rating them with dollar signs as well as the familiar system of stars indicating quality. The dollar-sign ratings are qualitative and subjective, but we have put them on a quantitative scale (and filled in some gaps) as consistently as possible with prices implicit in the few large transactions that have been publicly reported of late. Recent deals indicate that the average older (more than 10 years) feature film may be worth in the range of $150 to 200 thousand.[23] Package deals undoubtedly include many titles that are essentially worthless but, on the other hand, also include some fairly recent and successful ones, e.g., *When Harry Met Sally* and *The Graduate.* The higher end of values may be shown by the acquisition by Canal Plus of the Carolco Library, which were all fairly recent productions. These 24 titles brought $58 million, for an average of $2.4 million.

There are a few notable classics that would fall out of our assumed range but, working simply in terms of averages, we have assigned values ranging from $50 thousand for one dollar sign to $2 million for 3-1/2 or 4 $s. For our sample, the result is an average value of roughly $250 thousand. However, there is a trend during the period that we have approximated as follows: for 1926-1930, an average $175 thousand; for 1931-1934, $250 thousand; and for 1935-1941, $400 thousand. Combining these values with the foregoing probabilities of survival yielded estimates of the values of expiring copyrights that grew steadily from $13 million per year (expirations of 2002 to 2004) to $168 million per year from 2011 onward. To put these on a comparable basis with the other media, we convert the asset values to current revenues by dividing by a factor of 10.[24] The results are summarized in Table 4.

Table 4. Numbers and Annual Royalties of Commercially Viable Movies Projected to Enter Public Domain (under current law) During 5-year Period, 1998-2017

Copyrighted	Renewed	To expire	Titles renewed	Titles surviving to expiration	Royalties (million$)
1922-1926	1950-1954	1998-2002	2,840	72	1.2
1927-1931	1955-1959	2003-2007	5,636	918	16
1932-1937	1960-1964	2008-2012	5,562	1,934	48
1938-1941	1965-1969	2013-2017	5,378	2,095	61

Sources: Copyright renewal records, *BiB TV Programming Source Book,* calculations by CRS. See text.

[23] Rawsthorn, Alice. PolyGram Agrees Film Purchase. *Financial Times,* December 4, 1997. p. 13; Fabrikant, Geraldine. MGM Owner Said to Offer $300 Million to Buy Orion. *New York Times,* April 19, 1997. p. 14; Klady, Leonard. Big Boys Anteing Up to Get Library Cards. *Variety,* May 13, 1996. pp. 13, 16.

[24] A common rule of thumb would value mature media properties at about 10 times annual cash flow. In the table, we also give effect to a "decay" or disappearance factor of 1.8% per year (less than half the rate for books or music).

Outliers: Various "all time best" list were inspected to give form to the peak of popularity of old films. In particular, the American Film Institute has compiled 400 titles as a first cut toward naming the 100 best of the first 100 years.[25] Narrowing this further with our own subjective judgment of commercial potential, we have identified 32 titles from our study period (4 from the silent era, the rest after 1931) that appear to be of extraordinary continuing value.[26] If these had a capitalized value of $10 million each and a corresponding annual cash flow of $1 million, as a group this would come to $32 million/year, raising our estimated total almost 25%. However, a striking feature of this outlier list is how "back-loaded" it is: Almost half of these are from the final 3 years, 1939-1941.[27] Thus, the economic impact of copyright expiration, as currently scheduled, would occur toward the end of the projected 20-year period.

Summary

Table 5 combines the results for the three media considered here. Unlike the previous tables, it totals the estimated annual revenues from all works scheduled to expire up to the dates indicated. For example, the second line indicates potential royalties of $19 million in 1999 for copyrights in the three media scheduled to expire at the beginning of 1998 and 1999. (In doing so, it also continues the depreciation rates beyond the expiration years. This is why the figures for "works to date" are less than the simple sums of figures from works "of the year.") In order to understand this, it should be borne in mind that time is being measured in two dimensions. First is the year in which works are copyrighted—their vintage—which is associated with corresponding years of expiration 75 years later or extension to 95 years. The other dimension of time is the years in which royalties are collected. Table 5 shows royalty collections in indicated years, if terms were extended, for two kinds of vintages: The one which would expire that year without extension ("0f the year"), and the sum of all those that would expire starting 1998 ("of works to date"). The final line indicates the estimated value potential royalties that would be paid or collected in year 2017 due to extension of 20 years' worth of copyrights. Beyond that time, the total would not grow as rapidly, because the copyrights of 1922 and beyond would start to expire notwithstanding the extension and each, year by year, would be dropped from the tabulation.

---

[25] Available via World Wide Web (listed chronologically) at: http://ptd15.afionline.org/100/movies/directory.html

[26] The most notable of the 32, in our judgment, are *Wizard of Oz, Gone with the Wind, Citizen Kane, Maltese Falcon, Fantasia, Duck Soup, Night at the Opera, King Kong, and 42nd Street.*

[27] The streak continued into 1942 with classics like *Casablanca* and *Bambi.*

Table 5. Annual Royalties of Book, Music and Movie Copyrights, for Copyrights Expiring in Selected Years and Expiring from 1998 to Those Years (millions of 1997 dollars)

	Books		Music		Movies		All	
Year	of the year	of works to date	of the year	of works to date	of the year	of works to date	of the year	of works to date
1998	$9.1	$9	$0.7	$1	$0	$0	$10	$10
1999	9.2	18	0.7	1	0	0	10	19
2000	10.9	28	0.7	2	0	0	12	30
2001	10.5	38	0.7	3	0	0	11	41
2002	12.5	49	0.6	3	1.2	1	14	53
2007	10.6	90	0.5	5	5.4	16	16	111
2012	14.1	132	1.5	12	12.9	62	28	206
2017	12.7	178	6.1	24	11.8	115	31	317

Sources: Previous tables and further calculations by CRS.

In the initial years, almost all of the potential revenue is attributable to books. However, the book revenues subsequently grow only very slowly, rising from $8 million in the first year to $13 million for the books expiring in the 20th year. After five years, the movie revenues grow rapidly and each parity with books (in terms of the latest-year expirations) by 2012. Music revenues are smaller than the other media throughout the period but give indications of growing comparable to them with the works of the 1940s (expiring in the 1920s).

The recipients of this income can be characterized in general terms as follows. Quick perusal of the copyright renewal records indicates that the books are mostly registered in the names of the authors. Even when the works are still owned by publishers, though, authors usually retain an interest contractually, so royalties are in most cases going to their personal heirs. Movie copyrights are almost all owned by the studios and their successors. While modern contracts assign percentages of revenue from broadcast and video to certain key participants (directors, writers, lead actors, etc.), this is not the case with these older works. The owner will usually be the sole recipient of current revenues. Music ownership has many variations. Often it is vested in a publishing company, but this could be owned by the writer (who may also be the first recorded performer), a record company, or one of several large publishers that have brought up other companies or their catalogs of songs. The writer/composer is typically allocated 50% of the royalties contractually.

In terms of nationally, it appears that the great majority of owners are (or at least were at the time of renewal) domestic rather than foreign. The conspicuous least is classical music. In our sample, 6 out of the 26 works (23%) falling within the study period were by Americans. Eleven were by composers from what is now the European Union (mostly Britain, France and Germany); seven from other is now the European countries (mostly Russia), and two from South America. Looking with a slightly wider perspective—the 49 works in our sample by composers who were active during 1922-1941 regardless of timing of the particular works—we find only 16% attributable to Americans.[28]

FEES FOR TERM EXTENSION

Rationale

This section considers the idea of charging a user fee for gaining the gaining the proposed extra 20 years of copyright protection. It would be in an amount yet to be determined but supposedly greater than the administrative costs of registration, so that net proceeds would be generated for subsidizing the creators to "give something back." The lucky few whose work has survived over the long term would be required to share some of their good fortune to nurture a new generation of artists. (On the other hand, it could be argued that they have simply earned their due, and that if the arts are to be subsidized, the public at large should bear the cost). Another motivation for a user fee is that it could be a compromise between the two most divergent perspectives on intellectual property: That intellectual property is either a perpetual natural right of the creator (and heirs), or it is an institution created legally by the community for the benefit of the community. If term extension is seen to be privatizing more of the public domain, a user fee would be partially compensating the public for it.

Alternatively, and a little more skeptically, the concept envisions a situation where most lucrative older properties have been acquired by corporate interests, by recycling some of the benefits back to the "real" creators (albeit a new generation of them). As such, this echoes previous debates about *termination rights*.[29] It has been given further focus by the proviso that the user fee only be applied to *works made for hire.*

Effects

The economic values estimated in the preceding section represent the maximum amount that could be collected from copyright owners for the opportunity of extending the duration. That is, if there were a mechanism for requiring owners to either pay a certain amount (tailored to each owner) or forfeit future use of the work, theoretically they could be induced to pay virtually the entire value of their expected net revenues. However, a straight "one size fits all" user fee would not be an adequate mechanism to extract all of the value. A slightly more refined version would set different fees for each class of work, e.g., books, music, films. If judiciously set, these differentiated fees could collect more than a single level while

---

[28] Aside from the smallness of the sample, these results should be considered of limited precision, because there is a difficulty in appropriately categorizing the "nationality" of the composers. A number of prominent ones, such as Stravinsky, Hindemith and Schoenberg, emigrated mid-career. Furthermore, there is no telling without detailed investigation where the ultimate beneficiaries of their rights are located, a generation or two after their passing.

[29] "Termination rights were created in the 1976 Copyright Act as an agreed compromise between author and publisher-producer interests.... Without a reversion of rights, only the publisher-producer would benefit from the longer term." U.S. Library of Congress. Congressional Research Service. *Proposed U.S. Copyright Term Extension,* by Dorothy Schrader. CRS Report 95-799 S. 1995.

minimizing the number of non-renewals. Alternatively, an auction could yield even more revenue.[30] Many variations on such systems are possible. The point is that the entire value of the proposed copyright extensions represents a theoretical outer limit on what could be collected for public purposes.

Utilization of Works

Another important question about user fees is how they might affect the pricing, availability and utilization of copyrighted works. This depends critically on how the system is structured. We assume here a straightforward choice for owners: Either they pay the stated one-time fee (which may be differentiated by copyright type) and receive an extra 20 years of protection, or they turn their rights over to the public domain. (This differs from, say, *domaine publique payant*, where a fee is paid to the state per use.) Economic theory would suggest, in cases where the fee is paid and the term extended, that the entire cost would be born by the owner, i.e., he/she would not be able to users via a higher royalty. Consequently, there would be no change in utilization.

The conclusion that utilization would not change despite the payment of the fee rests upon basic price theory. Reduced to its essentials, the reasoning starts from the well-known dictum that price depends on supply and demand. And in this case, neither demand or supply is charged by the user fee; therefore, price does not change. First, demand is a constant: The amount that people are willing to pay presumably does not depend on who owns the copyright or indeed, on whether it is owned at all. Moreover, in the case at hand, supply is constant as well: The work in question may have taken considerable effort to produce, but that cost is "sunk" and hence irrelevant. The intellectual property exists and does not cost anything to produce in the present. In sum, the price to the users does not change. What changes is the net revenue of the owner, as he/she has to pay the user fee.

Another perspective on this may be gained by considering the distinction between cost and rent in their economic meaning. The cost of production consists of those expenses, if any, incurred in producing a tangible item, e.g., printing a book. The difference between price and cost is rent.[31] The significance of rent is two-fold: First, it does not affect price. On the contrary, causation is the other way around: Supply and demand determine price, and price minus cost (and normal profit) determines rent as the residual. Second, no matter what portion of the rent may be taken away from the owner, he/she will still continue to offer the work to users because he/she is still receiving something beyond cost, and something is better than nothing.

There is still the possibility that the required fee exceeds an owner's expected rent. In this case, he/she will forfeit the work to the public domain. The result for availability is that of expiration of copyright protection, with consequences as discussed at the beginning of this chapter.

An interesting feature of the assumed system (pay to play) is that no matter what the level of the fee, the system will not cause any loss of availability to the public nor increased pricing of any works. The foregoing reasoning of this section indicates that there is no effect on pricing when the fee is paid and the copyright extended. In the other case—where the fee is

---

[30] As in *domaine publique payant* type of system proposed in S. 2423 (Dodd) in the 103rd Congress.

[31] More precisely, there is a rate of profit called "normal profit," and rent is the net return in excess of that.

greater than the commercial possibilities would support—the work would be freed from the obligation of paying. The owner would suffer a loss through his/her forfeiture, but society as a whole would find the work still available for use, and probably at lower price.

Revenue Collected

As already noted, the maximum theoretical revenue collection is equal to the total expected rent, which is presumably reflected in the current capitalized value of the copyrights. This maximum would not be extracted by a simple pay-to-play system of user fees, because of the diversity of values of all of these works. Still, there is some one-fee level (which we do not have enough information as yet to estimate) that would generate the most possible revenue under the simple fee system. It could be determined by operationalizing the following. The amount collected as a function of the size of the fee, if graphed, would resemble the projectile of a cannonball. Starting with a zero fee, zero revenue would result. Then, if the fee were set at $100 (to pick an arbitrary figure), and if all currently viable works were extended, roughly $150 thousand could be collected over the first five years from books, $270 thousand from popular songs, and $7,000 from movies, based on data cited *supra.* If the fee is raised, revenue collected will rise approximately proportionally, but at some point, some owners will rather let their works lapse. Total revenue will then increase at a decreasing rate until it stops increasing and a maximum has been reached, beyond which total revenue will actually decrease. Ultimately, if the fee exceeds the value of every single work, no one would pay and revenue collected would be zero. The revenue collected as a function of the fee level follows a version of the Laffer Curve much discussed in the context of income taxes.[32]

The foregoing figures assume that the fee would apply to all works being extended. If the fee is applies only to works made for hire, revenue collected could be significantly less. A preliminary look at the renewal records indicates that about 35% to 40% of works renewed in the 1950s and 1960s were works made for hire. We do not have a precise breakdown by medium, but it appears that much of the revenue collected would be in the motion picture category. Works in the other categories studied here appear to be registered more often in the name of individual creators. A portion of the musical compositions were made for hire but, interestingly, most of these cases are where the music was written for movies. In books, rights would be typically be assigned to publishers initially but, if the copyright was renewed, it would be done in the name of the author. There is a class of literature that was done for hire, but apparently, most of these works were magazine articles or "pulp" novels that have not endured particularly well.[33]

---

[32] See, for example, Bender, Bruce. An Analysis of the Laffer Curve. *Economic Injury,* July 1984. pp. 414-420.
[33] Wineapple, Brenda. Grinding it Out. *New York Times* Book Review, January 18, 1998. p. 15.

COPYRIGHT RESTORATION FOR PUBLIC DOMAIN WORKS

Dorothy Schrader

COPYRIGHT RESTORATION FOR PUBLIC DOMAIN WORKS

The United States joined the Berne Convention for the Protection of Literary and Artistic Works in 1989[1] without making any provision for recapture of copyright in public domain works. The spirit, if not the letter, of Article 18 of the Berne Convention seems to require some copyright restoration. The North American Free Trade Agreement ("NAFTA") required the United States to allow copyright restoration for certain Mexican and Canadian films.[2] The NAFTA implementing legislation created a one-year window of opportunity to effect recapture of copyright in Mexican and Canadian films published without notice of copyright between January 1, 1978 and March 1, 1989. A broader recapture provision is now under consideration in the context of draft legislation to implement the trade agreements reached at the conclusion of the Uruguay Round of the General Agreement on Tariffs and Trade ("GATT 1994"),[3] although nothing in the GATT explicitly requires copyright restoration of public domain works.

This chapter reviews and analyzes the legal, constitutional, and practical issues relating to recapture of copyright in works residing in the United States public domain.

---

[1] The United States joined the 1971 Paris Act of the Berne Convention for the Protection of Literary and Artistic Works (July 24, 1971) effective March 1, 1989 (hereafter: "Berne Convention").

[2] For an analysis of the NAFTA provisions, see Intellectual Property Provisions of the NAFTA" CRS Report No. 94-59A by Dorothy Schrader at pages 11-13.

[3] GATT members are expected to complete domestic approval procedures by July 1, 1995, the scheduled date for entry into force of the GATT 1994. Implementing legislation for United States acceptance of the GATT 1994 is under discussion and at the drafting stage between the Administration and key congressional committees. For an analysis of the intellectual property provisions of the GATT 1994, see "Intellectual Property Provisions of the GATT 1994: 'The TRIPS Agreement'" CRS Report No. 94-302A by Dorothy Schrader.

BACKGROUND

Historically, until 1989,[4] the United States copyright laws embraced formalities as conditions on the enjoyment and exercise of copyright (e.g., notice of copyright; also, until 1992, renewal of copyright by registration).[5] Non-observance of certain formalities caused total loss of copyright protection—the work fell into the public domain. In only very rare instances did Congress legislate to permit recapture of works from the public domain. (Private laws were enacted in the 19th century restoring copyright in individual works; two public laws in this century authorized presidential proclamations to allow recapture of copyrights lost because of wartime conditions during World Wars I and II).[6]

In ratifying and implementing the Berne Copyright Convention in 1989, the United States postponed legislating on copyright recapture, even though the spirit and arguably the letter of Article 18 of the Berne Convention seems to require some nod in the direction of retroactive protection of works. In trade negotiation contexts, the United States Government has nevertheless sought retroactive protection for United States authors and copyright proprietors, especially from those countries who formerly extended no protection to American works.

Recent developments in trade-related contexts have required the United States to reconsider its position on copyright recapture. Mexico, in the North American Free Trade Agreement ("NAFTA"), successfully insisted upon inclusion of a provision permitting copyright recapture for certain motion pictures (and works embodied in the motion pictures). France reportedly has placed copyright recapture on the negotiating table in discussions about protection of audiovisual works. As the United States prepares its legislation to implement the 1994 Uruguay Round agreements under the General Agreement on Tariffs and Trade ("GATT 1994"), serious consideration is being given to general copyright recapture provision for foreign Berne or "GATT" works.

The copyright recapture idea propounded in the 1886 Berne Convention[7] made considerable practical sense: if the founding members had not agreed to retroactive application of the 1886 Convention, the benefits of the new Convention to authors and copyright proprietors would have been delayed in coming to fruition. For decades, the Convention might have been little more than a mantle for bilateral agreements. Moreover, the practical effect of the retroactivity provision was much less in 1886 because formalities could

[4] When the United States adhered to the Berne Convention, effective march 1, 1989, it eliminated its mandatory notice of copyright requirement, which had been a condition of American copyright protection since 1790. Berne Convention Implementation Act of 1988, Pub. L. 100-568, 102 Stat. 2853 (October 31, 1988). Article 5(2) of the Berne Convention prohibits a member country from conditioning the "employment and the exercise of these rights" on satisfaction of any formality, like the notice of copyright.

[5] More than three years after its adherence to the Berne Convention, the United States eliminated the last remaining formality from its copyright law. The Copyright Renewal Act of 1992, Pub. L. 102-307, 106 Stat. 264 (June 26, 1992) abolished mandatory renewal registration as a condition of securing copyright protection for the second term of copyright in works copyrighted before 1978.

[6] The Act of December 18, 1919, 41 Stat. 368, allowed copyright recapture for certain works that lost copyright during World War I (15 month "window" during which a claimant could apply for copyright restoration). The Act of September 25, 1941, 55 Stat. 732, allowed copyright recapture for certain World War II works (length of recapture "window" set by individual presidential proclamations). Private law examples include the Act of May 24, 1828, 6 Stat. 389; the Act of January 25, 1859, 11 Stat. 557; and the Act of May 24, 1866, 14 Stat. 587.

[7] The Berne Convention originated in 1886 and has been revised at periodic intervals since then. As discussed later, the copyright recapture provision (originally Article 14; now Article 18) remains essentially the same in the subsequent revisions of the Convention.

still be maintained in the country of origin, and the obligation to extend retroactive protection did not arise if the work fell into the public domain of the country of origin for any reason.

For these reasons, the practical and legal problems that copyright recapture present will be more difficult for the United States than other new adherents to the Berne Convention. The successful implementation of the NAFTA copyright recapture obligation[8] suggests that the problems can be overcome.

COPYRIGHT RECAPTURE UNDER THE BERNE CONVENETION

1. Overview

Article 18 of the Berne Convention contains rather vague, circular language that invites honest differences about its intended obligations. Most commentators seem to agree in the following interpretation: new adherents to the Berne Convention are obligated to accord some retroactive protection to works that remain under copyright in their countries of origin, even if those works, pre-adherence, resided in the public domain of the newly adhering country other than as a result of the expiration of a previously granted copyright term. No obligation exists to protect such works in the forum country, if the term has already expired under the forum country's law. Each Berne country has considerable latitude and discretion in implementing Article 18.

The full text of Article 18 of the 1971 Paris version of the Berne Convention reads as follows:

> 1) The Convention shall apply to all works which, at the moment of its coming into force, have not yet fallen into the public domain in the country of origin through the expiry of the term of protection.
>
> 2) If, however, through the expiry of the term of protection, which was previously granted, a work has fallen into the public domain of the country where protection is claimed, that work shall not be protected anew.
>
> 3) The application of this principle shall be subject to any provisions contained in special conventions to that effect existing or to be concluded between countries of the Union. In the absence of such provisions, the respective countries shall determine, each in so far as it is concerned, the conditions of application of this principle.
>
> 4) The preceding provision shall also apply in the case of new accessions to the Union and to cases in which protection is extended by the application of article 7 or by the abandonment of reservation.

---

[8] The North American Free Trade Agreement Implementation Act, Pub. L. 103-182 (December 8, 1993) SEC. 334.

In general terms, the first paragraph establishes an obligation to allow copyright recapture in works that fell into the public domain of the country where protection is claimed ("forum country") if the copyright term has not expired for that work in the country of origin (usually the country of first publication or for limited classes of works, the country of which the author is a national). The obligation attaches at the moment the Convention comes into force in the forum country.

Under paragraph two, however, the forum country is not required to restore copyright in a work that fell into the public domain through expiration of the term of copyright granted by its law.

Paragraph three introduces ambiguity by providing flexibility. The obligation of Article 18 is qualified by the possible development of "special conventions" between two or more Berne members—in general, bilateral agreements. If no special conventions exist, each country determines for itself the "conditions of application" of Article 18. This language extends virtually complete discretion to legislate at the national level concerning the details of copyright recapture. The scope of a recapture provision, the limitations to protect reliance rights, and any time limits, and the effective date apparently are within the discretion of each new Berne Member (absent any special agreements). All commentators seem to agree that zero copyright recapture, however, is not one of the options.[9] Everything else is discretionary.

The final paragraph of Article 18 confirms that the "obligation" applies to new members and to instances in which protection is extended through the copyright duration rules of Article 7, or by abandonment of a reservation (principally the 10 year translation right sanctioned by the Additional Act of 1896, to which a few countries cling, or possibly withdrawal of a reservation allowing a developing country under the Appendix to the 1971 Paris Act). The confirmation that the copyright recapture obligation applies to new adherents is important. The remainder of the paragraph has little significance now.

No copyright recapture is required for works already in the public domain of the country of origin by expiration of the copyright term. If the work fell in the public domain of the country of origin because of failure to comply with formalities, copyright recapture should be allowed by the forum country (unless the normal copyright term has expired in the forum country).

These general principles can become exceedingly complex in application to relevant facts and law. First, ascertaining the country of origin may require the Wisdom of Solomon. The law varies depending upon which act of the Berne Convention is binding between the forum state and the "country of origin."[10] Second, national copyright laws may be amended over time. Third, the facts may change: a country becomes a new adherent to the Berne Convention; an author changes his or her nationality; an unpublished work becomes a

---

[9] S. RICKETSON, THE BERNE CONVENTION FOR THE PROTECTION OF LITERARY AND ARTISTIC WORKS: 1886-1986, 675 (1987)(Hereafter: "Ricketson"); Nordemann, *et al.*, "International Copyright and Neighboring Rights Law: Commentary with Special Emphasis on the EC," (1990)(R. Livingston, translator).

[10] An analysis of which act of the Berne Convention applies between two member countries is beyond the scope of this chapter. Members are currently bound by one or more of four acts: Berlin 1908; Rome 1928; Brussels 1948; Paris 1971. Under one theory, two countries are bound by the latest common version to which they have adhered. This history, however, is not a matter of settled interpretation. The only clear provision governing which act to apply appears in Article 32(3) of the 1971 Paris Act. The Appendix for Developing Countries is applicable to a country not bound by the 1971 Paris Act only if that country agrees to its application.

published work. To examine the policy issues concerning recapture of works from the public domain, an understanding of the likely interpretation of the basic obligation is a mere first step. Also, where retroactivity questions arise, we quickly move to the realm of the theoretical and conjectural since there are few relevant precedents or experiences.

2. Country of Origin

Copyright recapture is not required by the Berne Convention if the work is in the public domain of its "country of origin" and of the forum state where protection is claimed by reason of expiration of the term of copyright. Ever since the 1908 Berlin Act of the Berne Convention abolished copyright formalities, expiration of the term is the one clear reason copyright recapture is not required pursuant to Article 18.

Copyright recapture should operate as a two-way conduit. Works originating in a newly adhering state should enjoy copyright recapture in every existing Berne Member, unless the term of copyright has expired. Conversely, works originating in existing Berne Members should enjoy copyright recapture in the newly adhering state, unless the term of copyright has expired.

Identification of the country of origin is the first step in permitting copyright recapture. The rules can be very complex in cases of simultaneous publication in two or more countries and for certain classes of works (motion pictures; works of architecture; applied works of art; sculptures). Two general principles cover the bulk of the works: for published works, the country of origin is the country of first publication of the work; for unpublished works, the country of origin is the country of which the author of the work is a national.

The definition of the "simultaneous publication" varies depending upon which version of the Berne Convention is applicable to the facts. If the Rome 1928 version applies, the publication must occur the same day in two or more countries to be considered simultaneous. Under the Brussels 1948 and Paris 1971 versions, the publication is simultaneous if the work is published in two or more countries with a 30-day period.

If the work is published simultaneously in a Berne country and a non-Berne country, the Berne country is the country of origin. If the work is published simultaneously in two Berne countries, the one granting the shorter term of the copyright is the country of origin.

Other special rules determine the country of origin for certain classes of works. Under the 1971 Paris Act, assuming the motion picture is not the first or simultaneously published in a Berne country, the country of origin of the motion picture is presumed to be the Berne country where the filmmaker has its headquarters or habitual residence. Under the 1948 Brussels and 1971 Paris Act, if an architectural, sculptural, or artistic work is erected or fixed.

The 1971 Paris Act has another special rule: if work is first published in a non-Berne country, the country of origin is determined by the nationality of the author.

Where the author's nationality determines the country of origin, further complications arise if the work owes its creation to two or more persons from different Berne countries. In that case, the work probably has at least two countries of origin, although Geller suggests the rule of the shorter term might be applied to settle on one country of origin.[11]

---

[11] M. NIMMER & P. GELLER, INTERNATIONAL LAW AND PRACTICE, Introduction, INT-115, Sec. 4[3][a][i](1990) (Hereafter: Geller).

Where the work is simultaneously published in two Berne countries, which apply the same copyright term, again the work probably has two countries of origin.

Only after applying these complex rules to determine the country of origin, can one evaluate which works might be subject to copyright recapture, depending upon special agreements or national laws.

3. Alternative Theories about the Recapture Obligation

While most commentators conclude that Article 18 requires some recapture of works from the public domain, alternative theories exist about the nature of the recapture obligation.

(1) **No retroactive protection.** Can the vague language of Article 18, which, admittedly, leaves wide latitude to its implementation in national laws, be stretched to an interpretation that denies any retroactive protection for public domain works? That is the interpretation adopted by the United States in adhering to the Berne Convention in 1989, at least as a provisional matter. The statute implementing the Berne Convention specifically denies protection for any public domain works.[12] The legislative history does imply, however, that the United States might consider copyright recapture at an indefinite time after adherence.[13]

(2) **Recapture subject to reliance rights.** Berne states have wide discretion to legislate in a variety of ways to protect the legitimate reliance rights of persons who made investments or otherwise relied on the public domain status of the works.

(3) **Recapture in moderation.** Berne states must give a reasonable amount of retroactive protection, for at least some, to appropriately defined works.

(4) **No recapture for zero-term works.** Under this theory, pursuant to Article 7(8), copyright recapture is not required for works that have a zero term of protection in the forum country. Article 7(8) provides that "the term shall be governed by the legislation of the country where protection is claimed." If the term of protection in the forum country is zero, this argument posits there is no obligation under Article 18 to allow copyright recapture. The weak point of this argument is paragraph (2) of Article 18. Only if a previously granted term has expired may the forum country decline to protect the work anew. The counter argument to the "zero-term" theory, therefore, insists that the provisions of Article 7(8) and Article 18 must be interpreted to give meaning to both, and the "zero-term" theory fails on this point.

---

[12] SEC. 12 of the Berne Implementation Act of 1988, Pub. L. 100-568, 102 Stat. 2853 (October 31, 1988).
[13] H.R. REP. 100-609, 100th Cong. 2d. Sess. 51-52 (1988).

4. Exceptions and Qualifications

On the assumption that Article 18 obligates a newly adhering Berne State to accord a moderate degree of copyright recapture, this chapter next explores the permissible exceptions and qualifications.

(1) **Previously granted copyright term.** Works that have enjoyed a normal term of copyright in the country of origin or in the forum country are not entitles to a "second bite of the apple" after copyright expires. Article 18(1) establishes that expiration of the copyright in the country of origin removes any obligation to allow recapture of the copyright. In like manner, Article 18(2) sets forth the rule that, after expiration of the copyright term in the forum country, the work shall not be protected anew.

Whether these rules include expiration of less than a full term of copyright, is subject to debate. Two cases arise under United States copyright law. An argument can be made that since the United States protected all unpublished works under common law before 1978, these works enjoyed a previously granted term of copyright, which expired upon publication. Arguably, no copyright recapture is required even if those works fell into the public domain upon publication for failure to comply with formalities. The second case also concerns pre-1978 works—works that were protected for the first term of copyright (28 years) and fell into the public domain for failure to comply with the renewal registration formality. Query whether Article 18(2) exempts these works from copyright recapture?

(2) **Special conventions or agreements.** The first sentence of Article 18(3) provides that the copyright recapture obligation is subject to existing or subsequent concluded "special conventions" between two or more Berne members. This phrase clearly includes bilateral as well as multilateral agreements, with an emphasis on bilaterals.

The copyright recapture agreements concluded between founding Berne members in the late nineteenth century are no longer in effect but have historical significance. The typical agreement permitted completion of printing and distribution of the copies in the process of reproduction when the bilateral affected copyright recapture.[14] Other bilaterals took various approaches: published musical works would be protected retroactively unless publicly performed in one of the countries;[15] persons who invested in public domain works were entitled to compensation through arbitration—otherwise, no liability for future infringements.[16] Other bilateral either excluded retroactive protection, were silent on retroactivity, or required retroactive protection, subject to various exceptions and conditions.[17]

German unification provides a modern example of a copyright recapture provision. Because of a 20-year difference in the copyright term under West and East German law, upon unification in 1990, retroactive protection was extended to East German works. All copyrights were extended to life of the author plus 70 years. Persons who had exploited the

[14] Ricketson, *supra* note 9 at 667.
[15] The 1884 bilateral between Germany and Italy is an example of this approach. Ricketson at 667.
[16] The law of Great Britain is an example of this approach. Geller, supra note 11, at INT-120.

public domain works before July 1, 1990, could continue exploitation provided they adequately compensated the copyright owners for use of the works.[18]

An argument can be made that the "special convention" qualification is broad enough to include a multilateral treaty such as the Universal Copyright Convention ("UCC").[19] Article VII of the UCC bars retroactive protection. Its application between members of both UCC and the Berne Convention arguably satisfies the language of Berne Article 18. Therefore, the United States arguably has no obligation to permit copyright recapture for works in its public domain when a Berne-UCC state became bound by the UCC. More than 50 countries are Berne-UCC states, including most countries in Europe, North America, and South America. As a founding member of the UCC, the United States became bound by it in 1995. If this interpretation of Berne Article 18 is valid, the United States has no obligation to permit copyright recapture of works in its public domain in 1955 that originated in 50-plus countries, including most of Europe and North and South America.

That the UCC is a special convention within the meaning of the Berne Article 18 is not, however, a settle interpretation. Some would argue that the UCC itself incorporates the firm principle that relations between states bound by both Berne and the UCC are controlled by Berne.[20] Also, pursuant to Berne Article 20, a special agreement is valid only if it grants authors more extensive rights than Berne or is not contrary to Berne. Query whether the UCC's flat prohibition of retroactive protection is "contrary to" the copyright recapture principle of Berne Article 18? Or is the UCC an Article 18 special convention, which may deal with copyright recapture by a complete denial of protection? Although complete denial of protection at first blush seems contrary to the principle in Article 18, the experience of the Berne founding members in concluding bilateral agreements suggests complete denial is an option. Some nineteenth century bilaterals between Berne members excluded copyright recapture.[21]

In any case, Article 18(3) apparently gives the discretion to member states to conclude bilateral agreements that exclude any retroactive protection, or that allow copyright recapture subject to a variety of limitations designed to protect the reliance rights of public domain entrepreneurs.

(3) **National Discretion if no Special Convention.** As noted, all of the early bilateral agreements between the founding Berne states have long since become moribund. Also, newly adhering states have apparently not resorted to the device of bilaterals to regulate copyright recapture.[22] If the newly adhering states have dealt with copyright recapture (and many have not), they have regulated it under the discretionary clause of the last sentence of Article 18(3): "the respective countries shall determine, each in so far as it is concerned, the conditions of application of this [copyright recapture] principle."

---

[17] Ricketson, *supra* note 19 at 667.

[18] Note, "Retroactive and Reliance Rights under Article 18 of the Berne Copyright Convention," 24 VAND.JOUR.TRANSNAT'L LAW 971, 984 (1991).

[19] *Id.* at 992.

[20] *See,* Art. XVII of the Universal Copyright Convention and the accompanying Appendix Declaration.

[21] Ricketson, *supra* note 13 at 666.

[22] As Ricketson notes, given current membership of the Berne Convention (90-plus members), it is no longer practical for a newly adhering country to enter bilateral arrangements with each of the other members. *Id.* at 674. A bilateral arrangement might be useful between the United States and a few other countries, but a regional approach, like NAFTA, is more likely.

Although the 1886 Berne Convention contemplated bilaterals as the primary device for effecting copyright recapture, a new adherent today would not be expected to enter separate bilateral agreements with the 90-plus countries now members of Berne. Therefore, retroactivity will be handled, if at all, by national legislation, usually without any bilateral or multilateral agreement.

Wide differences can be seen in the provision adopted by member countries to address copyright recapture.[23] The United Kingdom and Norway, for example, once maintained reservations about application of Article 18, that is, they delayed many years in providing for copyright recapture.[24] Norway made a commitment at the 1928 Rome Diplomatic Conference to withdraw its Article 18 reservation—after maintaining the reservation for 42 years.[25] The United Kingdom, when it finally legislated, required that the owners of the restored copyrights compensate those who held reliance rights. Persons who relied on the public domain of works and incurred expenses were entitled to compensation for that reliance under UK law, subject to arbitration; otherwise, there was no liability for post-adherence acts of exploitation of the restored copyrights.[26]

The United States recently legislated concerning copyright recapture of certain motion pictures pursuant to the North American Free Trade Agreement ("NAFTA"). The legislation allows copyright recapture in films published or fixed in Mexico or Canada, which fell into the United States public domain for failure to comply with the notice requirements in effect from January 1, 1978, (effective date of U.S. Berne adherence and U.S. abolition of mandatory notice). Copyright recapture is affected only if the copyright owner claims restoration rights by notifying the Copyright Office during calendar year 1994. The Copyright Office will publish a list of the restored copyrights early in 1995. Reliance rights are protected temporarily: no liability is incurred until one year after the publication of the list of restored copyrights.[27]

Works Affected by Copyright Recapture

Article 18 potentially impacts all works, originating in any of the 90-plus Berne member countries, which remain under copyright in the country of origin but reside in the public domain of a newly adhering Berne country.

The primary focus of Article 18 is on recapture of copyright in works that reside in the public domain of the newly adhering state, but whose country of origin is another Berne country.

In the case of the United States, however, many works originating in this country (whether authored by U.S. citizens or foreigners) fell into our public domain for failure to satisfy formalities. If the copyright term that would otherwise apply to these works has not expired, these works are also potentially eligible for copyright recapture under the law of the other Berne members.

[23] Ricketson, *supra* note 13 at 674.
[24] *Id.* at 676.
[25] *Ibid.*
[26] Geller, *supra* note 11, at INT-120.
[27] The North American Free Trade Agreement Implementation Act, Pub. L. 103-182 (December 8, 1993), SEC. 334.

It is therefore useful to analyze recapture of specific works from two standpoints: recapture from the United States public domain, and recapture from the public domain of other Berne countries.

1. Recapture from U.S. Public Domain

Because the United States maintained formalities as a condition of copyright for approximately 80 years longer than most members of Berne, the number of works potentially eligible for copyright recapture is great. Although notice of copyright was the predominant formality, works fell into the United States public domain for a variety of reasons. These reason include the following: publication of the work by a non-eligible foreign national in a non-UCC country; publication before 1978 in violation of the manufacturing clause applicable to certain books, periodicals, or graphic arts works; first publication anywhere complying with the notice provisions in effect from 1978 through March 1, 1989; and failure to effect timely renewal of the second term of copyright by registration with the Copyright Office.

United States adherence to the Universal Copyright Convention ("UCC") in 1955 established an important time line. The UCC significantly halted the flow of foreign works into the Unites States public domain in a number of ways. It increased the number of foreign authors eligible for U.S. copyright, abrogated the manufacturing clause for UCC works, and simplified and facilitated use of the copyright notice, thereby avoiding the entry of many works into the public domain. Also, since the core membership of the UCC overlaps with Berne membership, many fewer works originating in Berne countries fell into the U.S. public domain post 1955. Nevertheless, many works did lose copyright either be publication without notice or by failure to renew at the end of the original 28-year term.

In sum, a higher percentage of foreign works published between 1955 and 1978 in Berne-UCC states did not enter the U.S. public domain compared to works published before 1955. Probably, the more important copyrights were preserved, at least for the original 28-year term. The percentage of foreign-origin works that were renewed for the second term is substantially lower than the percentage of U.S. works renewed (which is approximately 15% of those registered for the first term). These works, published less than 40 years ago, would have remained under copyright but for the formalities of U.S. law and are potentially eligible for copyright recapture.

An even higher percentage of pre-1955 foreign works resides in the United States public domain. United States copyright obligations for foreign-origin works were determined primarily by bilateral agreements in the pre-1955 period. The bilaterals always required by bilateral observance of U.S. formalities as a condition of protection for foreign-origin works. Therefore, a very high percentage of pre-1955 foreign works entered the U.S. public domain upon their first publication. For some of these older works, of course, if copyright had been obtained, the term of copyright would have expired by now. Under United States law, the copyright in any work published before 1918 would have in any case expired by 1993. Article 18 does not require recapture of copyright in the latter works.

So far, this section of the report has focused on recapture of foreign works from the United States public domain. Those are the works directly impacted by Article 18. The Berne

Convention strictly only governs protection of foreign works.[28] The United States has no obligation under Berne with respect to works originating in the United States. If the United States should legislate to permit copyright recapture of foreign works, however, some interests (authors, for example) may seek to extend retroactivity to works of United States origin. Recapture of copyright in these works exceeds what would be required by Berne Article 18.

2. Recapture from Public Domain of Other Berne Countries

When we analyze the potential pool of United States origin works residing in the public domain of other Berne countries, the pre-1955 and 1955-1978 time lines remain significant but other considerations also become important. These include the "back-door" to Berne and each country's application of the comparison of terms option.

For Berne members, the 1908 Berlin Act abolished all formalities as a condition of the enjoyment or exercise of copyright. When the Berlin text became effective in the founding countries and when the new countries later adhered, all of these countries ceased to apply formalities against foreign Berne works. They could have maintained formalities against non-Berne works, but few have done so.

In general, for most Berne members after 1908, copyrights entered the public domain by reason of expiration of the copyright term, or because the work was first published in a non-Berne state and there was no other treaty obligation requiring protection.[29]

If the Berne country has a bilateral copyright relationship with a non-Berne state, like the United States before 1989, the United States authors presumably received formality-free protection from the Berne member. Absent a bilateral relationship, protection for the United States work must have been obtained, if at all, by means of the "back-door" to Berne, before Berne states also became members to UCC.

The Berne "back-door" refers to the country of origin principle that copyright protection attaches to a work based upon its first or simultaneous publication in a Berne country, irrespective of the nationality of the author of the work.[30] United States copyright owners and authors, especially of books, music, and motion pictures, have long sought to first publish in a Berne country like Canada. If there is adequate proof of first or simultaneous publication in a Berne country, the "back-door" to Berne is a solid method of obtaining protection in all countries of the Berne Union. The principle has been fully tested, however, in only a few instances, and the results have been mixed.

Resort to the Berne "back-door" became much less important for the United States authors when approximately 54 Berne countries became members of the Universal Copyright Convention[31] operated to apply the Berne copyright standards to UCC works in Country A where Country B is a member of both Berne and the UCC and country A is a member of only

---

[28] Art. 5(1) of the Berne Convention.

[29] As discussed earlier in the "country of origin" section of this chapter, the principal eligibility criterion for published works is the country of first publication. For certain categories of published works, however, different criteria apply. Also, in the case of unpublished works, the criterion of the nationality of the author applies.

[30] Art. 5(4) of the Berne Convention.

[31] Art. 5(1) of the Berne Convention.

the UCC. Moreover, Country B (the Berne-UCC state) did not impose formalities as a condition of protecting the UCC works because its national law reflected the Berne Convention prohibition for formalities. (The Berne-UCC state could have legislated to apply the UCC-permitted notice to non-Berne works, but none did.)

From these principles, we can discern that United States origin works presumably protected in Berne-UCC states from the date the other country became bound by the UCC, unless the term of copyright has expired. No U.S. origin works would have entered the public domain of a Berne-UCC state for reasons such as non-eligibility or failure to comply with formalities. There are more than 50 Berne-UCC countries, including the major copyright producing countries of Europe and North and South America.

Those Berne-only states that did not enter a bilateral relationship with the United States would have the greatest number of U.S. origin works in their public domains. Unless the "back-door" to Berne could be invoked to protect the U.S. works, such works would be in the public domain of the Berne-only states when the United States adhered to Berne in 1989 because there was no treaty obligation to protect U.S. works. Arguably, if the United States legislates to allow copyright recapture from its public domain, it will have substantial negotiating leverage to obtain reciprocal copyright restoration of U.S. works from the public domains of Berne-only states.

3. Categories of Works and Nature of Rights

The general provisions of Article 18 give no guidance about the categories of works or the nature of rights that should be subject to copyright recapture. Article 18 paints with a broad stroke. All of the important details are left to regulation by special conventions or to the discretion of national law. The sparse precedent of special conventions and national laws, and the opinions of commentators, are the only sources available to determine the application of the copyright recapture principle to categories of works and rights.

(1) **Full Recapture.** Certainly, one interpretation would allow full recapture of all works and complete restoration of rights, subject presumably to the application of the normal copyright term. According to Ricketson, this was the original intent of the 1886 Berne Act, Article 14 (precursor to Article 18).[32] The "reserves and conditions," if any, on full retroactivity, were to be narrow and were viewed as transitional in nature.

Very few states, however, have interpreted the copyright recapture obligation this broadly, notwithstanding the pressure from authors' groups to make retroactivity absolute.[33] The French Government, in preparing the first revision proposals to update the Berne Convention in 1896, proposed full retroactivity unless a state legislated exceptions under a short deadline. These proposals were dropped because of the strong opposition of the Germans and the British.[34]

---

[32] Ricketson, *supra* note 19, at 667.
[33] *Id.* at 669.
[34] *Ibid.*

(2) **Selective recapture of Certain Categories of Works.** Is the discretion to regulate copyright recapture by special conventions and national laws broad enough to allow selective recapture of copyright in certain categories of works and deny restoration to the remaining categories? For example, could the recapture be limited to music, motion pictures, and sound recordings? Or the books, periodicals, and other printed works?

At least one commentator, Ricketson, says no. You cannot deny copyright recapture for a particular class or classes of works.[35]

The early bilaterals of the founding Berne members, however, support the idea that you can select particular classes of works for recapture and, at least by silence, deny recapture for the remainder. The 1884 bilateral between Germany and Italy dealt with musical works.

The United States agreed to the NAFTA provision on copyright recapture as limited to motion pictures and the works embodied in them. The NAFTA is in effect a special convention within the meaning of Berne Article 18(3). The United States has acted on the assumption that Article 18 permits selective recapture of copyright in certain classes of works.

(3) **Selective Recapture of Certain Rights.** The wide discretion to regulate copyright recapture by special conventions and national laws under Article 18 has apparently also extended to selective recapture of certain rights. For example, the right to prepare derivative works might be limited to protect the reliance rights of those who prepared derivative works relying on the public domain status of the underlying work.

In general, the traditional rights of the copyright owner would be restored subject, however, to various limitations or qualifications on those rights to protect the reliance interests of public domain entrepreneurs and the public. It would be unjust to authors and copyright owners, and require complicated legislation, to extend certain rights and deny others completely, except to the limited degree necessary to protect legitimate reliance interests.

Policy Issues for the United States

In adhering to the Berne Convention in 1989, the United States elected to postpone to a future, undetermined time, the enactment of legislation effecting copyright recapture. Fiver years later, the issue may be addressed in the context of GATT implementing legislation. If the Congress decides to legislate, several difficult policy issues will probably have to be resolved. The major issues are:

- Scope of copyright recapture (works, duration, and deadlines)
- Rights of authors and copyright owners

[35] *Id.* at 675.

- Liabilities for post-recapture exploitation of pre-recapture copies
- Liabilities for post-recapture uses of public domain works
- Recapture of copyright for works that entered the public domain through failure of renewal registration
- Constitutional concerns

This chapter next explores the first five of the above issues. The constitutional concerns are of sufficient complexity to be addressed in a separate section.

1. Scope of Recapture: Works, Duration, and Time Limits

Congress will probably have to make decisions, if it legislates copyright recapture, about the specific works subject to recapture, the duration of the restored protection, and appropriate time limits to effect recapture from the public domain.

With respect to works, the possibilities are almost infinite. The NAFTA recapture provision, for example, applies only to a particular class of works (motion pictures, including the works embodied therein), if the work was produced or fixed in Mexico or Canada, and then only if the work entered the United States public domain between January 1, 1978 and March 1, 1989, because failure to comply with copyright notice requirements. Copyright is not recaptured in Canadian or Mexican motion pictures that entered the United States public domain before 1978, or that lost copyright for any reason other than nonobservance of the notice formality.

The discretion to include certain works and exclude others from copyright recapture is arguably broader in the case of special conventions than in the case of unilateral, national legislation. The special convention, whether bilateral or multilateral, is an agreement among sovereign nations, in which concessions have likely been made by each party to reach the agreement. If sovereign countries agree on the works subject to copyright recapture, that agreement is justification for exclusion of certain works from recapture. Presumably, each party has acted on the basis of its national interests, and has duly considered the claims of authors and copyright owners for broader copyright recapture.

Assuming that it is appropriate to allow copyright recapture only for certain works, the following general criteria might be applied to select the particular works:

- **by categories of authorship** (books, music, motion pictures, computer programs, etc.);

- **by points of attachment** (nationality of the author, place of first publication, place of fixation, place of making, etc.);

- **by the reason the work entered the public domain;** and

- **by the date of the publication or other date the work entered the public domain.**

After selecting the works eligible for recapture, the Congress would presumably address the questions related to duration of the restored copyrights.

The most common duration provision restores the ordinary term of copyright that would have applied to the work had it not fallen into the public domain. The years the work resides in the public domain are ordinarily lost years of protection. On copyright recapture, those lost years would not be added to the term of copyright in order to make up the lost time.

If the Congress did wish, as a matter of fairness to authors, to restore some of the "lost years," a period of 10, 15, or 20 years might be added to the term otherwise applied to restored copyrights. For some authors, an extension for a fixed term might provide a "bonanza;" for others, depending upon the years in the public domain, the extension may still fall short of full term protection.

Another approach would set a minimum period of years post-recapture during which the work would be protected, irrespective of the expiration of its normal term of copyright.

Finally, with respect to scope of copyright restoration, the Congress may wish to establish some procedures and time limits under which the specific restored copyrights can be identified. In implementing the NAFTA copyright recapture provision, the United States required the claimants of the works to file with the Copyright Office during a one-year period. The Copyright Office will then publish a list of the restored copyrights to confirm the restoration and give notice to the public.

2. Rights of Copyright Owners

Ordinarily, copyright recapture legislation would restore to authors and other owners of copyright the normal exclusive rights granted by the national copyright law to works in the same authorship category. Under United States law, those are the rights of reproduction, public distribution, adaptation, public performance, and public display.

There seems to be no reason to withhold from authors and copyright owners of restored copyrights the normal exclusive rights extended to other authors and copyright owners. Appropriate limitations on the rights to protect reliance interests can be addressed, as discussed below, without complete denial of a particular right.

3. Liability for Post–Recapture Exploitation of Pre-Recapture Copies

The most difficult copyright recapture policy issues concern the balance between the rights of authors-copyright owners, and the rights of the public freely to exploit the public domain. Those who relied on the public domain status of a work to invest money, time, and effort in marketing the work, and perhaps even prepare and market a copyrightable new version of the work, acquire reliance rights. Considerations of equity suggest that holders of reliance rights should generally be subject to reduced liability for copyright infringement post-recapture.

A "typical" provision to protect reliance rights allows completion of printing and distribution of copies in the process of reproduction, or already reproduced, when copyright recapture is permitted. Sometimes these exceptions to the distribution right of copyright owners are subject to strict time limits and/or to payment of some reasonable royalty.[36]

4. Liability for Post-Recapture Uses in General

In addition to the limitations on the distribution right with respect to pre-recapture copies, a variety of other limitations may be considered.

The most compelling cases involve derivative works prepared as new versions of public domain works, which are later subject to copyright recapture. Should an exemption from all copyright liability be accorded the creators of such derivative works? Or, should the derivative work creator be permitted to exploit the derivative work, subject to a reasonable royalty (fixed by arbitration or a court, if necessary)? Or, should the period of exploitation be limited to the term of years to recoup any investment and make a reasonable profit?

Other public domain entrepreneurs may have substantial investments in packaging and marketing the public domain works, although they did not contribute copyrightable authorship to the creation of derivative work. Should their reliance rights be recognized through reduced copyright liability? Again, the solutions include statutory licenses with a right of remunerable, or a grace period of non-liability for several years to recoup the investment with or without remuneration to the owner of the restored copyright.

5. Unrenewed Public Domain Works

The policy issues discussed above face any legislature when considering copyright recapture. The United States Congress will probably be asked to consider an additional issue, unique to the United States copyright system: copyright recapture of pre-1978 works not renewed for the second term of copyright.

Before 1978, copyright for an original term of 28 years from publication (or registration if copyright was obtained by registration of an unpublished work). The copyright expired after 28 years and the work fell into the public domain unless timely renewal registration was made with the Copyright Office during the last year of the original term.[37] Renewed copyrights enjoyed a second term of protection, which was originally 28 years and was extended to 47 years in 1978.

When Congress enacted the general copyright revision in 1976[38] (effective January 1, 1978), the term for newly copyrighted works became life of the author plus 50 years in general.[39] Pre-1978 copyrighted works, however, remained subject to the dual term, renewal registration system[40] until June 26, 1992.[41] Since only about 15-20 percent of works

---

[36] Ricketson, *supra* note 9, at 667.

[37] Section 24 of the 1909 Copyright Act, title 17 of the U.S. Code in effect on December 31, 1977.

[38] The Copyright Act of 1976, Pub. L. 94-553, 90 Stat, 2541 (October 19, 1976), codified as title 17 of the U.S. Code.

[39] Section 302 of the 1976 Copyright Act.

[40] Section 304 of the 1976 Copyright Act.

[41] Congress abolished the mandatory renewal registration system by the Act of June 26, 1992, Pub. L. 102-307, 106 Stat. 264. The law applies prospectively and provides for automatic copyright renewal of works originally

registered for the first term of copyright obtained renewal for the second term, before 1922 the bulk of copyrighted works entered the public domain of the United States after enjoying copyright for 28 years.

Should the United States restore the second term of copyright in foreign works that entered the United States public domain before 1992 because of failure to make registration for the second copyright term?

Under the theory for interpreting Berne Article 18, there is no obligation to permit copyright recapture of unrenewed works because they fell into the public domain by expiration of their term of copyright. In any case, the disparity in length of protection is addressed by the comparison of terms rules. The forum country can apply the shorter term.

The opposing view contends that the references in Article 18(1) and (2) to "expiry of the term of protection," clearly mean expiration of the full copyright term—not a term shortened by failure to satisfy a formality prohibited by the Berne Convention. Under this viewpoint, the comparison of terms rule may satisfy governmental notions of reciprocity, but fails to accord authors a reasonable term of copyright protection in the case of unrenewed works. Since a 28-year term is much shorter than the minimum Berne term (except for photographs and works of applied art), it is argued that, fairness to authors requires copyright recapture of the second term of unrenewed works.

The most compelling case for copyright recapture of unrenewed works exist for those foreign works that fell into the United States public domain between March 1, 1989 and January 1, 1992. (That is, those foreign works that should have been renewed in the years 1989, 1990, and 1991.) All commentators seem to agree that the United States renewal registration formality in effect until June 26, 1992, was inconsistent with the obligations under the Berne Convention,[42] which the United States assumed March 1, 1989. In general, those works should have enjoyed a term based on the life of the author plus 50 years[43] (or nearly equivalent 75 years), instead of a 28-year period of protection. This full-term protection should have been available since March 1, 1989, without compliance with formalities.[44]

Finally, even if the United States concludes that it has no legal obligation under Berne to restore copyright in unrenewed works, restoration may become a bargaining chip in trade-related negotiations. If copyright recapture were extended to unrenewed works of foreign origin, United States authors would not benefit from this restoration, unless Congress also were to take the highly controversial step of restoring copyright in United States origin works that were nor renewed for the second term.

CONSTITUTIONAL CONCERNS

In considering copyright recapture of public domain works, the United States faces several unique problems. In addition to the unprecedented number of works potentially eligible for

copyrighted between January 1, 1964 and December 31, 1977. The automatic extension of the term for 47 years creates a full copyright term of 75 years for these pre-1978 copyrights.

[42] "Final Report of the Ad Hoc Working Group on U.S. Adherence to the Berne Convention," 10 COL.VLA JOUR. LAW & THE ARTS 513, 581 (1986).

[43] Art. 7 of the Berne Convention.

[44] Art. 5(2) of the Berne Convention.

copyright recapture and the complications of unrenewed works, the Congress would need to consider possible constitutional limitations on its ability to take works out of the public domain.

Constitutional concerns about recapture of copyright in public domain works may arise under the First Amendment's Free Speech-Freedom of the Press Clauses; the Patent-Copyright Clause of Article 1, Sec. 8, Cl. 8; the Contracts Clause of Article 1, Sec. 10, Cl. 1; the Ex Post Facto Clause of Article 1, Sec. 9, Cl. 3; the Due Process Clause of the Fifth Amendment; or the Takings Clause of the Fifth Amendment. Of these, the most serious concerns relate to the Ex Post Facto and Takings Clauses.

1. Ex Post Facto Clause

The Ex Post Facto Clause [U.S. Const. Art. I, Sec. 9, cl. 3] prohibits retroactive application of the criminal law. The Copyright Act contains criminal infringement provisions, which are enforced by the Criminal Code, title 18 U.S.C. Any copyright recapture legislation would nee to make clear there is no criminal liability for acts of "copyright infringement" undertaken before recapture. Care also would need to be taken with respect to acts commencing before recapture and continuing after recapture.

2. Takings Clause

The Fifth Amendment of the U.S. Constitution prohibits the taking of "private property ...for use without just compensation." The "Takings Clause" presents the most significant potential hurdle for the Congress in legislating copyright recapture of public domain works. The clause operates to inhibit the Congress from placing burdens on some citizens that, in fairness, should be borne by the public as a whole.[45]

The government has broad discretion to regulate the appropriate balance between the interest of individual property holders and the public interest in achieving certain policy objectives. Not every taking requires compensation.

Two primary issues must be addressed in evaluating the likely constitutionality of copyright recapture legislation:

> First, to what extent would the recapture legislation affect a "property" interest?
>
> Second, does the governmental action amount to an unconstitutional taking of any property?

[45] *National Board of Young Men's Christian Association v. United States,* 395 U.S. 85 (1969); *Agins v. City of Tiburon,* 447 U.S. 255, 260-261 (1980).

(1) **Property interests affected by recapture.** Public domain works are exploited by the public in various ways, including reproduction of copies and their distribution, preparation of new versions, and public performance or public display. The possible property interest involved include expectancies; vested rights acquired by creation of new versions; rights acquired by inheritance, gift, or purchase; and investment-based rights. With the exception of expectancies, each of these rights categories may constitute a "property" interest whose uncompensated taking may be unlawful under certain circumstances.

A mere expectancy is not a property interest covered by the Takings Clause since reliance rights have not been established. *Freese v. United States,* 639 F. 2d 754 (Ct. Cl. 1981) (federal law terminating right of mining claimholders to "patent" title to federal land upheld since the opportunity to apply for a patent is not a vested right).

The Takings Clause applies most strictly to land-based property rights, but it is clearly not restricted to real property claims. In *Rchelshaus v. Monsanto Co.,* 467 U.S. 986 (1984), the Court protected trade secrets in health safety data against an uncompensated, retroactive taking, even though private competitors of Monsanto, and not the general public, were the direct beneficiaries. Since the governmental regulation required disclosure—an act that expunged any trade secret right—the private property was take for public use, for which the Fifth Amendment requires just compensation.

Copyright recapture legislation most clearly implicates the Takings Clause if the law expunges copyrights in derivative versions of works recaptured from the public domain. The constitutionality of the law may be established by providing "just compensation," perhaps through an arbitration procedure or a grace period during which the right in the derivative work can be exploited to recoup any investment.

(2) **Is the governmental action a taking?** The Supreme Court has eschewed development of any formula for identifying when an unconstitutional taking occurs. The Court relies instead on ad hoc, factual inquiries, which are influenced by the following factors: the economic impact of the governmental regulation on the claimant; the extent to which the governmental regulation interferes with distinct investment-backed expectations; and the character of the governmental action. *Connolly v. Pension Benefit Guaranty Corp.,* 475 U.S. 211, 225 (1986).

In cases of permanent physical occupation or intrusion of real property, the governmental action invariably is considered a taking without regard to the public interests intended to be served. *Loretta v. Teleprompter Manhattan CATV Corp.,* 458 U.S. 419, 426-27 (1982) (city ordinance requiring landlords to allow intrusion of cable wires in their buildings held taking requiring compensation); *Dolan v. City of Tigard,* 93-518, __S.Ct.__(decided June 24, 1994) (city's restriction on building permit for hardware store expansion requiring recreational easement for adjacent pedestrian/bicycle path constitutes uncompensated taking in violation of the Takings Clause); *Hodel v. Irving,* 481 U.S. 704 (1987) (federal law abrogating rights of descent and devise in small undivided property interests in Indian lands held unconstitutional taking).

Physical occupation or permanent regular use of real property constitutes a taking because the governmental use tends to exclude all other uses. The nature of real property lends itself to exclusionary use. If the governmental use does not "swallow up" the entire property right, the Court tends to find there has been no taking. *Hodel v. Indiana,* 452 U.S. 314 (1981) (regulation of surface mining of prime farmland not a taking because the law did not prohibit surface mining and did not deprive the owner of other economically beneficial uses); *Pennell v. City of San Jose,* 485 U.S. 1 (1988) (city rent control ordinance held constitutional even though board has power to reduce rent for hardship tenants).[46]

Copyright, an intangible property right consists of a bundle of separately exploitable rights. Governmental regulation of copyright can therefore be crafted to avoid a taking by leaving some economically beneficial uses untouched. Like the regulation of bird feathers in *Andrus v. Allard,* 444 U.S. 51 (1979), governmental regulation of copyrights may avoid characterization as a taking if the regulation does not destroy all the strands in the copyright bundle of rights. In *Andrus,* the Court upheld retroactive application of prohibitions on the sale of bird artifacts—the most economically beneficial use—on the ground that the owners retained the rights to possess (and therefore display publicly) and transport their property. Reduction in the value of the property is not necessarily a taking, and the "interest in anticipated gains has traditionally been viewed as less compelling than other property-related interests." 444 U.S. at 66.

Application of these general Takings Clause principles to recapture of copyrights in public domain works leads to these general conclusions:

1. Complete abrogation of intellectual property rights in copyrighted derivative versions of the public domain work without any compensation to the rights holder probably constitutes and unconstitutional taking;

2. Copyright restoration that retroactively destroys investment-backed interests in the exploitation of the public domain work may constitute an unconstitutional taking;

3. Copyright restoration that retroactively destroys expectancies or other anticipated gains not backed by investments does not constitute a taking;

4. Preservation of the physical property right in material objects embodying public domain works by itself may not be sufficient to avoid an unconstitutional taking;

5. The constitutionality of copyright recapture legislation can probably be assured in cases one and two above either by an arbitration-

---

[46] For a comprehensive analysis of the Takings Clause, see "When the United States Takes Property: Legal Principles," CRS Report No. 91-339A by Robert Meltz.

compensation provision or by a grace period of several years during which the category one and two claimants can exploit their rights in the works designated for copyright recapture without any liability for copyright infringement.

3. Contracts Clause

Article 1, Sec. 10, clause 1 (the Contracts Clause) provides that "[n]o State shall...pass any...Law impairing the Obligation of Contracts..." The literal text imposes an obligation on the States and not on the federal government. The Supreme Court in *Pension Benefit Guaranty Corp. v. R.A. Gray & Co.,* 467 U.S. 717 (1984) held the Contracts Clause does not apply to actions of the federal government. Therefore, federal legislation allowing the recapture of copyright in public domain works would not implicate the Contracts Clause.

Although federal recapture legislation would not be subject to the Contract Clause, the Congress may as a matter of good policy, nevertheless, wish to consider special provisions or exceptions to minimize the impairment of contracts. A general grace period of a few years duration would minimize any impairment of rights acquired by purchase.

4. Patent-Copyright Clause

Authority for Congress to legislate in the copyright field has its source in the Patent-Copyright Clause of the U.S. Constitution [art 1, Sec. 8, cl.8]. Congress has the power to "promote the process of science and useful arts, by securing, for limited times, to authors and inventors, the exclusive rights to their respective writings and discoveries."

Does the "limited times" constraint on congressional copyright authority inhibit the power to restore copyright in public domain works?

The few precedents that exist suggest the answer is "no," especially if the recapture legislation merely restores protection for the remainder of the normal term of copyright.

Congress passed public laws twice in this century to restore copyright in works that may have fallen into the public domain because wartime conditions made it difficult or impossible to comply with copyright formalities.[47] In each case, Congress provided a grace period or "savings clause" to protect those who had acted in reliance on the public domain status of the recaptured works. The constitutionality of these recapture laws was never challenged.

Nor does the "limited times" provision significantly inhibit congressional authority to extend the term of subsisting copyrights. In the 1976 general revision of the copyright laws, Congress extended the term of all subsisting copyrights by 19 years. No one has litigated the question of Congress' authority to extend the term of subsisting copyrights. Of course, the "limited times" provision would be violated presumably by an excessive term of protection.

[47] The Act of December 18, 1919, 41 Stat. 368 (World War I works); Act of September 25, 1941, 55 Stat. 732 (World War II works).

Recapture legislation to restore the normal term or add a few years to the copyright term, however, would not seem to violate the "limited times" provision.

5. First Amendment's Free Speech-Freedom of Press Clause

At least one eminent copyright authority, the late Melville Nimmer in his copyright treatise posits that retrieval of works from the public domain may violate the First Amendment rights of freedom of speech and of the press.[48]

This thesis is based solely on sweeping language in one patent case decided by the Supreme Court. In *Graham v. John Deere Co.,* 383 U.S. 1 (1966), the Court said that "Congress may not authorize the issuance of patents whose effects are to remove existent knowledge from the public domain, or to restrict free access to materials already available." 383 U.S. at 6. Patent protection however is broader than copyright protection. The former protects concepts, discoveries, and ideas in concrete applications. Copyright protects only against copying the protected expression. The ideas, concepts, discoveries, or facts are not protected by copyright. Copyright restoration arguably does not "remove existent knowledge from the public domain."

Copyright restoration does inhibit "free access to materials already available," but only with respect to the original expression in those materials. Recent copyright decisions of the Supreme Court indicate there is no conflict between the objectives of the First Amendment and the Patent-Copyright Clause. In *Harper & Row v. National Enterprises,* 471 U.S. 539 (1985), the Court said, "the Framers intended copyright itself to be the engine of free expression." 471 U.S. at 558. Also, "copyright supplies the economic incentive to create and disseminate ideas." *Ibid.*

Since the information and ideas contained in the recaptured works could be readily available, recapture of copyright in the public domain works would not seem to conflict with the First Amendment's freedom of expression principle. To the contrary, the Supreme Court has recognized that copyright is a positive force in the creation and dissemination of the ideas.

6. Due Process Clause of the Fifth Amendment

Challenges to retroactive legislation under the Due Process Clause are much less successful than challenges under the Taking Clause. The general standard applied by the Supreme Court is that the governmental action must be in furtherance of a legitimate legislative purpose and Congress must see rational means to achieve its purpose. *Pension Benefit Guaranty Corp. v. R.A. Gray & Co.,* 467 U.S. 717 (1984). Unless Congress is found to act in an "arbitrary and irrational way," legislation "adjusting the burdens and benefits of economic life" will pass constitutional muster. *Usery v. Turner-Elkhorn Mining Co.,* 428 U.S. 1, 15 (1976).

The individual who attacks the constitutionality of retroactive civil legislation on due process grounds bears the burden of showing Congress acted "arbitrarily and irrationally." *United States v. Locke,* 471 U.S. 84 (1985). The regulations on the exercise of rights need

---

[48] M. NIMMER, NIMMER ON COPYRIGHT, Sec. 1.05 at I-36.2 (1993).

only be "reasonable restrictions designed to further legitimate legislative objectives..." *Id.* at 104.

The obligations of the United States under the Berne's Article 18 arguably provide ample justification for any copyright recapture legislation to satisfy the Due Process Clause. Additional justification, if necessary, could be found in the public benefits of promoting the rights of American copyright holders and authors abroad, lowering the trade deficit, reducing piracy of American works abroad, and fostering international goodwill and comity.

CONCLUSION

The Congress may consider, as a part of the legislation to implement GATT 1994, a provision permitting recapture of copyright in certain public domain works. Such a provision is not required by the GATT 1994, but may be proposed to facilitate future bilateral and regional negotiations. Copyright recapture legislation, while not unprecedented, is a rare phenomenon. The proposal presents legal, constitutional, and practical issues, which have been analyzed in the report.

Article 18 of the Berne Convention contains rather vague, circular language concerning retroactive protection of works that remain under copyright in their countries of origin but reside in the public domain of a country when it adheres to the Convention. Despite the vague language, most interpreters agree that Article 18 creates an obligations to restore in at least some of these public domain works, if the ordinary term of copyright has not expired either in the country of origin or in the country where protection is sought.

The United States adhered to the Berne Convention on March 1, 1989, and enacted implementing legislation, which deliberately failed to allow recapture of any works from the public domain. The Convention clearly allows each country considerable latitude and discretion in carrying out the obligations of Article 18 through special conventions (that is, bilateral agreements generally) or, in their absence, national law.

There are few relevant precedents to serve as guidelines for the implementation of Article 18. In the end, each country's national self-interest, including the interests of those who benefit and those who are disadvantaged by copyright recapture, determine when to legislate, if at all. Those same national interests will determine the nature, scope, and duration of the restored copyrights and limitations thereon.

Because the United States maintained formalities as conditions of the enjoyment and exercise of copyright for nearly 80 years longer than most countries, the number of works in our public domain potentially eligible for copyright recapture greatly exceeds that of other recent adherents to the Berne Convention. In addition, Americans in greater numbers have tended to exploit the public domain and, therefore, may be thought to hold reliance rights that are entitled in some measure to compensation, if copyrights are restored. Our written Constitution also may restrict the power of the Congress to legislate retroactive protection of the public domain works.

Copyright recapture legislation most clearly implicates the Takings Clause if the law should expunge copyrights in derivative versions of works recaptured from the public domain. The constitutionality of the law may be preserved by providing "just compensation" for any taking. The most promising alternatives are: arbitration procedures to establish just compensation, or a grace period of non-liability during which the holder of reliance rights can exploit the former public domain works sufficiently to recoup any investment made before the effective date of the recapture legislation.

The treaty obligations of the United States under the Berne Convention arguably provide ample justification for copyright recapture legislation to satisfy any due process concerns and to establish the rational basis for the legislation. The public benefits engendered through the promotion of rights of American copyright holders and authors abroad, lowering of the trade deficit, reduction of piracy of American works, and advancement of international goodwill, provide additional justification for copyright recapture legislation. Congress will be asked to balance these benefits against the negative effects that may result from a diminished public domain.

THE "WORK MADE FOR HIRE AND COPYRIGHT CORRECTIONS ACT OF 2000"

Robin Jeweler

BACKGROUND

A "work for hire" under the Copyright Act makes an exception to the general rule that the person who creates a work is the author of that work for copyright purposes. If a work is made for hire, the employer or entity that commissioned the work—not the employee or creator—is considered the author.[1]

Section 101 of the Act defines the term in subsection (1) as embodying the product arising from an employer-employee relationship. If a work is created outside of the employer-employee relationship, it may still qualify as a "work for hire" under subsection (2) which deals with specially ordered or commissioned works.[2] Two requirements of works for hire under subsection (2) are that: (1) the work must come within one of the ten categories of work listed in the definition, and (2) the parties must have an express written agreement designating the work as one for hire. When a work qualifies, the employer is the "author" and the legal owner of the copyright interest.

The Copyright Act grants authors the right to transfer all of their exclusive rights, and in certain specific instances, a right to *terminate* the transfer. The termination right is intended to safeguard authors against unrenumerative transfers arising from an historic unequal bargaining power. It permits the author to determine the value of the work after it has been fully exploited and to renegotiate a transfer of exclusive rights to enable the author to share in

---

[1]U.S. Copyright Office, Circular 9, *Works made for Hire Under the 1976 Copyright Act* at [www.loc.gov/copyright].

[2]17 U.S.C. 101 provides that a "work made for hire" is:

a work prepared by an employee within the scope of his or her employment; or

a work specially ordered or commissioned for use as a contribution to a collective work, as part of a motion picture or other audiovisual work, as a translation, as a supplementary work, as a compilation, as an instructional text, as a test, as answer material for a test, or as an atlas, if the parties expressly agree in an instrument signed by them that the work shall be considered a work made for hire. For the purpose of the foregoing sentence, a "supplementary work" is a work prepared for publication as a secondary adjunct to a work by another author for the purpose of introducing, concluding, illustrating, explaining, revising, commenting upon, or assisting in the editorial notes, musical arrangements the greatly appreciated value of an important work. Works made for hire, however, are *not* subject to the termination right. Parties may, by express agreement, vary the rights, which would otherwise by owned by the employer in a work for hire under §101(1).[3] In settings other than an employer-employee relationship governed by § 101(1), however, if the relationship between the parties is not that will otherwise qualify as a specially commissioned work for hire under § 101(2), the agreement that the work shall be regarded as such will *not* be effective to avoid the creative author's termination right.[4]

Termination of grants copyright executed on or after January 1, 1978, could begin in 2013. Termination of transfers of copyrights in sound recordings executed before January 1, 1978, could be effective in 2028.[5]

SOUND RECORDINGS AS WORKS FOR HIRE

In 1999, in the Satellite Home Viewer Improvement Act,[6] Congress amended the definition of a "work made for hire" to include sound recordings. The amendment was made pursuant to the "Technical Amendments" Title of the Act. After enactment, however, the provision was criticized for being a "substantive" amendment effected without adequate public input and review.[7]

Prior to the amendment in 1999, sound recordings were *not* expressly included in the categories of work "specially ordered or commissioned" in subparagraph (2). Whether the change was "technical" or "substantive" proved to be controversial. The House Judiciary Subcommittee on Courts & Intellectual Property held a hearing on May 25, 2000, on the effect of the amendment. Witnesses were not generally in agreement. Distilled to its essence, the issue is as follows: The recording industry and its performing artist routinely treat sound recordings as works for hire. There are currently many sound recordings filed with the U.S. Copyright Office as specially commissioned works for hire. The U.S. Copyright Office, however, merely accepts the registration and does not inquire whether a sound recording meets all of the requirements of a work for hire.[8] Some argue that because a sound recording was not specifically listed in subparagraph (2) prior to the 1999 amendment, it *could not* be specially commissioned work for hire pursuant thereto.[9] Others contend that sound

---

[3] 1 Melville B. Nimmer & David Nimmer, NIMMER ON COPYRIGHT §§1.06[C] & 5.03[D](1999).

[4] 3 NIMMER OF COPYRIGHT §11.02[A][2] (1999).

[5] 17 U.S.C. §§ 203, 304. Sec. 203 allows specified transfers executed on or after January 1, 1978, to be terminated after 35 years. Therefore, termination of grants made in 1978 could begin in 2013. Sec. 304 applies to transfers executed before January 1, 1978. Because sound recordings were first eligible for copyright protection in 1972, terminations under § 304 could begin in 2028.

[6] P.L. 106-113 (November 29, 1999), the Intellectual Property and Communications Omnibus Reform Act of 1999, Title I, § 1101(d).

[7] *House Panel Considers Undoing 1999 Copyright Amendment,* BNA Patent, Trademark & Copyright J. 87 (June 2, 2000)

[8] *See* Testimony of Marybeth Peters, Register of Copyrights before the House Subcommittee on Court and Intellectual Property at [http://www.house.gov/judiciary/petework.htm], May 25, 2000.

[9] *See* Lulirama Ltd. V. Axcess Broadcast Services, 128 F.3d 872 (5th Cir. 1997)(musical jingles do not qualify as works specially commissioned for use as part of "a motion picture or other audiovisual work"); Staggers v. Real Authentic Sound, 77 F. Supp.2d 57 (D.C. 1999)(a sound recording does not fit within any of the nine pre-1999 categories of "specially ordered or commissioned works"). *See also* 1 NIMMER ON COPYRIGHT § 2.10[A][3](absent an employment relationship or express assignment of copyright from the performer to the

recordings already qualifies under subparagraph (2) as "contributions to collective works." Therefore, the addition of "sound recordings" as a discrete category did not materially change their status within the rubric of "work for hire."[10]

The question is ultimately an important one, because if they *are* works for hire under the Copyright Act, neither individual nor joint "authors" may exercise the termination rights that they might enjoy in the absence of work for hire status. And, because termination rights for authors of sound recordings will not mature until 2028, courts have not yet begun to consider the issue.[11] Yet, even though an author's termination rights in a sound recording are not likely to ripen before 2028, the question may reach the courts in other contexts before then. It is reported the MP3.com is challenging recording companies' work for hire ownership of sound recordings in connection with damages awarded by a court against it in ongoing copyright infringement litigation.[12]

Nevertheless, the broad question—whether, prior to the 1999 amendment, a sound recording qualified as specially commissioned work for hire for purposes of an author's termination right—is not settled.

Acknowledging the controversy generated by the amendment, Congress deleted "sound recordings" from the list of categories in §101(2) a year after they were added in the "Work Made for Hire and Copyright Corrections Act of 2000."[13] Interestingly, the corrective" legislation is definitive in *declining* to resolve the outstanding question whether sound recordings qualify as works for hire under other classifications of §101(2). The law adds new language to the definition specifying:

In determining whether any work is eligible to be considered a work made for hire under paragraph (2), neither the amendment contained in section 1011(d) of the Intellectual Property and Communications Omnibus Reform Act of 1999, as enacted by section 1000(a)(9) of Public Law 106-113, nor the deletion of the words added by that amendment—

(A) shall be considered or otherwise given any legal significance, or

(B) shall be interpreted to indicate congressional approval or disapproval of, or acquiescence in, any judicial determination, by the courts or the Copyright Office. Paragraph (2) shall be interpreted as if both section 2(a)(1) of the Work Made for Hire and Copyright Corrections Act of 2000 and section 1011(d) of the Intellectual Property and Communications Omnibus Reform Act of 1999, as enacted by section 1000(a)(9) of Public Law 106-113, were never enacted, and without regard to any inaction or awareness by the Congress at any time of any judicial determinations.[14]

---

record producer, ownership of a sound recording will either be exclusively in the performing artists, or ... a joint ownership between the record producer and the recording artist.)

[10]*See* Testimony of Paul Goldstein, Lillick Professor of Law, Stanford University, before the House Subcommittee on Courts and Intellectual Property at [http://www.house.gov/judiciary/gold0525.htm], May 25, 2000.

[11]Testimony of Marybeth Peters, *supra* note 8.

[12]*New Work-for-Hire Legislation Will Get Early Test in MPs Case,* 61 BNA Patent, Trademark & Copyright J., Number 1947 (Nov. 3, 2000).

[13]P.L. 106-379 (October 27, 2000).

[14]*Id.*, § 2.

Thus, at such time when a court is confronted with the question whether a sound recording can be a work for hire, it is directed to specifically *disregard* the 1999 and 2000 amendments as a component of the provision's legislative history evincing congressional intent.

Committee report language accompanying H.R. 5107, the bill enacted, explains that the purpose of the amendment "is to restore the status quo as it existed before November 29, 1999, as to the issue of whether a sound recording can qualify as a 'work for hire' under the second part of the definition of that term in section 101 of the Copyright Act, and to do so in a manner that does nor prejudice any person or entity that might have interests concerning this question."[15] The amendment made by the Act is expressly retroactive to November 29, 1999.

[15]H. Rept. 106-861, 106th Cong., 2d Sess. 1 (2000).

NEW YORK TIMES CO. V. TASINI: THE U.S. SUPREME COURT AFFIRMS "AUTHORIAL" RIGHTS IN COPYRIGHT

Robin Jeweler

BACKGROUND

Jonathan Tasini and five freelance writers brought suit against the New York Times, Newsday and Time, Inc. (Print Publishers) for copyright infringement as a consequence of the inclusion of their articles in electronic databases. The Print Publishers licensed rights to print and sell articles to LEXIS/NEXIS and University Microfilms International (UMI)(Electronic Publishers), who placed the articles in the electronic databases: LEXIS, the New York Times OnDisc (NYTO), and General Periodicals OnDisc (GPO). UMI issued CD-ROM products. NYTO is a text-only database containing Times articles presented in the same manner as they are displayed in LEXIS/NEXIS; GPO is an image-based system that reproduces the Time's Sunday Book Review and Magazine as they appear in the print editions, complete with photographs, captions, advertisements, and other surrounding material. In both NYTO and GPO, as in LEXIS/NEXIS, the articles retrieved by users appear individually, without links to the original publication.

The writers brought suit in a U.S. district court alleging copyright infringement by both the Print Publishers and the Electronic Publishers. Plaintiffs sought declaratory and injunctive relief and damages. As a defense, the publishers asserted the privilege to include a copyrighted work in a revision of the collective work. The privilege is accorded publishers under 17 U.S.C. §201(c) of the Copyright Act, which provides:

> Copyright in each separate contribution to a collective work is distinct from copyright in the collective work as a whole, and vests initially in the author to the contribution. In the absence of an express transfer of the copyright or of any rights under it, the owner of copyright in the collective work is presumed to have acquired only the privilege of reproducing and distributing the contribution as part of that particular collective work, any revision of that collective work, and any later collective work in the same series.

The district court issued a summary judgment in favor of the publishers, holding that the databases were "part of...[a] revision of that collective work." The Second Circuit Court of Appeals reversed, holding that the databases were not among the collective works covered by §201(c), and specifically were not revisions of periodicals in which the articles were originally published.

THE COURT'S DECISION

In a 7-2 decision prepared by Justice Ginsburg, the Court examined the legislative history of the authorial rights of freelance writers and explained why the electronic databases are not, in the Court's view, "revisions" of the original collective works.

Prior to enactment of the current copyright law in 1976, a freelance author's contribution to a collective work was preserved only if the article was published with a copyright notice in the author's name. Since this was rarely done—or because the notice appeared only in the publisher's name—a freelance author's contribution to a collective work could easily fall into the public domain. Thus, even though a freelance writer could theoretically retain a copyright interest in a contribution to a collective work, the right was easily relinquished or unenforceable.

In the 1976 Copyright Act, Congress acted to remedy this perceived inequity. The law specifies that a single notice applicable to a collective work as a whole is sufficient to protect the rights of freelance authors.[1] Further, it expressly provides that an exclusive right, including a subdivision of any right, may be transferred and owned separately.[2] And, the provision of § 201(c), quoted above, expressly provides that the copyright in a contribution of a collective work is *distinct* from the rights in the work as a whole. It describes and *limits* the "privilege" a publisher acquires regarding an author's contribution to a collective work. This adjustment in the rights between the freelance author and the publisher, the Court explained, is designed to accommodate a freelancer's copyright in her contribution. After authorizing the initial publication, the freelance author may resell the article to others. Because the 1976 Copyright Act clearly demonstrates congressional intent to protect the divisible but retained copyright interest of the freelancer in an article that is initially published as part of a collective work, the Court was not willing to interpret § 201(c) in a manner that is believed would diminish the authors' exclusive rights.

The Court acknowledged that there were no factual disputes regarding ownership of the freelancers' copyright interest. The sole question before it was whether the transmission by the Print Publishers to the Electronic Publishers, and their commercial use of the material, was encompassed by the § 201(c) privilege revision.

To determine whether articles were reproduced and distributed as part of a revision of the collective works, the Court focused on "the Articles as presented to, and perceptible by, the user of the Databases."[3] It lent great weight to the fact that when the user conducts a search, the electronic databases produce each article as a separate item. Despite the fact that the article notes its placement, page number, etc. in the publication, it is displayed with minimal

[1] 17 U.S.C. § 404(a).
[2] 17 U.S.C. § 201(d)(2).
[3] Slip opinion at 14.

connection to the original publication.[4] Indeed, the Court refused to view the vast scope of collected articles within each electronic database as in any way constituting a "revision" of the original newspaper or magazine from which the article was extracted:

> One might view the articles as part of a new compendium—namely, the entirety of works in the Database. In that compendium, each edition of each periodical represents only a miniscule fraction of the ever-expanding Database. The Database no more constitutes a revision" of each constituent edition than a 400-page novel quoting a sonnet in passing would represent a revision" of that poem. "Revision" denoted a new "version," and a version is, in this setting, a distinct form of something regarded by its creator or others as one work."... The massive whole of the Database is not recognizable as a new version of its every small part.[5]

The publishers argued that the databases were comparable to the permitted collections of periodicals maintained on microfiche or microfilm. But the Court rejected the analogy, distinguishing microforms because each article appears in context. Although a user can extract an individual article, she must manipulate the microform much as she may have used the original. That is, if an article appears on page A2 and is continued on page A12, the reader must view reproductions of those pages on film. The databases, in contrast, offer users *individual* articles, not intact periodicals.

The fact that a user can manipulate the database to generate search results consisting only of articles from a particular periodical edition did not sway the Court. Because a database can be used in a noninfringing manner does not immunize it from other infringing activity.

THE DISSENT

The dissenting opinion, written by Justice Stevens and concurred by Justice Breyers, expressed a far broader view of a possible "revision" of a collective work – one that would encompass the material on the electronic databases. In their view, the stand-alone aspect of the databases' document retrieval coupled with information identifying its context in the original publication *is* sufficient to support the publishers' revision privilege.

They based their conclusion on several principles. They felt that the argument of the publishers invoking the concept of "media neutrality," the principle that the transfer of a work between media does not alter its character for copyright purposes, was persuasive:

> No one doubts that the New York Times has the right to reprint its issues in Braille, in foreign language, or in microfilm, even though such revisions might look and feel quite different from the original. Such differences, however, would largely result from the different medium being employed.6

[4] The right to "display" a work publicly is one of the author's discrete rights in 17 U.S.C. § 106(5). The Register of Copyright suggested that the authors' display right was implicated in the litigation and therefore, the publishers' privilege of reproduction and distribution under § 201(c) need not be the legal fulcrum for resolving the issue. 147 CONG. REC. E182-3 (daily ed. Feb. 14, 2001). The Court did not reach this contention, which was not argued by the parties to the case.

[5] Slip opinion at 15. (Citation omitted.)

[6] Slip opinion at 8.

The majority viewed the stand-alone feature of the article in electronic databases as an integral feature of the medium employed, computer generated ASCII text files. They were not satisfied with the majority's distinction between permissible microfilm collections and electronic databases.

Nor do they believe that the majority adequately balances authorial copyright interests against the public's interest in broad availability of literature, music, and other arts. The paramount copyright goal created by the explicit reservation of the freelancers' copyright in a contribution to a collection is to ensure his or her ability to exploit its value in additional media venues: for example, by republication in a new collection such as the author's collected essays or from resale to different publications. They concluded that finding copyright infringement in the case before them is not likely to enhance the copyright value of the freelance author's relationship to the original publisher in a meaningful or permanent way.

First, according to the publishers, since 1995, the New York Times has required freelance authors to grant complete "electronic rights" in addition to print rights. But this has not had a discernable impact on the freelancers' compensation. Second, the dissenters presume that the vast majority of database users seek comprehensive and easily searchable collections of periodicals, not the individual writings of freelance authors. Therefore, they conclude that the Court's holding does not increase the value of the authorial right in a pragmatic way – other than their right to retrospective statutory damages for copyright infringement.

Impact of the Court's Decision

Great concern was expressed in many quarters — including many publishers, historians, and scholars — over the consequences of holding for freelance authors. The publishers contend that either a judicial injunctive remedy ordering the excision of the infringing articles from the databases, or their voluntarily removal by the publishers themselves in order to mitigate damages for infringement, would leave a great information void in the historic record encompassed by the databases. The Court, however, viewed the excision of the infringing material from electronic databases as unnecessary and undesirable. It suggested alternative scenarios such as negotiated agreements between the authors and the publishers to authorize continued electronic reproduction of the infringing articles, or blanket licensing agreements patterned after those utilized by the music industry. Regardless of the consequences, however, the Court would not subordinate its view of the scope and implementation of authorial rights under the Copyright Act to speculation about future harm. Or, as expressed by the Register of Copyright, the *Tasini* case should be about authorial rights and the compensation of authors, not the preservation of electronic databases.

The dissent expressed greater concern that the majority over the impact on the public, which, it believes, stands to lose many of the principle benefits from access to comprehensive electronic archives, with little, if any, benefit to either authors or readers.

COPYRIGHT AND FAIR USE AFTER ACUFF-ROSE AND TEXACO

Dorothy Schrader

COPYRIGHT AND FAIR USE AFTER ACUFF-ROSE AND TEXACO

Fair use is "an equitable rule of reason"[1] that constitutes an important limitation on the proprietary rights of authors and other copyright owners under the Copyright Act.[2] The doctrine has had a particular significance for educators, researchers, and other nonprofit users of copyrighted works, but it also may apply in some commercial contexts. The courts continue to develop the doctrine. Recent cases have involved the possible application of fair use to the photocopying practices of research corporations, reverse engineering of computer software, parody of a song by reproduction in a commercial recording, and copying via electronic bulletin boards.

Originally, common law courts developed the fair use doctrine as a reasonable limitation on statutory copyrights and to resolve the possible tension between copyright law and the First Amendment. Congress codified the doctrine in section 107 of the 1976 Copyright Act. The legislative history[3] clearly indicates, however, that the courts remain free to develop the fair use concept, principally but not solely within the bounds of the four statutory factors Congress established to guide the courts.

Congress may be asked to re-examine the fair use doctrine in the context of legislation to facilitate the use of copyrighted works on the national information superhighway.[4]

This chapter reviews recent developments in fair use doctrine, with emphasis upon the Supreme Court's application of fair use to a commercial rap version of a copyrighted song,

---

[1] *Harper & Row Publishers, Inc. v. Nation Enterprises,* 471 U.S. 539, 560 (1985).

[2] The Copyright Act of 1976, title 17 U.S.C. §§ 101 et. Seq. Future references to the Copyright Act or copyright law should be understood to mean the law as codified in title 17, unless the context provides otherwise.

[3] H.R. REP. No. 1476, 94th Cong. 2d Sess. 66 (1976).

[4] The draft report of the Clinton Administration on proposals to resolve the intellectual property issues relating to the national information infrastructure ("NII") by-passed the fair use issue, pending meetings with authors, publishers and other copyright owners, libraries, educational groups, and other users. The final report, which may be issued in August 1995, is expected to contain some recommendations about fair use.

and the Second Circuit's refusal to apply the fair use doctrine to justify photocopying by corporate research scientist.

BACKGROUND

As a judge-made equitable doctrine, fair use has been developed on an ad hoc, case-by-case basis. Bright line principles are not easily discerned. All fair use cases tend to be very fact-bound.

Ever since Congress codified the fair use doctrine in section 107 of the Copyright Act, the courts begin their consideration of a fair use case with an analysis of the four statutory factors—

1) **the purpose and character of the use,** including whether such use is of a commercial nature or is for nonprofit educational purposes;
2) **the nature of the copyrighted work;**
3) **the amount** and substantially of the portion **used in relation to** the **copyrighted work** as a whole; and
4) **the effect of the use upon the potential market** for or value of the copyrighted work.

In a preamble to these four factors, the statute emphasizes that fair use copying for "purposes such as criticism, comment, news reporting, teaching (including multiple copies for classroom use), scholarship, or research, is not an infringement of copyright." The last sentence of section 107, responding to some inconsistent court opinions, clarifies that the unpublished status of a work shall not itself bar a finding of fair use.[5]

In codifying the four fair use factors, Congress made clear that it intended "to restate the present judicial doctrine of fair use, not to change, narrow, or enlarge it in any way."[6] Congress also sought flexibility in the application of the doctrine. To this end, Congress gave the courts discretion to continue the common law tradition of fair use adjudication, observing that "there is no disposition to freeze the doctrine in the statute, especially during a period of rapid technological change.[7]

Two Supreme Court decisions in the 1980s initially appeared to give some bright-line guidance to the lower courts. In *Sony Corp. of America v. Universal City Studios, Inc.,* 464 U.S. 417 (1984), the Court held fair use justified the VCR copying of entire copyrighted works by television viewers of advertiser-supported programming for delayed viewing. The five-four majority observed, however, that "every commercial use…is

---

[5] The last sentence was added by the Act of October 24, 1992, Pub. L. 102-492, 106 Stat. 3145.
[6] H.R. REP. No. 1476, 94th Cong., 2d Sess. 66 (1976).
[7] *Ibid.*

presumptively...unfair."[8] This comment suggested that in weighting the first fair use factor, a commercial motive would weigh heavily against a finding of fair use.

Later decisions of the Court and the lower courts, however, modified the significance of finding a commercial motive for the copying. In *Harper & Row Publishers, Inc. v. National Enterprises,* 471 U.S. 539 (1985), the Court explained that the distinction between a for-profit and nonprofit motive" is not whether the sole motive of the use is monetary gain but whether the user stands to profit from exploitation of the copyrighted material without paying the customary price."[9] Then, most recently in *Campbell v. Acuff-Rose Music, Inc.,* 114 S.Ct. 1164 (1994), the Court devalued the significance of a commercial motive even further, when it sanctioned the application of fair use to a commercial parody of a musical composition.

Harper & Row also seemed to set forth a bright line principle initially. The Court rejected the *Nation* magazine's fair use claim for excerpting 300 words from President Gerald Ford's memoirs. In "scooping" the book and the authorized magazine excerpter, the *Nation* had published previously unpublished material, avoided paying a licensing fee for its use of the copyrighted material, and had interfered significantly with the market for the original. For the Court, the clearest evidence of market harm was shown by the authorized excerpter's cancellation of the licensing contract and its refusal to pay the remaining fee. *Time* magazine, the authorized excerpter, would pay only for exclusivity. Publishing exclusivity had been lost by the unauthorized copying by the defendant.

The *Harper & Row* decision seemed to stand for the principle that the fourth factor—market harm—was the most significant factor in the fair use calculus. Moreover, copyright owners need not show present of past harm. Market harm could be established by showing that if the challenged use should become widespread, this use could adversely affect the potential market for the copyrighted works. The case also seemed to imply that unauthorized publication of even small excerpts from *unpublished* works was likely to be an unfair use.

After some inconsistent lower court decisions, Congress amended the fair use provision[10] by legislating that the unpublished nature of the work is merely one element of the fair use equation. The importance of the market harm factor would also be modified or clarified by the later decision of the Supreme Court in *Acuff-Rose.*

PARODY AS FAIR USE: CAMPBELL V. ACUFF-ROSE MUSIC

The most recent fair use case to come before the Supreme Court[11] involved the alleged parodic use by the rap music group "2 Live Crew" of the musical composition first recorded 30 years ago by country music singer-composer Roy Orbison. The 2 Live Crew proceeded to record and sell its version of Orbison's rock ballad "Oh, Pretty Woman" even after denial of their request for a license from the copyright owner and notwithstanding their admission that their recording entitled "Pretty Woman" could not qualify for the compulsory license for recording music.[12]

---

[8] 464 U.S. at 451.
[9] 471 U.S. at 562.
[10] Pub. L. 102-492, Act of October 24, 1992.
[11] *Campbell v. Acuff-Rose Music, Inc.,* 114 S. Ct. 1164 (1994).
[12] Reproduction of musical compositions on records is subject to compulsory licensing pursuant to 17 U.S.C. § 115 (known as the mechanical reproduction license). After the music copyright owner has authorized or made a

When Acuff-Rose Music, the owner of the copyright on "Oh, Pretty Woman" sued for copyright infringement, 2 Live Crew defended with a claim that their recording is a parody of the copyrighted song.

The district court agreed with 2 Live Crew that the fair use doctrine justified their use of the song.[13] On Appeal, the Sixth Circuit reversed, finding that the alleged parodic motive was weak and that the blatantly commercial nature of the use weight too strongly against fair use.[14]

The Supreme Court reversed and remanded the case for further fair use findings. *Campbell v. Acuff-Rose Music, Inc.,* 114 S. Ct. 1164 (1994). In a case of first impression for the Supreme Court on the significance of a parodic purpose to a finding of fair use,[15] a unanimous Court held that the rap group's parody of the copyrighted song could qualify as a fair use, notwithstanding the commercial nature of the use.

Commercial Purpose and Transformative Use

The Sixth Circuit had erred, the Court said, by over-emphasizing the commercial nature of the use, which relates to only one of the four factors. All of the statutory factors "are to be explored, and the results weighed together, in light of the purposes of copyright."[16]

According to the Court, the central purpose of the first fair use factor is to determine whether to second work merely supplants the original work or whether and to what extent the use is transformative. Although a transformative use is not dispositive of fair use, the purpose of copyright law is furthered by a transformative use in contrast to a nontransformative use.

In a somewhat startling statement, the Court opines that "the more transformative the new work, the less will be the significance of other factors, like commercialism, that may weigh against a finding of fair use.[17]

The Court presumably does not mean that if the infringer paraphrases the copyrighted work with sufficient adroitness, the transformed "new work" is less likely to be an unfair use.

---

recording of the song, the owner cannot object to the recording of the song by another person if: the proper notice is served on the copyright owner (or sometimes the Copyright Office), the statutory fee for each record made and distribution is paid monthly (6.6 cents per song or 1.25 cents per minute of playing time), and the song is arranged no more than "necessary to conform it to the style or manner of interpretation of the performance involved" without changing "the basic melody or fundamental character of the work." 17 U.S.C. 115(a)(2). The 2 Live Crew admitted that it could not invoke this compulsory license because its arrangement changes the "basic melody or fundamental character" of the Orbison song. *Campbell v. Acuff-Rose Music, Inc.,* 114 S. Ct. 1164, 1169 (Footnote 4)(1994). The irony of the Supreme Court's decision is that a commercial recording company is allowed to by-pass the conditions Congress established for the mechanical reproduction compulsory license and thereby gets absolutely free use of the song. The Court incomprehensively did not discuss the section 115 limitation on arrangements other than to note in a footnote that 2 Live Crew conceded the compulsory license was unavailable to them.

[13] 754 F. Supp. 1150 (M.D. Tenn. 1991).

[14] 972 F. 2d 1429 (6th Cir. 1992).

[15] *Acuff-Rose* is a case of first impression on parody and fair use only because the Supreme Court was unable to decide and earlier parody case. The Court split 4-4, which resulted in the affirmance of the lower court decision in the "Gaslight" case. *Benny v. Loew's Inc.,* 239 F. 2d 532 (9th Cir. 1956), *aff'd sub. Nom. Columbia Broadcasting System, Inc. v. Loew's Inc.*, 356 U.S. 43 (1958). The 9th Circuit had held that Jack Benny and CBS infringed MGM's copyright in the motion picture "Gaslight" through a television comedy skit; Benny had copied more of the original motion picture than necessary for his parodic purpose.

[16] 114 S. Ct. at 1171.

[17] *Ibid.*

A bedrock principle of copyright law would otherwise be lost: an infringer cannot escape liability by pointing out how much has been added to the second work. Moreover, the Court arguably does not give enough weight in this decision to the ordinarily exclusive right of the copyright owner to prepare derivative versions. As noted earlier, the Court also does not discuss the limitation on musical arrangements under the mechanical reproduction license of section 115.

A parodic use was held to have an obvious claim to transformative value.[18] Since parody is a form of social criticism and "criticism" is included in the preamble to section 107, parody is considered a prime candidate for a favorable fair use finding. The Court did not attach any significance to the fact that the other socially favored uses (comment, news reporting, teaching, scholarship, or research) involve primarily factual works, which traditionally have the greatest fair use latitude. Parody alone of these socially favored uses tends to focus on entertainment-type works, and the parody cases that are litigated tend to involve highly commercial uses.[19]

The Court ironically embraces transformative use as a very important principle in evaluating a fair use claim. It had refused to apply this principle in *Sony v. Universal* even though the Ninth Circuit had found VCR copying an infringing use, in large part because it was a nontransformative use.

The *Campbell v. Acuff-Rose* Court, while it embraces the transformative use principle, does not establish transformative use as a new bright-line test. The main precedential value of Acuff-Rose is the re-emphasis on case-by-case decision-making. Judicial application of the fair use factors "is not to be simplified with bright-line rules, for the statute, like the doctrine it recognizes, calls for case-by-case analysis."[20]

The Court minimized the import of its earlier fair use cases. It said: A commercial use is not presumptively unfair. *Sony* stands for the proposition that a commercial as opposed to nonprofit merely tends to weigh against finding of fair use.[21] That "even the force of that tendency will vary with the context is a further reason against elevating commerciality to hard presumptive significance."[22]

Market Harm

The Court's review of the fourth factor—market harm—was hampered by the state of the record. The Sixth Circuit, applying *Sony*, had presumed harm because of the commercial purpose. It made no finding whether the market for the licensed rap version of "Oh, Pretty

---

[18] 114 S. Ct. at 1171. The Court notes that Acuff-Rose did not deny the transformative value of parodies. Acuff-Rose, however, did vigorously deny that 2 Live Crew's adaptation of the Orbison song was in fact a parody.

[19] Berlin v. E.C. Publications, Inc., 329 F. 2d 541 (2d Cir. 1964) (Mad magazine lampooned Berlin's "A Pretty Girl is like a Melody"); Benny v. Loew's Inc., supra (jack Benny in his popular television show purported to parody the Oscar-winning motion picture "Gaslight"); Columbia Pictures Corp. v. National Broadcasting Co., 137 F. Supp. 348 (S.D. Cal. 1955) (Sid Caesar in his popular television show burlesqued the Oscar-winning motion picture "From Here to Eternity"); *Campbell v. Acuff-Rose Music, Inc., supra* (2 Live Crew in a recording made for sale to a mass audience purported to parody a famous Roy Orbison song). Except for Benny's parody, each parody was held as fair use.

[20] 114 S. Ct. at 1170.

[21] 114 S. Ct. at 1174.

[22] *Ibid.*

Woman" had been harmed.[23] The Supreme Court remanded for evaluation of the amount of copyright in light of 2 Live Crew's parodic purpose, the transformative nature of the use, and for consideration of the potential for harm to the market for a licensed rap version.[24]

By way of guidance, the Court did make some observations about the fourth factor. It confirmed that the harm analysis must consider the potential harm if defendant's conduct were repeated by others on an unrestricted, widespread basis, which could result in a substantially adverse impact on the potential market.[25] This analysis must also include the harm to the market for derivative works.[26]

There is no presumption or inference of market harm, however, in a case involving a transformative use, even if there is a commercial purpose.[27] When "the second use is transformative, market substitution [for the original] is at least less certain, and market harm may not be so readily inferred.[28]

Concurring Opinion

Although a unanimous Supreme Court decided *Campbell v. Acuff-Rose*, Justice Kennedy had concerns about the sweep of the opinion, which he expressed in a concurring opinion. He had reservations about the legitimacy of the parodic purpose by 2 Live Crew. He was especially concerned that future courts "must take care to ensure that not just any commercial take-off is rationalized *post hoc* as a parody."[29] "More than arguable parodic content should be required to deem a would be parody a fair use."[30]

Justice Kennedy realized, as perhaps the rest of the Court did not, that is any weak transformation may qualify as a parody, copyright protection is significantly weakened.

Case Analysis

If the lower courts heed Justice Kennedy's cautionary words, the impact of *Campbell v. Acuff-Rose* may be limited to its insistence on the case-by-case nature of fair use adjudication, and the principle that, where the use is transformative, a commercial purpose carriers no

---

[23] 114 S. Ct. at 1179.

[24] 114 S. Ct. at 1176-77.

[25] 114 S. Ct. at 1177.

[26] *Ibid.*

[27] *Ibid.*

[28] *Ibid.* The Court went on to comment that "when a lethal parody, like a scathing theater review, kills demand for the original, it does not produce a harm cognizable under the Copyright Act." 114 S. Ct. at 1178. Potentially remediable displacement of the market for the original work must be distinguished from irremediable disparagement of the original work. For the latter, there is no copyright remedy. The Court announced "a rule that there is no protectable derivative market for criticism." *Ibid.* After appearing to give alledged parodies a presumption against market harm, the Court did observe that it had earlier been speaking of "parody pure and simple." If the second work has effects not only in the area of criticism but also contains non-parodic material that impacts the protectable market for derivative works, then analysis of the fourth factor may result in copyright liability. That is the main issue the lower court will consider on remand, if the case is not settled. It seems clear that the Court thought the lyrics had a parodic purpose, but the findings with respect to copying of the musical elements were less clear.

[29] 114 S. Ct. at 1182.

[30] 114 S. Ct. at 1181.

necessary inference of market harm. A commercial purpose is one factor to be weighed with the others. If the use is nontransformative and commercial, there is a tendency to weigh those facts against a finding of fair use.

Without bright-line tests, fair use doctrine arguably becomes less effective and less reliable in setting appropriate limits on the rights of copyright owners. As noted in the background section, fair use cases have always been fact-bound. The Supreme Court's renewed emphasis on ad hoc fair use decision-making suggest that we cannot realistically look to the Court for precedents that might make fair use analysis more predictable and coherent. It suggests that Congress may wish to consider legislating additional fair use principles for electronic uses in digital libraries, on electronic bulletin boards, and on the national information superhighway.

PHOTOCOPYING BY CORPORATE RESEARCHERS: THE TEXACO CASE

In *American Geophysical Union v. Texaco, Inc.*, 37 F. 3d 881 (2d Cir. 1994), a divided panel of the Second Circuit reached a long-awaited decision regarding the application of the fair use doctrine to photocopying by corporate scientists and other researchers. The court held two-to-one that fair use did not apply to excuse the photocopying by Texaco's researchers.[31]

The court minimized the significance of a commercial purpose for the copying (especially in light of *Campbell v. Acuff-Rose*). The majority held, however, that the nontransformative nature of the use, the copyright of entire journal articles for archival purposes, and the market harm to Copyright Clearance Center-member publishers who lost photocopying licensing revenues, resulted in a finding of unfair use.

The significance of this victory for publishers, in vindication of their quest for photocopying license fees, is somewhat blunted by the narrow language of the majority opinion and the force of the dissent.

The majority took pains to observe that it was not deciding "the broad issue of whether photocopying of scientific articles is fair use," or even "whether photocopying of such articles is fair use when undertaken by a research scientist employed at a for-profit corporation."[32] The court also expressly declined to decide the fair use balance in the case of publications not available through the Copyright Clearance Center ("CCC").[33] It also emphasized that application of fair use "always depends on consideration of the precise facts at hand."[34]

---

[31] The plaintiffs consisted of 83 publishers of scientific and technical journals who brought a class action against Texaco for unauthorized photocopying of their many journals. The parties made significant stipulations, however, which narrowed the scope of the case. They agreed that the "fair use" phase of the trial would focus exclusively on the photocopying of journal articles by one scientist-researcher, the plaintiffs selected photocopies of eight articles from one journal, the *Journal of Catalysis*. The articles are copied in their entirety. The photocopies were filed in order to have them available for later reference as needed. The evidence showed that the scientist never made use of five of the eight articles copied. The average monthly issue of *Catalysis* comprises 20-25 articles within 200 pages. Each article runs from 2 to 20 pages. The authors of the articles must assign their copyrights to the publisher for no compensation. Texaco employs 400-500 researchers nationwide.

[32] 37 F. 3d at 884.

[33] 37 F. 3d at 899. The CCC is a central clearinghouse established in 1977 primarily by the publishers of scientific and technical journals to license photocopying of their works. The CCC initially offered per use transaction-

Analysis of the Four Factors

Copyright articles from scholarly, scientific, and technical publications by Texaco corporate researchers are found to be an intermediate but nontransformative use for "archival" purposes. The commercial nature of a secondary use tends to weigh against a finding of fair use, but "the link between Texaco's commercial gain and its photocopying practices is somewhat attenuated."[35] Most secondary users seek some financial gain and Texaco certainly reaped indirect commercial advantage.[36] On balance, the nontransformative nature of the use coupled with indirect commercial advantage tips the first factor of the publishers.[37]

The second factor favors Texaco because the articles are predominately factual and Texaco's scientists are interested in the facts or ideas of the articles.[38]

Since Texaco copied entire journal articles (which are separate works), the third factor favors the publishers.[39]

While acknowledging the *Campbell v. Acuff-Rose* modifies the Supreme Court's earlier emphasis on the fourth factor,[40] the Second Circuit's analysis of market harm was clearly the deciding point in the case. Because of *Campbell v. Acuff-Rose*, however, the majority analyzed the significance of the absence of any derivative market for critical works and the absence of any traditional market for individual journal articles for scholarly works. Before photocopying became widespread, the journal publishers had not attempted to license secondary uses of scientific or scholarly articles.[41]

The majority concluded that "[o]nly an impact on potential licensing revenues for traditional, reasonable, or likely to be developed markets should be legally cognizable...[when evaluating market harm]."[42] The court concluded, however, that the publishers did create a workable market for institutional users to obtain photocopying licenses through the CCC.[43] These lost photocopying revenues demonstrated harm to the value of the publishers' copyrights as a result of Texaco's unlicensed photocopying.

Dissenting Views

The dissenting judge disagreed with the majority's analyses of the first and fourth factors. He would have held that photocopying for purposes of scientific research is a transformative and productive use of the copyrighted works, that the alleged adverse effect on the copyrighted works is illusory, that the researcher's file of photocopied articles is not archival

based licenses. Later, they developed a blanket license called an annualization fee, which is established by statistical sampling of photocopying activity.

[34] 37 F. 3d at 884.
[35] 37 F. 3d at 890.
[36] *Ibid.*
[37] 37 F. 3d at 892.
[38] 37 F. 3d at 893.
[39] 37 F. 3d at 894.
[40] *Ibid.*
[41] 37 F. 3d at 895.
[42] 37 F. 3d at 898.
[43] *Ibid.*

but is part of the transformative process of scientific research, and that there is no workable market for photocopying licenses.[44]

The CCC licensing system is neither traditional, reasonable, nor workable, according to the dissent.[45] Only a small fraction of the 200,000 periodicals in print are available through the CCC.

The authors of scientific and scholarly articles are required to assign their copyrights to the publishers. They receive no compensation for their writings. The authors seek publication to promote their writings, ideas, and reputations. Photocopying revenues, therefore, provide no incentive to create more works.[46] As long as there is enough revenue to publish the scholarly journal, the dissenting judge felt this would be sufficient incentive under the Copyright Act. The copyright law is not intended to assure maximum economic return to the copyright owner—only a fair return.[47] "[T]he law's purpose is to balance competing interests—assuring the author a *fair* return, while permitting creative uses that build upon the author's work."[48]

The dissent charged that the majority's ruling will require an attorney to monitor photocopying machines. The ruling "will add cost, time, and effort to the work of scientist-authors and will tend to *diminish* the only reward these authors seek from publication."[49]

Case Analysis

Unless the Texaco decision is overturned through further appeals, it should serve as a firm precedent in future licensing negotiations between publishers and other corporations with extensive research activities. Although the closeness of the decision and the narrowness of its language would ordinarily mute the precedential effect, in the corporate world, settlement of disputes may be less costly than litigation.

The narrow language of the majority opinion and the forceful dissent should mean that the case will not serve as any precedent outside the field of photocopying for corporate research. The opinion would seem, for example, to have little significance, if any, for library and educational photocopying by teachers, students, and non-corporate researchers including government researchers.[50]

It is significant that the majority emphasized the fact-bound nature of fair use analysis, denied that its decision affected the broader world of photocopying for research purposes even by for-profit organizations in general, and expressly stated it was not deciding the fair use balance in the case of journal articles not available through the CCC. With these limitations on the scope of the opinion, the publishers still prevailed only by one vote.

[44] 37 F. 3d at 900-904.
[45] 37 F. 3d at 904-905.
[46] 37 F. 3d at 906-907.
[47] 37 F. 3d at 907-908.
[48] 37 F. 3d at 908 (emphasis in original).
[49] 37 F. 3d at 907 (emphasis in original).
[50] This observation seems confirmed by a report subsequent amendment of the majority opinion filed July 17, 1995. National Law Journal, July 31, 1995, at A8, col. 3. According to this chapter, the amended opinion "states in at least two places that its closely watched conclusions concern 'institutional, systematic copying,' not copying by individual researchers or professors." *Id.*

The case turned primarily on the issue of market harm: did the publishers create a viable, reasonable market for photocopying licenses through the CCC? The two-judge majority said "yes." The CCC was created at the urging of Congress to provide a negotiated, licensing solution to the impact of photocopying technology on copyrighted works. Since a license is available through reasonable procedures at least to corporate research entitles, the market harm factor tips in favor of the publishers in the case of photocopying by such entities.[51]

OTHER FAIR USE DEVELOPMENTS

Other important fair use cases decided just before or after *Campbell v. Acuff-Rose* involved off-campus document delivery services, uploading and downloading video games on an electronic bulletin board, and reverse engineering of composer programs.

Document Delivery

An off-campus, for-profit document delivery service that prepared course packs for students by photocopying 5-30 percent of many copyrighted works was held a willful infringer of copyright. *Princeton University Press v. Michigan Document Services,* 855 F. Supp. 905 (E.D. Mich. 1994).

The for-profit document delivery service attempted to assert a fair use privilege on behalf of the students it served.[52] The document service argued that if it had to pay photocopying fees, these costs would be borne by the students. The document service argued that its whole purpose was to serve students. The service also argued that sale of the course packs stimulated sales of the original works.

The court dismissed these arguments handily. It found that competitors pay licensing fees and that there are relatively simple procedures in place to get permission and pay royalties. The use was held nonproductive, "pure copying for profit,"[53] and harmful to the market for the original works. If the document service's "practice of photocopying without permission became widespread, there would be a significant loss of publishers' revenues."[54]

[51] The dissent had an entirely different view of market harm, of course. Judge Jacobs believes there is no appreciable impairment of publishers' revenues from subscription sales since publishers capture additional revenue from institutional users by charging double the ordinary subscription price.

[52] 855 F. Supp. at 908.

[53] 855 F. Supp. at 909.

[54] 855 F. Supp. at 911.

Electronic Bulletin Boards

In *Sega Enterprises, Ltd. V. MAPHIA,* 857 F. Supp. 679 (N.D. Cal. 1994), the court granted a preliminary injunction to stop the unauthorized uploading of Sega's video games to defendant's electronic bulletin board[55] and their downloading by MAPHIA users.

The operators of the bulletin board attempted to justify a fair use defense, asserting that they did not download or retain copies of any Sega video games. They tried to persuade the court that they did not upload or download Sega's games themselves and should not be responsible for the activity of independent users of the bulletin board.

Like the document delivery case, the court readily rejected the fair use defense of the bulletin board operators. It held that MAPHIA's role in providing the bulletin board facilities and its directions, knowledge of the activities, and actual encouragement to MAPHIA users to exchange video games, amounted to contributory infringement.[56]

MAPHIA users had a commercial purpose: to avoid buying an original copy. The MAPHIA operators had a commercial purpose: a direct fee for downloading the games was sometimes charged; other times items were bartered for the privilege of downloading games. Since 45,000 bulletin boards like MAPHIA operate in the United States, the court concluded that, if unauthorized copying of video games through bulletin boards becomes widespread, "there would be a substantial and immeasurable adverse effect on the market for Sega's copyrighted video game programs."[57]

Reverse Engineering

While Sega prevailed against bulletin board operator in MAPHIA, it lost a major fair use case against a video game developer one year earlier. The Ninth Circuit held that reverse engineering of a copyrighted computer program by a direct competitor could under certain circumstances be justified as a fair use. *Sega Enterprises Ltd. V. Accolade, Inc.,* 977 F. 2d 1510 (9th Cir. 1993).

The defendant had reverse-engineered Sega's video game programs to discover the operational requirements for compatibility with the hardware, the Sega Genesis console. The process required making entire copies of the programs for study and analysis. After isolating the bytes that controlled interoperability, the defendant created its own, original video games without reproducing the Sega program code, except for the few bytes that controlled interoperability.

[55] An electronic bulletin board ("EBB") is a system for exchanging information to remote points by means of a computer and modem devices. The EBB consists of an electronic storage medium (computer memories or hard disks), which is attached to telephone lines via modem devices—all controlled by a computer.

[56] 857 F. Supp. at 687.

[57] 857 F. Supp. at 688. On the surface, it may seem that the electronic copying held infringing in this case is similar to the VCR copying held a fair use in *Sony v. Universal.* There are several compelling distinctions: the broadcasts in *Sony* were licensed and available for public viewing whereas uploading the Sega games were unauthorized; Sony knew that VCR users would copy television programs but the Betamax could be used also for non-infringing copying whereas only infringing copying took place in MAPHIA; the encouragement to copy was somewhat more blatant in the case of the MAPHIA operators who often received either a fee or value through barter for facilitating the copying whereas Sony profited only from the sale of its VCR machine; and, most significantly, the VCR copying in Sony was justified only on the basis of delayed viewing ('time-shifting") whereas permanent copies were made by MAPHIA users.

The Ninth Circuit found this process to constitute "intermediate copying," which could constitute infringement, unless the copying was justified by a legitimate need for access to the otherwise inaccessible program ideas and functions. The court decided that disassembly of Sega's object code programs was necessary in order to understand the functional requirements of the hardware for playing the video games.[58] Computer programs, the court said, are in essence utilitarian articles that accomplish tasks.[59] "Because Sega's video game programs contain unprotected aspects that cannot be examined without copying, we afford them a lower degree of protection than more traditional literary works."[60]

Fair use justifies the wholesale copying[61] by a direct competitor because the copying is intermediate, productive, and necessary to gain access to the unprotected aspects. The copying comports with the purpose of copyright law to promote progress of science and the useful arts. "If disassembly of copyrighted object code is *per se* an unfair use, the owner of the copyright gains a *de facto* monopoly over the functional aspects of the work—aspects that were expressly denied copyright protection by Congress."[62] Therefore, reverse engineering to discover the unprotected aspects, which are otherwise inaccessible, is a permissible fair use of the copyrighted computer programs.

CONCLUSION

Fair use is an equitable rule of reason that constitutes an important limitation on the property rights of authors and other copyright owners under the Copyright Act. Originally, common law courts developed fair use as a reasonable limitation on the exclusive rights granted by copyright law and as an accommodation between the goals of copyright law and First Amendment free speech rights.

Congress codified the fair use doctrine in the 1976 Copyright Act, by establishing four factors to guide the courts in deciding fair use cases.

A unanimous Supreme Court in *Campbell v. Acuff-Rose Music,* 114 S. Ct. 1164 (1994) held that a rap group's commercial parody of a song fixed in a record for mass distribution may qualify as a fair use. Although commercial purpose tends to weigh against a finding of fair use, this is only one factor to be weighed with the others. A parody is a transformative use of a copyrighted work. This type of use is favored because it advances the purposes of the Copyright Clause of the U.S. Constitution. When the use is transformative, there can be no presumption or inference of market harm from a commercial purpose. Even if the parody destroys the market for the original by its criticism, fair use will apply unless the alleged parodist also copies expressive elements unnecessary to the critical purpose, and this copying impacts the protectable market for derivative works.

---

[58] 977 F. 2d at 1526.

[59] 977 F. 2d at 1524.

[60] 977 F. 2d at 1526.

[61] Although defendant Accolade made many complete copies of Sega's computer code for study and analysis to find the interoperability code, the latter was the Sega code reproduced in the final Accolade video games. This interoperability code consisted of about 20-25 bytes; an entire game program contained between 500,000 and 1,500,000 bytes.

[62] 977 F. 2d at 1526.

In another important fair use case, the Second Circuit in *American Geophysical Union v. Texaco,* 37 F. 3r 881 (2d Cir. 1994), declined to justify photocopying of scientific journal articles by corporate research scientist as a fair use. In a narrow two-to-one opinion, the court found the photocopying was a nontransformative, archival use for indirect commercial advantage. It also found that the journal publishers have created a workable market for institutional users to obtain photocopying licenses the Copyright Clearance Center. The loss of photocopying revenues as a result of unlicensed photocopying by the corporate researcher harmed the value of the publishers' copyrights.

Other courts recently denied the fair use claims of an off-campus document delivery service that photocopied course packs for university students, and the operators of an electronic bulletin board that facilitated the unauthorized uploading and downloading of video games. Another court applied fair use, however, to justify the intermediate copying of entire computer game programs for purposes of study and analysis ("reverse engineering") to isolate the computer code that controls operation of the video games on the hardware console. This copying was a fair use since the unprotected ideas and functions of the programs were otherwise inaccessible to the public. Fair use also applied to the replication of the 20-25 bytes of code required for interoperability since an adverse ruling would have given patent-like protection to the code.

As a judge-made equitable doctrine, fair use has developed on an ad hoc basis. The cases tend to be very fact-bound. Bright-line principles have been difficult to discern, and now, the Supreme Court, in its most recent fair use decision, states that application of the four fair use factors is not to be simplified with bright-line rules.

In either this or the next session, Congress may decide to consider legislative proposals submitted by the Clinton Administration to resolve the intellectual property issues relating to implementation of the National Information Infrastructure (or national information superhighway). Application of fair use doctrine to electronic and computer uses of copyrighted works will of fair use doctrine to electronic and computer uses of copyrighted works will probably be one of the most contentious and difficult issues in that legislation.

If, as the Supreme Court indicates in *Campbell v. Acuff-Rose,* we cannot expect the courts to develop bright-line fair use tests, the existing fair use doctrine arguably becomes less effective and less reliable in setting appropriate limits on copyright owners' rights. Fair use doctrine may lack sufficient predictability and coherence to facilitate access to the information superhighway, while assuring adequate protection of copyrights.

Congress may decide to legislate additional fair use guidelines to govern electronic uses of copyrighted works in digital libraries, on electronic bulletin boards, in computers, and on the national information superhighway.

CRIMINAL COPYRIGHT INFRINGEMENT: PROPOSAL TO IMPOSE CRIMINAL LIABILITY ON NONPROFIT INFRINGERS AND FELONY LIABILITY FOR TRANSMISSIONS

Dorothy Schrader

CRIMINAL COPYRIGHT INFRINGEMENT HISTORY

Traditionally, the rights conferred on copyright owners have been enforced by the rights holders in civil infringement suits. The existing penalties for civil copyright infringement are strong[1] and provide as many remedies as, or greater remedies than, those found in the copyright laws of other countries.

Criminal Penalties 1897-1974

Criminal penalties for copyright infringement were added to the copyright law in 1897, but originally applied only to violation of the public performance right in musical and dramatic works.[2] The 1897 Act also established the *mens rea* standard that has not been

[1] Unlike the criminal provisions, it is not necessary to prove willfulness or non-profit motive for civil infringment. Civil remedies apply in case of "unconscious" or "innocent" infringement, although the penalties may be diminished for "innocent" infringers. Vicarious and contributory infringers are also liable. The civil remedies include an injunction, actual damages and the infringer's profits, or in lieu of actual damages and profits at the option of the copyright owner, statutory damages. The statutory damages ordinarily range from $500 to $20,000 for each work infringed, as the court considers just. If the infringement is willful, the statutory damages limit is increased to $100,000 for each work. The court may reduce the award to $200 for "innocent" infringers and may even remit damages for nonprofit educational users who acted under a reasonable belief the fair use defense applied to their copying activities. Infringing articles, copies, or phonorecords are subject to seizure and forfeiture. 17 U.S.C. §§ 501-505; 509. A prevailing copyright owner in an infringement suit may be awarded costs and attorney's fees, if the work infringed was timely registered with the Copyright Office. 17 U.S.C. §§ 412 and 505.

[2] The main purpose of the Act of January 6, 1897, was to grant copyright owners of musical compositions a public performance right for the first time. A public performance right for dramatic works has been granted more than 40 years earlier by the Act of August 18,1856. The civil damages remedy of the 1856 Act was extended

substantively changed since then: the government must prove that the infringer acted "willfully" and for profit." "Willfully" has never been defined in the copyright statutes. The "for profit" element is now expressed in the phrase "for purpose of commercial advantage or private financial gain," and is also undefined in the statute.

Until the advent of audio and video taping technology in the 1060s and 1970s, criminal prosecutions for copyright infringement were exceedingly rare. Even in the case of second or subsequent offenders, or damages involving hundreds of thousands of dollars, the maximum, general penalties before 1974 were a fine up to $1000 or one year in prison, or both. Any criminal copyright infringement could be punished only as a misdemeanor before 1974.

Criminal Penalties 1974-1992

In the 1970s, Congress perceived that commercial piracy of records and motion pictures could not be controlled simply by civil remedies and misdemeanor penalties. Congress recognized that "record piracy is so profitable that ordinary penalties fail to deter prospective offenders."[3] In 1974, the maximum fine for criminal infringement of recordings alone was increased to $25,000 for first offenders and $50,000 for second offenders. Also, for the first time ever in copyright law, felony charges could be brought against second offenders of sound recording copyrights.[4]

In the Copyright Act of 1976, a general provision of the copyright law,[5] Congress extended the increased penalties for record piracy of motion pictures. For works other than sound recordings and motion pictures, the offense of criminal copyright infringement remained a misdemeanor, although the maximum general fine was increased from $1,000 to $10,000.

The 1976 Copyright Act went into effect on January 1, 1978. Within just a few years, motion picture and sound recording copyright owners petitioned Congress to increase the criminal penalties once again. Congress responded with the Piracy and Counterfeiting Amendments Act of 1982.[6] Although the maximum fines were increased for all copyrighted works, the most significant changes were limited to sound recordings and motion pictures. For the first time in United States copyright law, certain *first* offenders faced felony prosecution.

---

in the 1897 Act to musical compositions: $100 for the first infringing public performance for profit and $50 for a second and subsequent infringements. When the public performance right was granted to musical compositions, the performing rights societies later created to enforce this right did not exist. For example, the American Society of Composers, Authors, and Publishers ("ASCAP") was established in 1914. The public performance right in musical works is much more difficult to administer and enforce than the comparable right in dramatic works. In the absence of a collective mechanism to enforce the music performance right, its advocates successfully petitioned the Congress to add the first criminal remedy for copyright infringement.

[3] H.R. REP. 93-1581, 93rd Con., 2d. Sess. 4 (1974).

[4] Act of December 31, 1974, Pub. L. 93-573, 88 Stat. 1873 (up to two years in prison for second offenders). This Act, in addition to increasing the penalties for record piracy, made sound recording copyright protection permanent. Copyright had been granted to sound recordings in the Sound Recording Act of 1971, effective February 15, 1972. Act of October 15, 1971, Pub. L. 92-140, 85 Stat. 391. The 1971 Act had extended criminal liability for violation of the mechanical reproduction license of §1(e) of the Copyright Act of 1909, 33 Stat. 1075, but merely made applicable the misdemeanor penalty and $1,000 maximum fine.

[5] Copyright Act of 1976, Pub. L. 94-553, 90 Stat. 2541, codified at title 17 U.S. Code §§ 107-803.

[6] Act of May 24, 1982, Pub. L. 97-180, 96 Stat. 91, 93.

Under the 1982 Act, the general maximum fine was increased from $10,000 to $25,000 for first and subsequent offenses involving any copyrighted work other than a sound recording or motion picture. First and subsequent offenses remained punishable only as misdemeanors for works other than sound recordings and motion pictures.

In the case of record and film piracy, the 1982 Act created three penalty categories based upon new statutory thresholds. If the offense involved multiple copyright/distribution, within a 180-day period, of 1,000 or more phonorecords of sound recordings, or 65 or more copies of motion pictures, the maximum fine was $250,000, or five years, or both, even for a first offender. These penalties also applied to a second or subsequent offense for record or film piracy. If the multiple copying/distribution activity within a 180-day period fell between 101-999 phonorecords, or 8-64 copies of motion pictures, for a first offense the penalties were a maximum $250,00 fine, two years, or both. First offenses involving less than 101 phonorecords, or less than 8 copies of motion pictures, or copyright/distribution activity that fell outside the 180-day range, were subject to the general penalties applied to other works--$25,000 fine, one year in prison, or both.

The heightened penalties for record and film piracy applied only to infringement of the reproduction or distribution rights. They did not apply to infringement of the adaptation right, or in the case of motion pictures, of the public performance and public display rights. Criminal infringement of these rights was subject to the $25,000 fine and misdemeanor penalty. In actuality, criminal prosecutions have been attempted for decades for infringement of rights other than the reproduction and distribution rights.

Finally, the 1982 Act made a structural change in criminal copyright law. The Act moved the criminal penalties to title 18 U.S.C.—the Criminal Code—in a new section 2319. The criminal offense and the *mens rea* standard, however, continued to be set by section 506(a) of title 17 U.S.C.—the Copyright Code.[7]

EXISTING CRIMINAL INFRINGEMENT PENALTIES

Summary

The existing criminal penalties for copyright infringement were legislated in a 1992 Amendment of 18 U.S.C. §2319 described simply as the "Criminal Penalties for Copyright Infringement."[8] Some refer to the Amendment as the "Copyright Felony Act," since for the first time infringement of works other than sound recordings and motion pictures became a felony offense.

The Amendment also effected a ten-fold increase in the maximum general fine for individual infringers of works other than sound recordings and motion pictures (from $25,000 to $250,000) and ten-fold increase in the possible prison sentence (from one year to 10 years).

[7] This migration of the criminal penalties for copyright infringement to title 18 was done for the purpose of highlighting the serious nature of the crimes of record and motion picture piracy. It was also hoped that federal prosecutors and judges, accustomed to working with title 18 offenses, would be more likely to treat the copyright infringement offense more seriously, if it were part of the Criminal Code.

[8] Act of October 28, 1992, Pub. L. 102-561, 106 Stat. 4233.

The 1992 Amendment established new statutory thresholds to distinguish misdemeanor and felony offenses. If fewer than 10 copies/phonorecords are involved in a first offense, or the retail value of the copies/phonorecords are $2,500 or less, or the 180-day criterion is not met, maximum penalties are a fine up to $250,000 for an individual and $500,000 for a corporate offender, or one year, or both. The offense is then a misdemeanor.

If 10 or more copies/phonorecords, having an aggregate retail value of more than $2,500, are reproduced/distributed within a 180-day period, a first offender is subject to the same fines described above, but the offense becomes a felony. The offender may be sentenced up to five years in prison, fined, or both. For a second or subsequent offense meeting these statutory thresholds, the offense is a felony. The same fines apply, but the maximum prison sentence can be 10 years.

As under the pre-1992 law, criminal infringements of rights other than the reproduction and distribution rights are subject to the misdemeanor penalty (i.e., one year in prison). The new increased fines apply, however.

Legislative History

Although public hearings were conducted on a bill to extend the felony provisions of the 1982 Act to computer software piracy, extension of the felony provisions to works other than sound recordings, motion pictures, and computer programs was not publicly debated.

The original proposal, S. 893, 102d Congress, First Session (1991), as passed by the Senate in June 1992 only applied the 1982 Act's penalties for record and film piracy to computer programs. No bill was pending in the House of Representatives. After the House Subcommittee on Intellectual Property and Judicial Administration held public hearings on S. 893, the House Judiciary Committee, on recommendation of the Intellectual Property Subcommittee, amended the Senate bill to "harmonize [] the felony provisions in section 2319 to apply to all types of copyrighted works, as is currently the case for misdemeanor violations."[9] The Senate acceded to the House substitute. For the first time, infringement of literary, musical, dramatic, graphic and visual art works became subject to possible felony prosecution.

Before 1992, Congress had refrained from using felony penalties against copyright infringers other than record or film pirates. As the Supreme Court observed in *Dowling v. United States,* 473 U.S. 207 (1985), "Congress hesitated long before imposing felony sanctions on copyright infringers." 473 U.S. at 225. Congressional concerns primarily focused on the intangible nature of the copyright interest; the potential use of copyright as a means of censorship; tensions between the First Amendment and rights under copyright; and the relative lack of public understanding of the heightened concern." 473 U.S. at 225.

In 1992, Congress abandoned a piecemeal, calibrated approach to felony copyright infringement in favor of harmonization of the criminal penalties.

[9] H.R. REP. 102-997, 102d Cong., 2d Sess. 4 (1992).

Mens Rea Standard

The statutory thresholds of existing law continue to insulate less substantial copyright/distribution activities from felony prosecution. Arguably, however, the $2,500 retail limit on misdemeanors is reached easily in today's marketplace. On the other hand, all offenses infringing exclusive rights other that the rights of reproduction and distribution are misdemeanors.

The principal limit of existing law on the scope of criminal liability, however, rests upon the *mens rea* standard. To be subject to criminal liability, the infringer[10] must act willfully and for purpose of commercial advantage or private gain, i.e., "for profit."

Willfulness

The Copyright Act does not define "willful." The Supreme Court has never defined the term in the context of the Copyright Act, although it has elaborated on the term as applied in other criminal contexts.

Some assert that a "split" exist among the Circuit Courts of Appeal about the meaning of "willful" in criminal copyright infringement.[11] According to one commentator: "The majority of courts have said that the language of the Copyright Act makes criminal copyright infringement a 'specific' intent crime; in other words, a prosecutor must show that the accused specifically intended to violate the copyright law."[12]

The *minority* view seems to be that "willful" means an intentional, voluntary doing of an act that violates the copyright statute, without specific knowledge that the act is a copyright infringement.[13]

The Courts of Appeal do not, however, themselves acknowledge the existence of a "split." *United States v. Moran,* 757 F. Supp. 1046, 1049 (D. Neb. 1991). The paucity of criminal cases makes it difficult to reach a firm conclusion on the existence of a "split."

Cases decided under the 1976 Copyright Act, uniformly seem to fall within the "majority" view, which requires proof of specific intent to infringe. *United States v. Cross,* 816 F. 2d 297, 300 (7th Cir. 1987) (defendant knowingly and voluntarily violated the copyright laws); *United States v. Moran,* 757 F. Supp. 1046, 1050 (D. Neb. 1991) (defendant not guilty because he lacked requisite specific intent—that is, voluntary, intentional violation of a known legal duty).

Even the cases decided under the 1909 Copyright Act in the 1970s, seem to adhere to the specific intent interpretation. In one of the first convictions for record piracy, *United States v.*

---

[10] Conviction of criminal infringement requires proof beyond a reasonable doubt of those statutory elements that constitute civil infringement: subsistence of a valid copyright and unlawful copying by the defendant. Civil infringement principles are used to establish these elements in a criminal case, but the prosecution must meet the higher burden of proof required for criminal liability.

[11] Saunders, *Criminal Copyright Infringement anf the Copyright Felony Act,* 71 DENVER UNIV. L. REV. 671, 688 (1994).

[12] *Ibid. See also, United States v. Moran,* 757 F. Supp. 1046, 1049 (D. Neb. 1991) M. NIMM. NIMMER & D. NIMMER, NIMMER ON COPYRIGHT, §15.01[C] at 15-10, n. 13 (1995).

[13] Saunders, *ibid.,* attributes this minority view to the Second and Ninth Circuits. As discussed later in this chapter, this observation does not seem warranted by the more recent cases in those circuit. The opinion may rest on

Heilman, 614 F. 2d 1133 (7th Cir. 1980), the court applied the specific intent standard of *United States v. Murdock,* 290 U.S. 389, 394-95 (1993). It upheld the conviction because defendant "chose to persist in the conduct which he knew had 'a high likelihood of being held by a court of competent jurisdiction to be a violation of a criminal statute.'" 614 F. 2d at 1138.

In *United States v. Wise,* 550 F. 2d 1180 (9th Cir 1977), the Ninth Circuit upheld the conviction of a film collector who had intentionally and knowingly sold unauthorized copies of films to "friends." The district court had earlier found that defendant "knew what he was doing and did it with a bad purpose to disobey the law or disregard the law, and that he had the specific intent."[14]

One of the earliest criminal copyright cases from the Second Circuit implies, however, that intent to copy a copyrighted work might satisfy the willfulness standard. In a highly unusual criminal prosecution of someone who copied the designs of two related statues or figurines, the Second Circuit upheld a criminal conviction on the basis that the defendant "deliberately had the copies made and deliberately sold them for profit." *United States v. Backer,* 134 F. 2d 533 (2d Cir. 1943). Although the court did not mention a specific intent requirement, it is clear from the facts of the case that the defendant had knowledge of the copyright law, instructed his manufacturer to adapt the copies enough to avoid copyright infringement, but otherwise intended to copy designs the defendant knew were copyrighted.

In probably the strangest criminal copyright infringement case, two of the Marx Brothers (Groucho and Chico) were convicted of infringing and aiding and abetting the infringement of copyright in a dramatic composition (a radio script). *Marx v. United States*, 96 F. 2d 204 (9th Cir. 1938). An indictment was upheld that merely charged willful infringement by the intentional copying. Evidence that the Marx Brothers met with the author one year before the infringing broadcast, discussed the use of the script in a radio broadcast, and knew the script was copyrighted was sufficient to prove willfulness.

The *Marx* case appears to be an aberration. The proof adduced to establish "willful" infringement is a kind of proof normally submitted to prove ordinary civil infringement. This case does not represent the law of the Ninth Circuit now. Cases like *Wise, Drebin, and Atherton*—all decided towards the end of the 1909 Copyright Act—require specific intent to infringe.

The Government argued for the lesser "deliberate intent to copy" standard *United States v. Moran,* 757 F. Supp. 1046, 1048 (1987) and was rebuffed. Although *Moran* was a district court case, it seems to reflect at least the prevailing and perhaps consistent view under existing law.

---

two pre-1945 cases, one in each circuit, that may imply an intent to copy establishes willfulness. *United States v. Backer,* 134 F. 2d 533 (2d. Cir. 1943) and *Marx v. United States,* 96 Fed. 204 (9th Cir. 1938).

[14] 550 F. 2d at 1194, fn. 27. *Accord, United States v. Drebin*, 557 F. 2d 1316, 1324 (9th Cir. 1977) (overwhelming proof of willfulness in evidence defendants familiar with motion picture industry practices and copyright law and knew it was a Federal offense to copy motion picture prints); *United States v. Atherton,* 561 F. 2d 747, 752 (9th Cir. 1977) (willfulness established by proof defendant intentionally sold unauthorized motion picture prints and knew that these sales in violation of the copyright law were illegal); *United States v. Sherman*, 576 F. 2d 292, 297 (10th Cir. 1978) (proof of specific intent to infringe established by evidence defendant reproduced record tapes he knew were actual recorded performances of famous artists); *United States v. Whetzel*, 589 F. 2d 707 (D.C. Cir. 1978) (past infringements relevant to show knowledge of copyright law and intent to infringe); *United States v. Rose*, 149 U.S.P.Q. 820 (S.D.N.Y. 1966) (an act is done willfully if done voluntarily and purposely and with specific intent to do that which the law forbids—that is, with bad purpose either to disobey or disregard the law).

To support this argument, the Government cited *United States v. Backer* (discussed above) and *United States v. Taxe,* 540 F. 2d 961 (9th Cir. 1976). In *Taxe*, the court did not discuss willfulness other than to note the trial judge had instructed the jury that in determining willfulness it should consider the fact that defendant acted on counsel's advice that his planned copying of the recordings was non-infringing. 540 F. 2d at 969. The court in this case was dealing with a prototypical record pirate who was found with 19,000 infringing recordings in his possession. He knew about the Sound Recording Act of 1971 (and the 1974 Act making sound recording copyright permanent). He attempted to circumvent the copyright law on advice of counsel by making minor technical adjustments and allegedly "re-recording" the sounds. He hoped thereby to argue he did not "duplicate" the "actual sounds" of the recordings he copied.[15] The court rejected these arguments and, in effect, found specific intent to infringe.

In summary, alleged interpretive "split" in the Courts of Appeal on the term "willful" in 17 U.S.C. §506(a) is not clearly discernible. Interpretation under the 1976 Copyright Act appears to require specific intent, that is, as intentional, voluntary violation of a known legal duty—a deliberate intent to infringe the copyright and not merely to deliberate intent to copy. There are few decisions discussing willfulness, however; therefore, an interpretation that criminal copyright infringement requires specific intent may not be firmly established.

Purpose of Commercial Advantage

That an infringer must have a "for profit" motive to be prosecuted for criminal copyright infringement has essentially been part of the copyright law from the beginning of criminal infringement in 1897.

Congress made a slight language change effective January 1, 1978, which is embodied in existing law. The phrase "for purposes of commercial advantage or private financial gain" replaced the "for profit" terminology. The change does not appear to have substantive significance,[16] but simply better reflects the case law interpretation of the "for profit" element. One need not "profit" from the infringement; one must simply make an attempt to profit, or have a hope that commercial gain will be realized from the infringement.[17]

Traditional, a for-profit motive has been required to criminalize copyright infringement for two principal reasons: 1) To avoid subjecting teachers, professors, librarians, researchers, scholars, and other nonprofit users to the threat of criminal liability; and 2) to avoid the potentially chilling effect on free expression that exposure to criminal liability could have on

---

[15] The Second Sound Recording Act of 1971, 85 Stat. 931, extended a narrow reproduction right to sound recordings. The right was "limited to the right to duplicate the sound recording in a tangible form that directly or indirectly recaptures the actual sound fixed in the recording." That the right was limited to duplication of the actual sounds was emphasized by a proviso that specified that "this right does not extend to the making or duplication of another sound recording that is an independent fixation of other sounds, even though such sounds imitate or simulate those in the copyrighted sound recording..." Section 1(f) of the Copyright Act of 1909, in effect on February 15, 1972. Richard Taxe and other "record pirates" attempted to evade civil and criminal liability by making minor changes in the course of "duplicating" records. The courts rejected these evasive tactics.

[16] *United States v. Moran*, 757 F. Supp. 1046, 1049-1050, fn. 2 (D. Neb 1991).

[17] *United States v. Cross,* 816 F. 2d. 297, 301 (7th Cir. 1987).

nonprofit writers and publishers (e.g., university publications, symposia, professional society publications, etc.).

The *United States v. Steele,* 785 F. 2d 743 (9th Cir. 1984), a film collector attempted to argue he had no motive of "commercial gain" but merely exchanged or swapped videotapes with "friends." The evidence showed sales of 20-25 copies to one "friend" and two copies to another for prices from $10-$80. This was sufficient evidence that defendant "was in business for commercial or private financial gain." 785 F. 2d at 749.

The requisite "commercial/financial gain" motive can exist with respect to an employee who knowingly participates in a copyright infringing activity that is for the purpose of financial gain. *United States v. Cross,* 816 F. 2d 297 (7th Cir. 1987)(chief clerk—resident female companion of co-worker of infringing video rental business has requisite commercial purpose).

Because prosecutors determined that he lacked the requisite "commercial purpose," criminal copyright charges were not filed against M.I.T. student David LaMacchia when he established an electronic bulletin board on the Internet and encouraged others to upload popular computer software for downloading by others. Instead, federal prosecutors attempted to convict LaMacchia under the wire fraud statute. 18 U.S.C. §1343. A district court judge dismissed this indictment, however, on grounds that the wire fraud statute does not reach copyright-related infringing conduct. *United States v. LaMacchia,* 871 F. Supp. 535 (D. Mass. 1994).

In an effort to provide criminal penalties against *LaMacchia*-type activities on the Internet and other computer networks, Senator Leahy has introduced a bill (S. 1122), which would effect major changes in criminal copyright liability.

ANALYSIS OF S. 1122

Summary

The pending bill proposes to change the *mens rea* standard for criminal copyright infringement and thereby extend criminal liability to new classes of users of copyrighted works, specifically nonprofit users and those who barter or exchange copyrighted works. It also lengthens the period for criminal prosecution by changing the statute of limitations, revises the statutory thresholds for distinguishing between misdemeanor and felony offenses, and makes an infringing transmission a felony offense for the first time.

The most important changes that S. 1122 would effect in the scope of criminal liability are:

- Criminal prosecution of nonprofit users of copyrighted works made possible for the first time ever (if $5,000 threshold is met)

- Criminal prosecution of users who barter/exchange copyrighted works is made possible apparently for the first time, without any minimum retail value for the goods

- Felony prosecution of nonprofit users of copyrighted works is made possible (if $10,000 threshold is met; no 180-day limit)
- Felony prosecution of users who barter/exchange copyrighted works is made possible (if statutory thresholds are met: 10 or more copies/phonorecords reproduced/distributed/transmitted within 180-day period, having a retail value of more than $5,000)
- Felony prosecution is possible against someone who transmits, or assists others in reproducing/distributing copyrighted works (if statutory thresholds are met)[18]
- Statute of limitations for criminal prosecution increased from three to five years
- The statutory thresholds distinguishing between misdemeanor and felony offenses are revised; different standards are set for nonprofit infringers and "commercial purpose" infringers[19]

Discussion

1) Nonprofit Infringers

The single most important and consequential change proposed in S. 1122 is modification of the *mens rea* standard to eliminate a "commercial purpose" as an *essential* element of criminal copyright infringement.

The change is effected by amending 17 U.S.C. §506(a) to create two copyright infringement offenses. One offense requires proof beyond a reasonable doubt of willful infringement for purposes of commercial advantage or private financial gain.[20] The second, entirely new offense, requires proof beyond a reasonable doubt of willful infringement by the reproduction, distribution, or transmission (including assisting others in reproduction or distribution) of one or more copies[21] of one or more copyrighted works having a total retail value of $5,000 or more.

This new criminal offense is a misdemeanor if the retail value of the works infringed falls between $5,000 and $10,000. If the value exceeds $10,000, the offense becomes a felony. Unlike existing law and unlike the modifies "commercial purpose" offense, the "nonprofit" offense lacks a 180-day limit for aggregating the infringing activity. Infringing activity that is spread out over the five-year period of the new statute of limitations (discussed below) could be aggregated to reach the $5,000 threshold for a misdemeanor offense or the "more than $10,000" threshold for a felony offense.

---

[18] In the case of nonprofit infringers, the felony threshold is the $10,000 retail value, without any minimum number of infringing copies and without any time limit. In the case of "commercial purpose" infringers, the felony thresholds are the 10 copies or phonorecords within a 180-day period having a retail value of more than $5,000.

[19] *Ibid.*

[20] This "commercial purpose" offense is also modified by defining "financial gain" to include barter or exchange for value, including receipt of copyrighted works.

[21] A drafting adjustment should probably be made in proposed §506(a)(2)—the nonprofit criminal offense. The bill refers only to infringement by one or more "copies". It should read "copies or phonorecords."

The sponsors of S. 1122 made clear in their introduction of the bill that they see the "commercial purpose" element of the existing law as an "enormous loophole in criminal liability for willful infringers…"[22] The main thrust of the bill is to "close this loophole" and make possible the criminal prosecution of nonprofit infringers like M.I.T student David LaMacchia.[23]

Undoubtedly, if the Congress decides that criminal copyright liability is necessary to deter willful nonprofit infringers (notwithstanding the historical arguments against criminal liability for these infringers), an amendment similar to S. 1122 will achieve that objective. It should be clear, however, from any review of the history of criminal copyright liability that the "commercial purpose" element of the offense has not previously been considered a "loophole." The "commercial purpose" element of the offense has not been deliberately chosen by Congress for nearly 100 years to insulate nonprofit infringers from the threat of criminal prosecution. Until now, the possibility of civil liability has been considered adequate and fair in response to the economic impact of nonprofit infringement.

In comparison with other forms of intellectual property, an argument can be made that exposure to criminal *copyright* liability is already strong. For example, there is no criminal liability for violation of the digital audio recording statutory license of 17 U.S.C., chapter 10; for infringement of the semiconductor chip/integrated circuit design rights of the title 17 U.S.C., chapter 9; or for infringement of any patent rights in title 35 U.S.C. Criminal liability for trademark infringement has existed only for 11 years, since enactment of the Trademark Counterfeiting Act of 1984, 18 U.S.C. §2320(a). Within the copyright law itself, there is no criminal liability for infringement of the software and record rental rights. 17 U.S.C. § 109(b)(4).

In essence, Congress has proceeded cautiously in creating criminal liability for infringement of intellectual property. Some major intellectual property rights are enforced only through civil remedies. The criminal remedies for willful copyright infringement for profit have a longer history than criminal remedies for other violations of intellectual property rights, but Congress has always proceeded cautiously in the copyright field also.

Under S. 1122 large new classes of users of copyrighted works risk exposure to the threat of criminal prosecution, depending upon the enforcement policies of the Justice Department and local United States Attorneys. These nonprofit users include teachers, professors, students, librarians, researchers, scholars, Internet users, and member of the general public.

To the extent that "willful" is interpreted as requiring a specific intent to infringe the Copyright Act, the true exposure to criminal liability is significantly reduced. However, threats may be made by copyright proprietors against nonprofit groups. Also, the government in criminal prosecutions in the past has argued for the lesser "intent-to-copy" standard of willfulness,[24] which broadens the risk of criminal liability for ordinary citizens.

---

[22] 141 CONG. REC. S11451, S11452 (daily ed. August 4, 1995) (Statement of Sen. Leahy).

[23] *Unites States v. LaMacchia*, 871 F. Supp. 535 (D. Mass. 1994) (wire fraud indictment dismissed; nor criminal copyright liability for nonprofit infringer).

[24] *See, United States v. Moran,* 757 F. Supp. 1046, 1048 (D. Neb. 1991) (Government's "intent-to-copy" standard rejected).

2) Definition of Financial Gain

In a change related to the extension of criminal liability to nonprofit infringers, S. 1122, while retaining a separate "commercial purpose" offense, would define "financial gain" to include receipt of anything of value. The purpose of this amendment is to equate barter or exchange with sale of the copyrighted works establishing a "commercial purpose." The existing Copyright Act does not define the phrase "for purposes of commercial advantage or private financial gain" or any of its constituent parts.

The modified "commercial purpose" offense applies to any such willful copyright infringement. As under current law, this offense would be a misdemeanor except where certain statutory thresholds are met. The "commercial purpose" offense is subject to felony charges for reproduction or distribution, including by transmission or assisting others, of 10 or more copies or phonorecords during a 180-day period of one or more copyrighted works having a total retail value of more that $5,000. The retail value represents an increase from the "more than $2,500" value of existing law.

The inclusion of barter or exchanges of value, including receipt of other copyrighted works, apparently represents a significant broadening of the "commercial purpose" offense compared to existing law. One can argue that the existing law could have been stretched to include the value of bartered works, to satisfy the "for profit" element, but criminal prosecutions have generally been confined to attempts to sell unauthorized copies or phonorecords.

3) Felony Charges for Transmissions

In a change that is almost as consequential as the extension of copyright liability to nonprofit infringers, S. 1122 for the first time makes possible felony prosecutions for unauthorized transmission of copyrighted works.

"Transmission" of a copyrighted work is not expressly designated as one of the exclusive rights of the copyright owner under existing law.[25] It is generally understood that "transmissions" are a subset of the public performance right under existing law. Satellite transmissions, cable transmissions, and presumably computer network transmissions are subject to the public performance right and the limitations on that right.

If the transmission is private, there is no copyright liability—civil or criminal. The same result follows if one of the exemption from, or limitations on, the public performance right is applicable.[26]

If copyright liability arises under existing law for an unauthorized transmission, criminal liability is subject only to misdemeanor charges. This is because only infringements of the rights of reproduction or distribution are subject to felony charges under existing law. The difference in penalties has existed since felony charges first became possible for second offenses of record piracy in 1974.

---

[25] In its final report, the Working Group on Intellectual Property Rights of the national Information Infrastructure Task Force recommends amendment of the Copyright Act to grant an exclusive transmission right by redefining the distribution right of 17 U.S.C. 106(3) (Commerce Department, September 1995), page 213. (Hereafter, "NII Working Group Report").

[26] For example, the exemption of 17 U.S.C. §110(2) for performance of a non-dramatic literary or musical in the course of instructional broadcasting; the exemption of §110(5) for public reception of radio and television signals on home-style receiving equipment absent a direct charge for the reception; the cable compulsory license of 17 U.S.C. §111(c)-(f); the satellite carrier compulsory license of 17 U.S.C. §119.

S. 1122 equates "transmissions" with reproductions and distributions. A new offense of "assisting others" in the infringing reproduction of distribution of copyrighted works is also created by the bill.[27] The proposal concerning transmissions is consistent with the civil liability recommendations of the Report of the NII Working Group on Intellectual Property Rights.[28] One possible legislative choice would be to delay consideration of new felony liability for transmissions until the issue can be considered in the context of the proposal for broader civil liability.

4) Statute of Limitations

The bill would increase from three to five years the statute of limitations on commencing criminal prosecution for copyright infringement.

Under existing law, the limitation on commencing civil or criminal infringement is essentially the same: three years after the cause of action arose (criminal action) or three years after the claim accrued (civil action).[29]

Lengthening the period for commencing a criminal action would make criminal prosecution easier. The government could take a longer time to investigate the case. The longer period, coupled with the absence of a 180-day limit for the nonprofit infringer's offense, would substantially increase the exposure of certain classes of citizens to criminal liability. The longer period could also be used to delay prosecution until the statutory threshold could be met for felony charges against nonprofit infringers.

5) Victim Impact Statements

For the first time, the bill proposes to add provisions relating to victim impact statements to the criminal copyright penalty provisions,[30] the criminal penalties for unauthorized fixations of live music,[31] and the criminal penalties for trafficking in counterfeit goods or services.[32]

With respect to each criminal offense, the producers and sellers of legitimate works/products, holders of the relevant intellectual property rights, and legal representatives of such producers, sellers, and rights holders would have the right to present a victim statement during preparation of the pre-sentence report pursuant to rule 32(c) of the Federal Rule of Criminal Procedure. The statement could identify the victim of the offense and describe the extent and scope of the injury and loss suffered by the victim, including the estimated economic impact of the offense.

The bill also directs the Sentencing Commission to ensure that the applicable guideline range for a defendant convicted of an intellectual property offense is sufficiently stringent to

---

[27] The Copyright Act of 1909, effective until December 31, 1988, had included an offense of knowingly and willfully aiding or abetting in an infringement. This offense was eliminated by the Copyright Act of 1976.

[28] The Report of the Working Group also expressed general support for the amendments of the copyright law set forth in S. 1122, but did not specifically address the significance of creating a felony for transmission of works. NII Working Group Report at 229.

[29] 17 U.S.C. §507.

[30] 18 U.S.C. §2319.

[31] 18 U.S.C. §2319A.

[32] 18 U.S.C. §2320.

deter such a crime, and to reflect adequately the retail value and quantity of the legitimate items that are infringed.

ARGUMENTS FOR AND AGAINST INCREASED CRIMINAL COPYRIGHT LIABILITY

Supporting Arguments

The principal supporters of the legislation are copyright owners of computer software, databases, and other works likely to be distributed or transmitted through the Internet, other computer networks, and electronic bulletin boards. Copyright owners are likely to support the bill.

The sponsors of the bill see the "commercial purpose" element of the offense as an "enormous loophole in the criminal liability for willful infringers who can use digital technology to make exact copies of copyrighted software and other digitally encoded works, ad then computer networks for quick, inexpensive and mass distribution of pirated, infringing works."[33]

The case of *United States v. LaMacchia,* 871 F. Supp. 535 (D. Mass. 1994) is cited as an example of the problem the bill addresses. It is alleged that LaMacchia's nonprofit, but infringing, activities "resulted in an estimated loss to the copyright holders of over one million dollars over a 6-week period."[34]

In the past, civil remedies for copyright violations were considered adequate to deter nonprofit infringers. It is argued that computer networks, like the Internet, now enable anyone to engage in mass distribution/transmission of digitized copyrighted works, sometimes at virtually no cost. The potential for mass infringement by, for example, intellectual property "vandals," it is argued, can be deterred only be criminal penalties. Civil remedies are inadequate because many nonprofit infringers, like the student LaMacchia, are "judgment-proof"—they cannot pay large civil damages. It is too expensive to bring civil infringement suits merely to enjoin the infringer, if there is no realistic possibility of collecting a monetary judgment.

Supporters of the bill argue that the "monetary thresholds, combined with the scienter requirement, would ensure that criminal charges would only apply to willful infringements, not merely casual or careless conduct, that result in a significant level of harm to the copyright holder's rights."[35]

---

[33] 141 CONG. REC. S11451, S11452 (daily ed. August 4, 1995) (Statement of Sen. Leahy).
[34] *Ibid.*
[35] *Ibid.*

Opposing Arguments

Opposition to S. 1122, or at least serious concern, has been expressed within the education community. It is likely that the concern will increase as more segments of the nonprofit communities become aware of the bill.

Opponents would argue that S. 1122 is no a bill that merely closes a "loophole" in the criminal law of copyright infringement. It proposes the most radical change in the *mens rea* standard since criminal copyright liability was created in 1897. The bill removes the one safeguard that the library and educational communities have had against possible threats of criminal liability.

Copyright owners, it is argued, do not need the luxury of criminal penalties against nonprofit users. Without commercial purpose, virtually any infringing activity would have only a slight impact on the copyright holder's rights. If there is significant economic impact, the copyright owners should enforce their rights through civil remedies.

Opponents see. S. 1122 as an overreaction to an isolated, exceptional action by a student computer "hacker." They argue there is no justification for exposing millions of ordinary citizens to criminal liability. The copyright law is a mystery to ordinary citizens. The intangible nature of the complex rights means that they can be "intentionally" infringed through mistakes or misunderstandings. If there is a mistaken but possibly "intentional" distribution through a computer network, criminal liability for nonprofit infringers could theoretically ensnare millions of ordinary citizens.

The standard of "willfulness" as interpreted by prosecutors is not an adequate safeguard against excessive criminal liability for nonprofit users.

Even if the courts uniformly interpret "willful" to require specific intent to infringe, a point not clearly settled, factual issues will arise as a whether or not the standard has been satisfied. Under S. 1122, it is argued, nonprofit users will face the risk of criminal prosecution, or threats of prosecution, in the form of intimidation tactics by rights holders and perhaps government authorities.

The statutory thresholds of $5,000 for misdemeanor offenses and $10,000 for felony offenses are no safeguards against overzealous invocation of criminal liability, opponents argue. In today's marketplace, these amounts are easily aggregated, especially since nonprofit infringers do not have the benefit of the 180-day time limitation that is granted to "for profit" infringers. Also, the lengthening of the statue of limitations period to five years substantially increases citizen exposure to criminal copyright liability.

Opponents of S. 1122 would also argue that imposition of a felony liability for transmissions is at best premature and at worst unjustified. At a minimum, it is argued, felony liability for transmissions should be thoughtfully examined as part of the consideration of the recommendations of the Working Group on Intellectual Property Rights of the National Information Infrastructure Task Force.

CONCLUSIONS

Congress has until now concluded that nonprofit infringers are adequately deterred by civil remedies. S. 1122 would extend criminal liability to willful nonprofit infringers if the retail value of the works infringed is $5,000 or more. The bill also makes infringement by transmission a felony offense for the first time.

Proponents of S. 1122 argue that criminal penalties are necessary in the digital world and cyberspace. They assert that the potential for mass copying/distribution/transmission of digitized works over the Internet, other computer networks, and electronic bulletin boards cannot be controlled merely with civil remedies. Unauthorized copying can, within a short time frame and at little cost to the infringer, cause millions of dollars of damages to rights holders. Proponents say criminal penalties are needed to highlight the seriousness of the violation, deter potential infringers, and provide remedies against those who are "judgment-proof."

Opposition to S. 1122, or at least serious concern, has been expressed within the education community. Copyright owners, it is argued, have strong civil remedies and do not need the luxury of criminal penalties against nonprofit users. Without a commercial purpose, virtually any infringing activity would have only a slight impact on the copyright. Where there is an economic impact, copyright owners should enforce their rights through civil remedies. Opponents see S. 1122 as an overreaction to an isolated, exceptional action by a college student. They are concerned that the bill exposes teachers, librarians and other nonprofit users to the threat of criminal liability for the first time. They doubt that the statutory thresholds and standard of willfulness are sufficient safeguards against overzealous rights holders and prosecutors.

Legislative options to address the concerns of the education community might include: an exemption for teachers and librarians; clarification of the willfulness standard to require a specific intent to infringe; substantial upward revision of the statutory thresholds for nonprofit infringers; or express exemption for persons acting on a belief that their activity is non-infringing.

Another alternative approach would be to consider the proposed changes in criminal liability in tandem with the legislative recommendations of the Working Group on Intellectual Property Rights, National Information Infrastructure Task Force.

As another alternative, Congress might consider amendment of the wire fraud statute rather than the copyright law. Under this approach, Congress could establish criminal liability under 18 U.S.C. §1343 for using wires, radio, television, satellites, or other transmission facilities with the intent to deceive or defraud someone with respect to an intellectual property interest.

COPYRIGHT TERM EXTENSION AND MUSIC LICENSING: REVIEW OF RECENT DEVELOPMENTS

Dorothy Schrader

SUMMARY

Duration of copyright is one of the major parameters for establishing the amount of protection accorded authors and other owner of copyright. It is also the principal dividing line between the property rights of these owners and the public domain—that is, the domain of unprotected works, which are available to the public for unrestricted, uncompensated use.

Under the United States Constitution, Art. I, Sec. 8, Cl. 8, Congress is authorized to grant copyright only for "limited times." Under current law, copyright in post-1977[1] works endures generally for the life of the author plus 50 years for personal works, or the shorter of 75 years from publication or 100 years from creation in the case of works made for hire, anonymous works, or pseudonymous works. If a personal work is created jointly by two or more authors, the term is measured by the life of the last surviving author. Copyright in pre-1978 works endures generally for 75 years from publication with notice of copyright or registration in Copyright Office as an unpublished work.

---

[1] The last general revision of the copyright law was enacted in 1976 and took effect on January 1, 1978. Public Law 94-553, Act of October 19, 1976, codified as Title 17, U.S. Code, §§101 *et seq.* This general revision effected many important changes in the law, including a change in computation of the copyright term. For various reasons, including fairness and possible impairment of contracts, Congress changed the basis for computing the copyright term only for post-1977 works, that is, works in which copyright is secured under the conditions of the law effective January 1, 1978. For personal works (i.e., works created by known authors who are not employees of another person or entity) copyrighted after 1977, the term is based on the life of the author plus 50 years. For impersonal works, the term is a fixed period, which is the shorter of 75 years from publication or 100 years from creation. For pre-1978 copyrighted works, the term is also a fixed period of 75 years—computed from the date copyright was secured. All of an author's post-1977 copyrights expire (and enter the public domain, therefore) at the same time. Copyright in pre-1978 works expires individually for each work.

MOST RECENT DEVELOPMENTS

Bills pending in Congress (S. 505 and H.R. 2589) would extend the existing copyright terms generally by an additional 20 years. The extended terms would apply retroactively to all works in which copyright no exists.

On March 25, 1998, the House of Representatives passed H.R. 2589 with several amendments. Title II of H.R. 2589 contains three of the core provisions of a separate bill, H.R. 789, known as the "Fairness in Musical Licensing Act." H.R. 2589 and S. 505 are under consideration by the Senate Judiciary Committee.

This chapter summarizes H.R. 2589 as passed by the House of Representatives and reviews and summarizes the arguments for and against the term extension and the music licensing proposals.[2]

SUMMARY OF COPYRIGHT TERM-EXTENSION PROVISIONS

Title I of H.R. 2589 would increase the term of existing and future copyrights by 20 years. Essentially the same term-extension proposals were considered but not enacted in the 104th Congress.[3] The House Judiciary Committee reported favorably on H.R. 2589 with amendments on March 18, 1998.[4] The House passed the bill with further amendments, including the music licensing provisions of Title II, on March 25, 1998.

Title I of H.R. 2589, in addition to adding 20 years to the term of existing and future copyrights, would: 1) grant a new, limited termination right[5] with respect to the 20-year period; 2) expand the classes of persons eligible to terminate licensing contracts; 3) grant libraries and nonprofit educational institutions a narrow exemption to use copyrighted works during the 20-year period if the works are not commercially exploited and copies are not available at a reasonable price; 4) express a "sense of Congress" view encouraging private sector interests to negotiate voluntary agreements to establish an audiovisual works fund allocating royalties received from the exploitation of motion pictures during the 20-year period; and 5) require the assumption by transferees of motion picture rights of certain collective bargaining contractual obligations.

---

[2] This chapter does not discuss S. 505 further, but notes that the basic term-extension provisions of S. 505 and H.R. 2589 are identical. The music licensing provisions are not included in S. 505. For a more detailed analysis of the term-extension issues, see a separate report by D. Schrader, "*Proposed U.S. Copyright Term Extension*," CRS Report No. 95-799 S. For a more detailed analysis of the musical licensing issues, see a separate report by D. Schrader, *'Music Licensing Copyright Proposals: An Overview of H.R. 789 and S. 28*, "CRS Report No. 97-789 A.

[3] S. 483 and H.R. 989. Hearings were held on H.R. 989 by the House Subcommittee on Courts and Intellectual Property on June 1, 1995 and July 13, 1995. Senate hearings were held on September 20, 1995. The Senate Judiciary Committee reported an amended version of S. 483. S. REP. 104-315, 104th Cong., 2d Sess. (1996). No further action occurred on either bill in the 104th Congress.

[4] H.R. REP. 105-452, 105th Cong., 2d Sess. (1998).

[5] A "termination right" is an inalienable right granted by the copyright statute to authors and their heirs to revoke an earlier contract assigning or licensing fights to another party, after a certain period of years.

Copyright Term Extensions

- For post-1977 personal works, the copyright term would become life of the author plus 70 years.

- For post-1977 works for hire, anonymous or pseudonymous works, the term would become the shorter of 95 years from publication or 120 years from creation.

- For pre-1978 works, the term would become 95 years from the date copyright was secured either by publication with notice of copyright, or, in the case of unpublished works, be registration.

All of the extended terms would apply retroactively to any work in which copyright now exists, and to the works that have been retrieved from the public domain by the 1994 law implementing the General Agreement on Tariffs and Trade (GATT).[6]

Another special provision would extend the term of works created but not copyrighted before 1978 (i.e., unpublished, unregistered works) by 20 years (by increasing their expiration date from 2027 to 2047), provided the work is published by December 31, 2002.[7] Preemption of common law/state law copyright in pre-February 15, 1972, sound recordings is also delayed 20 years from February 15, 2047, to February 15, 2067.

Termination Provisions of H.R. 2589 (Title I)

Termination provisions affect transfer and ownership of the rights granted to authors under the copyright statute. They are a means for regulating who benefits from a statutory increase in the length of the copyright term. The exercise of termination rights essentially effects a reversion of the copyright (or other partial rights) back to the original author-owner (or the heirs of the author) notwithstanding a contractual assignment of the property to another.

Existing copyright law contains two termination provisions. One termination clause applies to "old law works" (i.e., works copyrighted before 1978), which is found at section 304(c) of the 1976 Copyright Act. It applies to grants (i.e., licensing agreements) executed before January 1, 1978, by the author or any statutory renewal claimant. The holder of the

---

[6] Uruguay Round Agreements Act, Pub. L. No. 103-465 (December 8, 1994). For eligible works, copyright restoration occurred automatically one year after the effective date of the entry into force of the World Trade Organization. Therefore, these copyrights were restored effective January 1, 1996. While the eligibility rules are complicated, in general copyright is restored for "foreign-origin" (i.e., non-United States origin) Berne Convention works. The Berne Convention is the major international copyright treaty, of which the United States became a member on March 1, 1989.

[7] The general revision of the copyright law effective January 1, 1978, preempted common law and state statutory copyrights in unpublished works. Congress granted these works a minimum federal term of 25 years. The term can be increased to 50 years by publication on or before December 31, 2002. H.R. 2589 fixes a 70-year term, if the work is published before 2003. The purpose of the existing law was to provide minimum federal protection for pre-1978 common law works, in order to assure the constitutionality of federal preemption, and to encourage early publication of unpublished works. Since common law copyright was apparently perpetual, many of these works had been protected already for decades or hundreds of years by the states before 1978. No change is proposed to the 25-year term for works created before 1978 if they are not published by December 31, 2002.

termination right can terminate the pre-1978 grant with respect to the 19-year period added to the copyright term for "old law works" by the 1976 Act.

The second termination clause of existing law applies to "new law works" (i.e., works copyrighted on or after January 1, 1978). Under section 203 of the 1976 Copyright Act, grants by the author relating to new law works can be terminated 35 years after their execution.

H.R. 2589 would give a new termination right[8] to the author or other owner of a termination right in a pre-1978 grant, whose right to terminate under section 304(c) has already expired without being exercised. The basic structure of the existing "304(c)" termination right is retained by SEC. 102(d) of H.R. 2589. The time limit for exercising the right is changed, however, and the new "304(d)" termination right applies to the 20-year extension legislated by the bill. Termination could be effected at anytime during a 5-year period beginning at the end of the 75-year copyright term.

The new "304(d)" termination right would apply only to grants executed before January 1, 1978.

If the existing section304(c) termination right has already been exercised, the holder of the exercised termination right would own the copyright in the 20-year added period, unless the copyright has already been re-assigned post-termination. Such re-assignments are not terminable. In that case, the assignee would own the copyright during the 20-year added period.

SEC. 103 of H.R. 2589 makes a second change in the termination provisions of existing law. Unlike the first, above-discussed change, the amendment effected by SEC. 103 applies both to "old law" and to "new law" works. Under existing law, the author's executor under a will, administrator, personal representative, or trustee have no termination right. The next of kin have a termination right in transfers, which they may have granted with respect to "old law" works but have no termination rights in "new law" works. SEC. 103 of H.R. 2589 grants termination right to the author's executor to terminate the author's interest, if the author, spouse, children, and grandchildren are deceased. Also, in the absence of a will and no surviving author, spouse, child, or grandchild, the administrator, personal representative, or trustee of the author's estate would own the author's termination interest in the case of both "old law" and "new law" transfers by author.

Reproduction by Libraries and Archives During the 20-Year Added Period

Libraries, archives, and educational groups expressed concerns about diminution of the public domain as a consequence of adding 20 more years to the copyright term. In partial response to these concerns, SEC. 104 of H.R. 2589 could amend 17 U.S.C. 108 to limit the rights of copyright owners against libraries, archives, and nonprofit educational institutions during the 20-year period for preservation, scholarship, or research purposes, if the works are not being commercially exploited and copies or phonorecords cannot be obtained at a reasonable price.

This exemption does not apply after notice by the copyright owner that the conditions for use are not satisfied or to subsequent users other than the exempt entities.

---

[8] The new termination fight would be codified as section 304(d) of 17 U.S.C.

Motion Picture Contracts: Division of Royalties During the 20-Year Added Period

Term-extension proponents place great emphasis on the need to harmonize U.S. copyright terms with European Union terms. They argue that this harmonization will result in increased economic benefits through the additional 20 years of royalties from foreign licensing of commercially valuable U.S. works.

In the case of motion pictures, it is not certain that term extension will result in 20 years of added royalties abroad. The question arises because of the treatment of impersonal works, works made for hire, and "related rights" in the European Union, in comparison with the treatment of these works or rights in the United States.

Under existing U.S. law, virtually all commercially significant theatrical motion pictures are "works made for hire." The copyright endures for the shorter of 75 years from publication or 100 years from creation.

The Berne Convention (to which the United States and the European Union States are bound) sets a minimum term for motion pictures at either i) life of the author plus 50 years, or ii) 50 years from making the motion picture publicly available (or if not publicly available, 50 years from the making).

Article 2(2) of the European Union Directive on Copyright Duration sets the term for "cinematographic or audiovisual works" at the life of the author(s) plus 70 years after the death of the last of four contributors to survive—the principal director, the author of the screenplay, the author of the dialogue, and the composer of the music specifically created for the motion picture. This life-based term is established in the context of another provision that mandates that at least the principal director shall be considered the author.[9] Article 3(3) of the European Union Directive provides that the "related rights" of the film is lawfully published or lawfully communicated to the public during that period, 50 years from the first publication or communication to the public, whichever is earlier. The term "film" specifically designates a "cinematographic or audiovisual work," according to Article 3(3) of the Directive.[10]

Under these standards, what European Union terms applies to U.S. motion pictures and who is entitled to collect licensing fees for uses of the motion picture in European Union countries during the extended 20-year period? The answers are not self-evident. These issues will likely be the subject of future trade negotiations between the United States and the European Unions.

The fundamental conflict between U.S. and European treatment of motion picture copyrights arises because, in general, the Europeans believe that, at least some of the principal, individual creative artist who contribute to the creation of the motion picture, should be considered authors and owners of copyright. United States law, on the other hand, rests on the view that theatrical motion pictures are usually corporate, collaborative creations,

---

[9] Article 2(1) of the European Union Directive on Copyright Duration (effective July 1, 1995) (hereafter, the "EU Directive").

[10] The optional term of a fixed 70 year period for certain copyrights owned by legal persons does not seem to apply to U.S. motion pictures. The requirement of Article 2(1) to make the director an author seems to foreclose application of the "legal person" provision to theatrical motion pictures. Since the director of a theatrical motion picture is given screen credit, the naming of this "author" on the work means the "legal person" option cannot be applied.

and therefore the production company is generally considered the author (of a work made for hire) and the owner of copyright. Further, in the United States, the rights of the creative talent are recognized through collective bargaining agreements between the motion picture producers and the unions or guilds representing the creative artists rather than through rights under the copyright law.

In an effort to clarify further the rights of contributors to U.S. motion pictures, H.R. 2589 contains two sections dealing with licensing of motion pictures during the 20-year period.

SEC. 105 expresses a "sense of Congress" viewpoint. It is intended to encourage voluntary agreements between the producers and the various contributors to a motion picture leading to the establishment of a fund or other mechanism for the division of royalties accrued during the 20-year period.

SEC. 106 of H.R. 2589 amends Part VI of title 28 U.S.C. by adding a new Chapter 180 dealing with the assumption of contractual obligations when transferring motion picture rights. The contractual obligations referenced are those that attach to motion pictures because of collective guilds or unions representing various contributors to the creation of motion pictures such as directors, screenwriters, actors and actresses, composers, lyricists, musicians, and other artistic talents. With the exception of collective bargaining agreements limited to the public performance right, SEC. 106 requires that the transfer of motion picture rights shall be deemed to incorporate the collective bargaining agreements negotiated after the enactment of H.R. 2589, if the transferee knew or had reason to know about the agreements, or if there is an existing court order against the transferor which the latter is not able to satisfy within 90 days after the order is issued.

If the transferor of the motion picture rights fails to notify the transferee of the collective bargaining obligations and the transferee becomes bound by a court order to make payments under the collective bargaining agreement, the transferor is liable to a damages claim by the transferee.

SUMMARY OF MUSIC LICENSING PROVISIONS—TITLE II

Under the existing law—Copyright Act of 1976[11]—the owner of copyright in a musical work is granted the exclusive right to perform the work publicly [17 U.S.C. 106(4)], subject to specific limitations and exemptions.

A musical work is "publicly performed" if it is rendered or played directly or by means of any device or process either i) at a place open to the public or any place where a substantial number of persons outside of the normal circle of family and social acquaintances is gathered, or ii) by transmission to a place open to the public or to the unassembled public which is capable of receiving the performance (for example, by radio, television, cable, or satellite).

Performances at "semi-public" places are generally considered public performances. These places include "clubs, lodges, factories, summer camps,...schools;[12] daycare, seniors,

[11] Public Law 94-553, 90 Stat. 2541, Act of October 19, 1976, codified as title 17 of the U.S. Code, sections 101 *et seq.*

[12] H.R. REP. 1476, 94th Cong., 2d. Sess. 64 (1976) (hereafter, the "1976 House Report").

and other recreational centers; and possibly the common areas of hospitals, nursing homes, and other care facilities.[13]

Performances of music at public places such as restaurants, bars, taverns, nightclubs, conventions, and stores are public performances, whether the music is performed live, or by recordings or transmissions, and whether the music is used as background, incidental, or theme music. Of course, performances of music in concert halls, opera houses, stadiums, outdoor arenas, and similar places open to the public are public performances.

Although the above examples constitute public performances, the need to obtain a music performing license hinges upon the availability or absence of an exemption, limitation, or exception to the music copyright owner's public performance right. If the performance is neither exempt nor subject to compulsory licensing, the music user must obtain permission or a license to perform the music by negotiating the terms and conditions with the music copyright owner or an authorized agent. With few exceptions, music-performing licenses are obtained from the performing rights societies ("PRS"), who represent music copyright owners.[14]

The principal exemptions or limitations to the music performing right are set forth in section 110 of the Copyright Act, or in the compulsory licensing sections.[15]

The existing music performing right was enacted as part of the last general revision of the copyright law in the Copyright Act of 1976. Under former law, the Copyright Act of 1909, nonprofit performances of non-dramatic music were exempt. The statute did not define "nonprofit." The term was given meaning by the courts. Although the line drawn between "for-profit" and "nonprofit" performances was not always clear, in general the nonprofit exemption was applied fairly broadly. Musical performances by public broadcasting and by religious broadcasters were arguably exempt.

In the Copyright Act of 1976, Congress dropped the broad exemption for nonprofit musical performances and replaced it with a broad performance right, which is subject to specific, more narrowly drawn exemptions.

The 1976 Act also legislated a broad definition of the term "public," which results in application of the music licensing rights to "semi-public" contexts that formerly were arguably considered private performances of music (e.g., performances at membership clubs, fraternal organizations, lodges, summer camps, and perhaps private schools).[16]

The general effect of these changes from the Act of 1909 was to create a need to obtain a music performing right license on a broader basis than under the law in effect before 1978.

---

[13] Whether common areas of care facilities are "public places" has been debated but not litigated. It is likely that the private or semi-private rooms of residents or patients of care facilities are not public places.

[14] By custom and practice, music publishers and composers-lyricists generally share the) royalties obtained under the music performing fight equally – that is, 50-50 – after the PRS deducts its administrative costs. Currently, there are two major PRS who control virtually all of music licensing: the American Society of Composers, Authors, and Publishers ("ASCAP") and Broadcast Music Inc. ("BMI"). Both PRS operate under antitrust consent decrees.

[15] The Copyright Act has 5 active compulsory licenses: section 111 (cable retransmissions); section 114(f) (subscription digital audio transmissions of sound recordings); section 115 (mechanical reproduction of music); section 118 (public broadcasting license); and section 199 (satellite television license). All of these compulsory licenses affect public performance of music except the section 114(f) subscription transmission license and the section 115 recording license.

[16] *See, Metro-Goldwyn-Mayer Distributing Corp. Wyatt*, 21 C.O. BULL. 203 (D. Md. 1932). The House Report accompanying the bill later enacted as the Copyright Act of 1976 explicitly states the congressional intent to broaden the public performance right "to put performances at semi-public places under the control of the copyright owner. 1976 House Report at 64.

Since January 1, 1978, the performing rights societies have gradually extended their music licensing efforts to take full advantage of new rights granted to their members (composers, lyricist, and music publishers). The expansion of music licensing efforts has generated opposition and counter legislative proposals from groups impacted by the broader music performing right.

H.R. 789, the "Fairness in Musical Licensing Act," proposes several changes in music licensing by expanding certain exemptions to the public performance right; by requiring new licensing practices (such as arbitration of licensing rates); by establishing statutory conditions for radio per program licenses; by requiring access to PRS repertories and licensing information; and by eliminating the vicarious or contributory infringement liability of landlords and other event sponsors for the musical performances by tenants or lessees, under certain conditions.

The supporters of this music-licensing bill have linked their legislative effort with the copyright term extension bills for at least two reasons. Music licensing supporters argue that the additional 20-year period of copyright protection should be balanced by some concessions to music users. Secondly, supporters of music licensing reform argue that music copyright owners are principal beneficiaries of the term extension bill.

Music and other copyright owners deny there is any appropriate link between the copyright term extension proposals and the music licensing proposals. Copyright owners support term extension but oppose the music licensing proposals of H.R. 789 and S. 28.

Over the objections of copyright owners, H.R. 2589 was amended during floor debate in the House of Representatives to include three of the core provisions from the music-licensing bill in H.R. 2589 as Title II. The three music licensing provisions assed to H.R. 2589 are: I) additional exemptions in section 110 for performance of music by means of playing a radio or television in a public place ["business exemptions" of SEC. 202]; binding local arbitration to review the reasonableness of the rates charged by ASCAP and BMI [SEC. 203]; and elimination of vicarious or contributory infringement liability for landlords under certain conditions [SEC. 204].

Business Exemptions

Current law exempts performances of any work by public reception of broadcasts or other primary transmissions, if—reception occurs by means of receiving equipment commonly used in private homes, there is no direct charge to see or hear the transmission, and the transmission is not further distributed.

SEC. 202 of H.R. 2589 would expand the exemption for public performances of non-dramatic music in business contexts to apply to—

i) Areas of less than 3500 sq. feet where a transmission is intended to be received (excluding the customer parking area),

ii) Areas greater than 3500 sq. feet (A) if there is an audio only performance by means of not more than 6 speakers (and no more than 4 speakers in any one room) or (B) in the case of an audiovisual performance, any visual portion is communicated by no more than two devices each with a diagonal screen size no greater than 55 inches and the audio portion is transmitted under the same standards as an audio only transmission (i.e., no more than 6 speakers; no more than 4 speakers in any one room).

In addition, there can be no direct charge to see or hear the transmission, the transmission must not be further transmitted, and it must be licensed.

Amendments are also made to the existing section 110(7) exemption for performance of music in stores as part of promotional efforts to vend music and records. These changes broaden the exemption to cover audio, video, and other devices used to promote retail sales of physical equipment for playing or recording music. Other relatively small amendments strike the limited word "sole" before purpose and strike the limitation to performances "within the immediate area where the sale is occurring."

Local Arbitration of Rate Disputes

In accordance with the existing antitrust decrees[17] governing the two major performing rights societies ("PRS")—ASCAP and BMI, disputes about the rates the PRS charge music users to pay for performing right music licenses can be challenged and reviewed only in designated Rate Court in the federal district court for the Southern District of New York. Although rates must be challenged in the S.D.N.Y., the PRS can be sued for antitrust violations in any federal district court.

SEC. 203 of H.R. 2589 requires binding local arbitration of rate disputes at the option of persons or entities defined as "general music users." Local arbitration could be demanded either prior to any court action, or, in the context of an infringement suit, by annexation to the judicial proceeding. A "general music user" is defined to include persons who perform musical works publicly other than by transmission (unless the transmission occurs within a single commercial establishment or establishments under common ownership or control). Radio and television broadcasters, cable operators, and satellite service providers would not be able to invoke binding arbitration.[18]

Pre-litigation arbitration can be invoked by a general music user in cases of a rate dispute with a PRS. Court-annexed arbitration can be invoked by a general music user who is sued for infringement of the music performing right and admits the prior public performance of the music but contest the amount of the licensing fee.

The arbitrator fixes a "fair and reasonable fee," and is authorized to make infringement determinations about past performances as well as fix the fee for future performances for a period of not less than 3 years or more than 5 years (if the music user requests the arbitrator to set a fee for future performances).

---

[17] ASCAP is governed by a 1950 consent decree. BMI is governed by a 1966 consent decree, which was modified only in 1994 to establish the district court for the S.D.N.Y. as the forum to review BMI music licensing rates. A different judge would be assigned to the BMI proceedings than the judge who presides at the ASCAP proceedings.

[18] The exclusion of broadcasters, cable, and satellite providers from court-annexed arbitration is a change from the original music-licensing bill, H.R. 789. Under H.R. 789, broadcasters and other transmitters were excluded from pre-litigation arbitration but they could have invoked arbitration if they were sued for copyright infringement.

If the arbitrator makes a finding of infringement, the arbitrator can impose a penalty, which, in pre-litigation arbitration, "shall not exceed the arbitrator's determination of the fair and reasonable license fee." In short, the PRS could recover the licensing fees determined to be fair and reasonable and nothing more. In the case of court-annexed arbitration, however, greater damages are permitted. The arbitrator's award for past infringements "shall not exceed two times the amount of the blanket license fee" during the years the performances occurred.

Prohibition of Vicarious or Contributory Liability of Landlords and Event Sponsors

Under the judicially created doctrines of vicarious or contributory infringement,[19] in addition to the actual performer of musical works, the landlord, sponsor/organizer of an event, or the owner of the facilities where unlicensed music is performed, is generally liable for the infringing performance. Liability attaches if there is a financial benefit to the landlord or other facility provider, even if the contract with the performer gives the landlord no right to select the music and requires the performer to obtain a performing right license.

By custom and practice, individual performing artist ordinarily do not obtain music performing right licenses. The PRS seek to license the landlord, event sponsor, or other owner of the facilities instead of the performer. The doctrines of vicarious and contributory infringement underwrite this practice.

SEC. 204 of H.R. 2589 would amend 17 U.S.C. 501 to eliminate this vicarious or contributory infringement liability of the landlord, event sponsor/organizer, or other owner of the premises where copyrighted works are performed by a tenant or other user of the space, if the contract with the performer prohibits infringing performances and the landlord-facility provider does not exercise actual control over selection of the copyrighted works performed.[20]

Arguments for and Against Copyright Term-Extension

The arguments in favor of term extension distill to two main points: 1) economic fairness to the heirs of authors in view of increased longevity since the life-plus-50 standard was "adopted" in 1908;[21] and 2) the "economic necessity" of matching the European Union standard of life-plus-70 in order to i) avoid application of the rule of the shorter term for musical works and other personal works[22] and ii) to enhance the bargaining position of the

[19] The Copyright Act does not refer to vicarious or contributory infringement. The basic infringement provision, 17 U.S.C. 501(a), simply provides that "[a]nyone who violates any of the exclusive fights of the copyright owner.., is an infringer of the copyright...."

[20] H.R. 2589 substantially broadens the elimination of vicarious or contributory infringement liability compared to H.R. 789 (the music licensing bill) since H.R. 2589 eliminates vicarious or contributory liability for public performances of any works; H.R. 789 eliminates this liability only for musical works.

[21] Although the Berne Convention recommended a term of life-plus-50 years as early as 1908, that term did not become mandatory until the 1948 Brussels Act.

[22] The direct benefit of term-extension appears limited to these categories since the European Union accords lesser protection than existing U.S. law in the case of corporate works and works made-for-hire. The "rule of the shorter term" means that a country is entitled to compare the copyright term of its law with that of another

U.S. Government and U.S. copyright industries in international trade negotiations, both bilateral and multilateral.

Those who oppose term-extension, in addition to denying the validity of the proponent's arguments, argue that the public domain will be diminished to the detriment of the public and new authors, and that there is no proof (or reason to believe) that a 20-year extension of the term will motivate any author to greater creativity. Therefore, opponents assert, any possible benefits of an improved international trade position are far outweighed for the public by the added costs of 20 more years of restricted access without more creativity to balance these costs.

The argument based on increased longevity and economic fairness to authors' heirs assumes that it is appropriate to provide sufficient copyright duration to provide an income to authors' children and grandchildren. A subsidiary argument about economic fairness notes that modern technologies have increased the value of copyright properties for longer periods. The authors' heirs, it is asserted, should have the benefit of this extended value.

Opponents of term-extensions argue that increased longevity has already extended the period of copyright duration under the life-based system that is the international standard. Authors live longer, and their copyrights therefore endure for additional years. With respect to income for children and grandchildren, opponents argue that many authors do not have heirs, and, even if there are heirs of the author, the real beneficiaries of the copyright in the fixed years after the death of the author are corporate interests or persons other than the heirs. With respect to the increased value of works for longer periods, opponents assert this value accrues only for a relatively small number of commercially significant works; the overwhelming bulk of works lose economic significance a few years after their public availability. While authors need copyright protection during their lifetimes as an incentive to create, opponents contend that there is no proof that 70 rather than 50 years of copyright after the death of the author has any positive impact on creativity. In fact, opponents argue that the longer term may even stifle additional creativity—older works are favored by term-extension and the added protection may depress the market for new works; also corporate authors may be more inclined to market older works whose marketability is known rather than risk capital on the creation of new works.

Supporters of term-extensions counter these points by emphasizing that copyright protection—not free use—is the engine for the creation of new works. The whole theory of property rights in copyrightable subject matter is that the grant of rights induces creativity for the benefit of the public. Also, proponents contend that this copyright incentive applies both to creators and disseminators of works. The Copyright Clause of the Constitution is intended both to stimulate creativity and to encourage distribution of works to the public. Term-extension, it is asserted, will encourage copyright owners to continue to market their works for maximum public availability. This added protection will encourage further investment and lead to the creation of new works and jobs. Even if individual authors are not stimulated to greater creativity by term-extension, copyright industries will be encouraged to invest in the distribution of old and new works and in the creation of new works.

Opponents of term-extension view the argument that we need to conform to the European union standard to protect U.S. works abroad as either a baseless or not proven contention.

---

country and apply the term that is shorter. This form of reciprocity is permitted by Article 7 of the Berne Convention.

Since most economically significant U.S. works, other than music, are works made-for-hire, the existing U.S. term of 75 years already exceeds the new European Union terms of 50 years (for the rights of motion picture producers and recorder producers) or 70 years (for legal persons who own computer software). Even in the case of personal works, the benefit from avoiding application of the rule of the shorter term is arguably very slight. As practical matter, the shorter term will not apply significantly to life-based copyrights until about the year 2040.

Supporters of term-extension respond that it would be economically foolish for the United States to allow copyright terms in U.S. works to expire before terms set by the European Union, and that the additional years of protection are needed to enable the U.S. to bargain successfully for adequate protection of U.S. works in foreign countries.

Arguments For and Against Music Licensing Reform

The music licensing provisions of Title II of H.R. 2589 are supported by a range of music users including operators of restaurants, bars, taverns, hotels, and retail stores; by general music users (as defined in the bill); by landlords or other owners of facilities where works are performed; and by sponsors and organizers of conventions, meetings, or events where works are performed.

The music licensing provisions of H.R. 2589 are opposed by music copyright owners, copyright owners in general, and music performing rights societies.

Proponents of music licensing reform make the following arguments—

- Music licensing payments by small businesses for public reception by means of playing radios or televisions represents unfair "double dipping" by copyright owners who have been paid already for licensed broadcasts;

- The 1976 Copyright Act failed to strike a balance between the rights of music copyright owners and the needs of music users; removal of the 1909 Act's general exemption for nonprofit public performance of music failed to take account of the needs of incidental music users who do not directly profit from performance of music;

- Small music users have no relief from PRS rates and licensing requirements since it is too expensive to challenge music rates in the Southern District of New York Rate Court; arbitration rates would be less expensive, fairer, and more convenient and would not burden the PRS since they license and enforce music performing rights in all regions of the U.S;

- Performing rights societies exercise their monopoly power to set arbitrary rates; the outdated antitrust consent decrees do not adequately restrain the PRS' anti-competitive licensing practices;

- The limitations and exceptions to the music performing right proposed in the bill are consistent with exceptions found in foreign copyright laws and with the obligations of the Berne Convention; the proposed exceptions can be justified as "minor reservations" to the performing right, especially in light of the broad U.S. public performance right in comparison to the lesser rights granted by the laws of many foreign countries, including Berne Convention member industrialized countries.

Opponents of the music licensing provisions of H.R. 2589 make the following arguments—

- Business establishments play music via radios and televisions for their customers because music is good for business; the creative output of American songwriters is used by restaurants, bars, hotels, taverns, retail stores, and other commercial enterprises because the business people know music attracts customers and makes money for business;

- The Copyright Clause of the Constitution empowers Congress to legislate authors' rights because our Founders understood that fair economic reward is the engine of creativity; all of our society benefits from the creative output that is sustained by fair compensation to authors for use of their creations;

- Business establishments pay food distribution, electric and telephone companies, equipment suppliers, and other vendors for a range of products and services; musical performances in small or large businesses should be paid for since music attracts customers to the business;

- The proposed "business exemption" would exempt nearly all musical performances by commercial establishments; this proposal would cost songwriters and music publishers tens of millions of dollars in lost income annually;

- The music licensing proposals would overthrow the commercial stability that has existed for nearly 50 years under the 1950 ASCAP consent decree; some of the changes (e.g., the elimination of vicarious and contributory infringement liability) would destroy basic principles of copyright law that have been settled for 50 years or more;

- Local arbitration of rates would be costly and lead to inconsistent rates and licensing practices; the general music user is encouraged to infringe rather than agree to a license since the arbitrator in a pre-litigation context can only award a reasonable license fee as a penalty for any infringement; review of licensing rates by an expert Rate Court is more efficient, less expensive, and more reliable a method of regulation than a new, untried system of arbitrated rates; the likely result of arbitration would be different rates for identical uses of music;

- Legislation is not needed to address any perceived anti-competitive behavior of the PRS; Justice Department review, copyright infringement litigation, and Rate Court proceedings are more than adequate to restrain any anti-competitive behavior;

- The music licensing proposals may undermine the collection of performing rights revenues from foreign PRS, since foreign royalties are negotiated on the basis of revenue collections in each country; the proposed "business exemption' is inconsistent with the obligations of the United States under the Berne Convention.[23]

CONCLUSION

As passed by the House of Representatives, H.R. 2589 increases the term of copyright by an additional 20 years and enacts significant reforms of music licensing practices. Three of the core provisions of H.R. 789 (the "Fairness in Musical Licensing Act") are included as Title II of H.R. 2589: 1) "business exemption" for public performances of music via radio or television; 2) local arbitration of disputes between general music users and the performing rights societies over licensing fees; and 3) elimination of the vicarious or contributory infringement liability of landlords and other owners of facilities where music is performed.

---

[23] The opponents' argument about a violation of the Berne Convention presents a difficult analytical issue. Treaty obligations, of course, are to be respected in enacting domestic legislation. Since the United States has been a member of the Berne Convention only since March 1, 1989, however, United States courts have had very little opportunity to interpret the treaty obligations. There has been no decision interpreting the public performance rights. Also, it is difficult, and perhaps impossible, to discern a consensus interpretation by reference to foreign laws and court decisions. The public performance rights mentioned in the Berne Convention have been added incrementally throughout the 100-year history of this treaty. The rights vary depending upon the nature of the performance (i.e., whether live, recorded, or transmitted). The basic terms are undefined in the treaty. The Berne Convention permits compulsory licensing of retransmissions of broadcasts. Under Article 10(2), national legislation may exempt certain educational uses that are "compatible with fair practice." In addition, many Berne countries assume there is an implied exception regarding performances at certain religious, cultural, and patriotic events. These countries rely upon the recognition by the 1948 Brussels Revision Conference of the so-called "minor reservations" understanding concerning exceptions to the public performance rights. The General Report on this Revision Conference expressly recognized the legitimacy of exemptions for incidental or relatively minor performances of music that do not detract from the essence of the right. General Report of the 1948 Brussels Conference at 263-4.

Proponents of copyright term-extension include authors, copyright owners, publishers, performing rights societies, and authors' heirs and other representatives of authors' estates. These groups are opposed to the music licensing reforms in Title II of the bill.

The music licensing reforms (Title II of the bill) are generally supported by operators of business establishments such as restaurants, bars, taverns, hotels, retail stores, and other places where music is performed publicly by means of radios or televisions. Supporters also include general music users and landlords or other owners of facilities where music is performed in a variety of contexts.

COPYRIGHT ISSUES IN ONLINE MUSIC DELIVERY

Robin Jeweler

INTRODUCTION

Among online music services, Napster seems to capture the public's fancy. For many, especially young people and college students, Napster almost became synonymous with online music. If popularized music delivery over the Internet; it demonstrated the ease and convenience with which consumers could select songs from vast music repertoires; and, it made what had been the unrealized notion of completely customized, personal music CDs a reality. Unfortunately, the federal courts have ruled that its operation violates the copyright interest of the music industry and performing artist whose songs were being freely exchanged. It was a sad day for many—if not a surprising one—when the Ninth Circuit Court of Appeals affirmed the U.S. district court's issuance of a preliminary injunction against Napster for contributory and vicarious copyright infringement.[1]

But the widespread popularity of Napster made its mark. As a result, the avowed goal of those within and without the music industry is to see the development of convenient, meaningful, and *lawful* access to services on the Internet.[2]

On April 3, 2001, the Senate Judiciary Committee held a hearing entitles "Online Entertainment: Coming Soon to a Digital Device Near You."[3] The Committee took testimony from representatives of the music industry and online music services. The Committee's aim was to elicit information about the interaction of technology and business surrounding the development of online music delivery, not to formulate new legislation to regulate it.

Among those who testified were Hank Berry, Interim CEO of Napster, and Robin Richards, President of MPS.com. Both companies were sued successfully by the music industry for copyright infringement. Attempting to comply with the court's orders, Mr. Berry addressed the difficulty of obtaining information on copyright ownership rights and the general complexities of music licensing.

---

[1]A&M Records, Inc. v. Napster, Inc., 239 F. 3d 1004 (9th Cir. 2001).

[2]*Copyright Conference Panelists Say Digital Rights Management, Education, Access Key to Content Protection,* 61 BNA PATENT, TRADEMARK & COPYRIGHT J. 625 (Apr. 27, 2001).

[3]The House Subcommittee on Courts, the Internet and Intellectual Property held an oversight hearing entitled "Music on the Internet" on May 17, 2001.

Robin Richards of MP3.com discussed the difficulties obtaining copyright clearance faced by his company's music storage "locker" service, MyMP3.com. MyMP3.com is designed to allow consumers to use Internet-connected devices to listen to CDs that they have previously purchased. With respect to the Internet music transmissions, Mr. Richards referred to several different copyright authorizations required:

> [A]though we disagree with the interpretation of the copyright law put forward by the record labels and publishers, our desire to get our service back up and running led us to enter into very costly agreements covering all their claims. We have agreed to pay for performing both the sound recordings and the songs contained on those CDs. And we have even agreed to pay the publishers for the temporary, momentary "buffer" copy that automatically is made (and deleted) each time someone listens to their own music out of their MyMp3.com locker. Yet, today, nearly six months after signing the last of these agreements, we have not been able to obtain all of the licenses that the copyright owners insist we must have before we can fully re-launch the MyMP3.com service.[4]

The multiplicity of licensing requirements for online music led several business consumers and online music services to call for simplified music licensing on the Internet through "compulsory licensing." The recording industry expressed their concerns over the necessity of a secure means to transmit music electronically; and members of the general public (and the Congress) expressed their impatience with the pace of development for online music delivery.

When the law creates a compulsory license, parties thereto need not negotiate its availability or terms. When statutory requirements are satisfied, a compulsory license is available at statutory rates. Many copyright owners, and the U.S. Copyright Office, however, are generally against expanding compulsory licensing, particularly with respect to valuing rights in a cyberspace.[5] They contend that establishing the commercial market value of the property is best established through contract negotiation, not regulatory ratemaking.

Although there are several types of "compulsory" or "statutory" licenses created by U.S. copyright law, 17 U.S.C. § 101 *et seq.,* there are not, at this time, any legislative proposals to create a *general* compulsory license for transmission of music over the Internet.

Two relatively recent laws, however, the Digital Performance Right in Sound Recordings Act (DPRA),[6] which was amended by the Digital Millennium Copyright Act (DMCA),[7] presently control several aspects of compulsory licensing necessary for digital music transmission. 17 U.S.C. § 114 establishes statutory licenses for the public performance of qualified digital audio transmissions. 17 U.S.C. § 115 creates a compulsory license, referred to as a "mechanical" license, for reproductions of songs and digital phonocord deliveries over the Internet. Implementation of these provisions is proving difficult given their complexity and the challenge of applying them to new and evolving technologies and businesses.

---

[4] Statement of Robin Richards before the Senate Judiciary Committee at www.senate.gov/~judiciary/te04030/rr.htm.

[5] *Leave Webcasting to the Marketplace Government, Industry Witness Tell Panel,* 60 BNA PATENT, TRADEMARK & COPYRIGHT J. 164 (June 23, 2000).

[6] P.L. 104-39 (Nov. 1, 1995).

[7] P.L. 105-304 (Oct. 28, 1998).

Indeed testimony before the Senate Judiciary Committee evidences a lack of consensus over many of the basic components of copyright rights relative to online music transmission. For example, parties disagree over the "new" statutory language of digital audio transmission and how traditional, protected activities such as "reproduction" and "public performance" should apply in an Internet environment.

This chapter gives a brief overview of the basic elements of music licensing and surveys recent developments in the U.S. Copyright Office's interpretation of compulsory licensing provisions under 17 U.S.C. §§ 114 and 115.

BACKGROUND: THE COMPLEXITIES OF MUSIC LICENSING

While almost all people acknowledge an intellectual property ownership interest in those who contribute their creative talents to the world of music, few outside the business side of the music industry appreciate the legal complexity of copyright interests and responsibilities. The Copyright Act confers discrete exclusive rights on different types of expressive media.

The owner of a musical composition (which is the underlying song on a sound recording) has the exclusive right to do or to authorize

- *Reproduction* of the copyrighted work;
- *Preparation of derivative* works based on the copyrighted work;
- *Distribution of copies* to the public by sale, rental, lease, or lending;
- *Performance* of the work *publicly;* and,
- *Display* of the work *publicly.*[8]

The owners of rights in sound recordings have an exclusive right to control reproduction and distribution of their recording, but they do *not* have the same public performance right as composers. In the case of sound recordings, the public performance right is qualified and limited. It covers

- *Performance of the work publicly by means of a digital audio transmission.*[9]

Cole Porter, Frank Sinatra, and "I've Got You Under My Skin"

Different exclusive rights attach to different uses and expressions of copyrighted work. The convergence of copyright interests in a sound recording is a prime illustration. An oft-cited example is that of Cole Porter's composition, the song *I've Got You Under My Skin.*[10]

[8] 17 U.S.C. § 106(1)-(5).
[9] 17 U.S.C. § 106(6).
[10] Kohn, *A Primer on the Law of Webcasting and Digital Musical Delivery*, 20 ENT. L. REPTR. 7 (1998).

The copyright to a song is most often owned by the composer or music publisher, in this case, Warner/Chappell Music, Inc.[11] In order to record a version of *I've Got You Under My Skin*, permission must be obtained from Warner/Chappell. Many performers have recorded different versions of it.

The copyright in a sound recording is most often owned by the recording artist or the recording studio. Frank Sinatra recorded a version in 1956, the copyright to which is owned by Capitol Records. Now assume that one wished to use the Frank Sinatra 1956 recording. How is it to be used? One way might be a radio station's over-the-air (analogue) broadcast of it. Since a broadcast is essentially a "public performance," the station would obtain permission, i.e., pay a royalty to Warner/Chappell. But because sound recording copyright holders do *not* have control over "public performances" of the recording, the radio station wishes to reproduce and distribute copies of Frank Sinatra's recording of *I've Got You Under My Skin* for promotional purposes. The composer/music publisher has the right to control the reproduction and distribution of the underlying composition (the song). And the sound recording copyright holder has the right to control reproduction and distribution of the sound recording. Hence, permission would be needed from both rights holders. Obtaining permission to use a song is a separate undertaking from permission to use a sound recording.[12]

In addition to what can be a complicated matter of identifying rights holders, one seeking permission to use copyrighted music may negotiate a wide variety of different types of licensing agreements. Again, the license will reflect which of the rights holder's exclusive rights are implicated depending upon the nature of the intended use.[13] In most instances, the negotiation of permission—that is, the licensing agreement—is a private, contractual matter between the parties. By contrast, when the law creates a compulsory or statutory license, no negotiation is necessary. The user, *i.e.*, the licensee, simply complies with the statutory conditions to use the work and pays the statutory rate or royalty for the benefit of the rights holder.

With respect to online music delivery, however, the relative newness of both the technology and the law itself suggests the precise copyright law principles that will govern online music transmission.

---

[11]Many writers and music publishers are represented by "performance fights societies" such as the American Society of Composers, Authors and Publishers (ASCAP), the Broadcast Music, Inc. (BMI), or the Society of European State Authors and Composers (SESAC).

[12]2 MELVILLE NIMMER & DAVID NIMMER, NIMMER ON COPYRIGHT § 8.22[A][3][b]: "Either [music or sound recordings] may be used as applicable, by compulsory license, by direct license, by statutory exemption, by virtue of the fair use doctrine, or because of its public domain status, in any permutation or combination. The point is that each exercise must be undertaken independently."

[13] The variety of music licenses is extensive, including, for example, print licenses, mechanical licenses, electrical transcription licenses, synchronization licenses, videogram licenses, musical product licenses, performance licenses, dramatic performance licenses, and grand performance licenses. AL KOHN & BOB KOHN, KOHN ON MUSIC LICENSING 428-431 (2d ed. 1996).

STATUTORY AND COMPULSORY LICENSES UNDER 17 U.S.C. §§ 114(D) AND 115.

Statutory Licensing for Performance Rights for Digital Audio Transmissions, 17 U.S.C. § 114

When Congress adopted the DPRA in 1995, it created a new but limited public performance right for digital audio transmissions. Rather than add a broad, comprehensive new performance right similar to that enjoyed by composers, Congress created many exemptions to the performance right.

Among the *exemptions* to a sound recording owner's exclusive right under 106(6), pursuant to § 114(d)(1) are:

- A non-subscription broadcast transmission, i.e., traditional radio and television broadcasts and qualified retransmission; and

- Internal transmissions by a business on or around its premises, including "on-hold music" transmissions via telephone to a caller waiting for a response.

These services are exempt from the performance rights and do not need to obtain a license are pay royalties for digital transmissions.

Congress also provided for statutory licensing for some, but not all, digital transmissions.[14] The nature of the digital public performance right requires the licensing parties to distinguish between "subscription" and "interactive" digital transmissions. Subscription services involved controlled transmissions that are limited to paid recipients, while an interactive service enables a member of the public to request a particular sound recording.[15]

The legislative history of the DPRA expresses congressional concern that interactive services had the greatest potential to impact traditional record sales. Therefore, copyright owners were to have the exclusive right to control the performance of their work on interactive media through negotiated contracts.[16] Thus, subscription transmissions may qualify for compulsory licensing, but interactive subscription services must be "voluntarily licensed."[17]

---

[14] 17 U.S.C. § 114(d)(2).

[15] 17 U.S.C. § 114(j)(7) & (14). Although subscription and interactive services may be related, some guidelines for determining what a service is are established by the statute. The ability of an individual to request that a particular sound recording be performed for the public at large, for example, or for members of a subscription service, does not render it an interactive one if the song is not performed within one hour of the request.

[16] S. Rept. 104-128, 104th Cong., 1st Sess. 16 (1995).

[17] 2 NIMMER ON COPYRIGHT § 8.22[A][1].

Statutory License for Subscription Transmissions

Unless a subscription service is exempt from the public performance right, it may qualify for a statutory, *i.e.,* a compulsory license, if detailed statutory requirements are complied with. Among the requirements for a statutory license is adherence to the "sound recording performance complement."[18] The sound recording performance complement is a complex protocol, adapted from traditional radio broadcast practice, which limits the number of selections a subscription service can play from any one phonorecord by the featured artist. The goal of the protocol is to prevent a pre-announced play schedule that facilitates copying of albums, or the work of individual performers, in their entirety.

Limitation on Exclusive Licenses for Interactive Services.

Although the DPRA requires negotiated licensing for interactive services, it does limit the duration of an exclusive license for the performance of a sound recording to prevent copyright owners of the recordings from becoming monopolistic "gatekeepers" and limiting opportunities for public performances.[19]

Compulsory or "Mechanical" Licenses for Reproduction and Distribution Rights Under 17 U.S.C. § 115.

The mechanical license in copyright law was enacted in 1909, in response to a U.S. Supreme Court decision which held that "mechanical" devices such as piano rolls were *not* copies of musical compositions. Hence, to reproduce a song on a piano roll or on a phonograph record would no result in an infringement of the composer's copyright.[20] Acting to overturn the Court's decision, to reverse its impact on owners of copyright interests in musical compositions, and to thwart a potential music monopoly by a large manufacturer of piano rolls, Congress created the compulsory license provision that is currently embodied in 17 U.S.C. 17 §115. The license protects the composer's right to control reproductions of the work but permits the recording of a song, by a third-party on "mechanical" media like a piano roll or record, hence the term "mechanical license."[21] In its present form, it essentially allows reproduction of music that may be heard with the aid of a mechanical device.[22] The mechanical license is validly obtained only after a song has been initially distributed publicly under the authority of the copyright owner. The license is authorized when the licensee's primary purpose is to distribute the work publicly for private use.

The § 115 mechanical license compensates the rights holder in the musical composition for reproduction and distribution rights; it does *not* authorize the duplication of a sound

[18] 17 U.S.C. § 114(d)(2)(B)(i).
[19] 17 U.S.C. § 114(d)(3).
[20] White-Smith Music Pub. Co. v. Apollo Co. 209 U.S 1 (1908).
[21] 2 NIMMER ON COPYRIGHT § 8.04[A].
[22] KOHN ON MUSIC LICENSING, *supra* at 653.

recording.[23] Permission to duplication a sound recording must be obtained from whomever owns the copyright, the recording artist or record studio.

Digital Phonorecord Deliveries

In 1995, the DPRA amended § 115 to include "digital phonorecord deliveries" or "DPDS.[24] DPDS were included in the mechanical license to compensate composers for an anticipated offset in revenues from record sales as songs become more frequently transmitted digitally:

> Among other things, [§ 115] is intended to confirm and clarify the right of musical work and sound recording copyright owners to be protected against infringement when phonorecords embodying their works are delivered to consumers by means of transmissions rather than by means of phonorecord retail sales. The intention in extending the mechanical compulsory license to digital phonorecord deliveries is to maintain and reaffirm the mechanical rights of songwriters and music publishers as new technologies permit phonorecords to be delivered by wire or over the airwaves rather than by the traditional making and distribution of records, cassettes and CD's. The intention is not to substitute for or duplicate performance rights in musical works, but rather to maintain mechanical royalty income and performance rights income for writers and music publishers.[25]

Hence, a mechanical license is available: to compensate the rights holders in the musical work when the license makes or distributes a phonorecord of the work; to compensate the musical composition rights holder when the licensee has obtained permission from a sound recording holder to duplicate the sound recording; and, to compensate the rights holder in the musical work for a DPD transmission of the work.

To summarize, there are many copyright requirements for both permission and licensing which must be observed before music can legally be transmitted over the Internet. These include:

- Permission from the rights holder in the musical composition to duplicate, distribute, and/or to perform the song publicly;

- Permission from the rights holder in the sound recording to duplicate and distribute it and/or to perform it publicly via a digital audio transmission.

---

[23] 2317 U.S.C. § 115(a)(1), "A person may not obtain a compulsory license for the use of the Work in the making of phonorecords duplicating a sound recording fixed by another, unless (i) such sound recording was fixed lawfully; and (ii) the making of the phonorecords was authorized by the owner of copyright in the sound recording...."

[24]A DPD is defined as "each individual delivery of a phonorecord by digital transmission of a sound recording which results in a specifically identifiable reproduction by or for any transmission recipient of a phonorecord of that sound recording, regardless of whether the digital transmission is also a public performance of the sound recording .... " 17 U.S.C. § 115(d).

[25]S. Rept. 104-128, 104th Congress, 1st Sess. 37 (1995).

In most cases and contexts, parties will negotiate licensing agreements. However, statutory and compulsory licenses are available in limited circumstances:

- A third party may obtain a compulsory license to compensate composers/music publishers when the licensee mechanically reproduces a song or transmits it digitally as a DPD;
- With respect to the public performance of a digitally transmitted sound recording, some transmissions are subject to a digital performance right, some are exempt, and yet others are entitled to the statutory license to compensate the sound recording rights holder.

RECENT AND ONGOING INTERPRETATIONS BY THE U.S. COPYRIGHT OFFICE

Recent actions and determinations by the U.S. Copyright Office illustrate the complexity of many of the legal issues affecting online music delivery.

Webcasting by Broadcast Radio

As discussed earlier, the DPRA's public performance right for digital transmissions of sound recordings *exempts* "non-subscription broadcast transmissions."[26] Radio broadcasters assert that this exemption covers broadcasters who stream their radio signals over the Internet.

The question, which arose in the course of rate adjustment proceedings for the § 114 statutory license, is whether FCC-licensed broadcasters' simultaneous transmissions of radio broadcasts via the Internet are exempt from the limited sound recording performance rights.

On December 11, 2000, the Copyright Office issued a final rule holding that, with the exception of over-the-air digital radio broadcasts, all other digital transmissions, including streaming over the Internet or "webcasting," *are* subject to statutory licensing under § 114(d)(2).[27] Broadcasters, believing the law exempts them, have filed suit challenging the rule.[28]

Rulemaking to Determine whether Service is Interactive

On the same day as the Copyright Office issued its webcasting rule, it denied a petition filed by the Digital Media Association (DiMA) to initiate a rulemaking to determine when an

---

[26]17 U.S.C. § 114(d)(1)(A).

[27]Public Performance of Sound Recordings: Definition of a Service, 65 Fed. Reg. 77292 (2000)(to be codified at 37 C.F.R § 201.35). The notice is also available on the Copyright Office's web site, www.copyright.gov.

[28]Bonneville International Corp. v. Peters, E.D. Pa. No.___, complaint filed 1/25/01, cited in *Broadcasters Challenge Webcasting Ruling*, 61 PATENT, TRADEMARK & COPYRIGHT J. 329 (Feb. 2, 2001).

online music delivery service is "interactive."[29] Interactive services must conduct arms-length negotiations with a sound recording copyright owner for a license before making a digital transmission that constitutes a public performance. Non-interactive services may qualify for a statutory license under § 114(d). Although the term "interactive service" is statutorily defined,[30] the Copyright Office noted that neither the statutory definition nor the legislative history "draws a bright line delineating just how much input a member of the public may have upon the basic programming of a service.[31] DiMA sought a rulemaking to attempt to clarify that some expression of consumer preference in audio digital transmissions will not necessarily render a service "interactive" and thus ineligible for a statutory license. Nevertheless, the Copyright Office found that a rulemaking is not necessary or appropriate because "[I]n light of the rapidly changing business models emerging in today's digital marketplace, no rule can accurately draw the line demarcating the limits between an interactive services and non-interactive service."[32]

Application of 17 U.S.C. § 115 to Certain Digital Music Service: What Constitutes an "Incidental" DPD?

On March 9, 2001, the Copyright Office issued a "Notice of Inquiry" requesting public comment on whether it should conduct rulemaking on the question of what constitutes an "incidental" DPD in order to determine royalties for a mechanical license.[33] When Congress amended § 115 to include DPDS, it made a statutory reference to—but did not define—"incidental" DPDS. Specially, when a Copyright Arbitration Royalty Panel (CARP) is convened to establish a statutory royalty rate for the mechanical license, it is directed to "distinguish between (i) digital phonorecord deliveries where the reproduction or distribution of a phonorecord is incidental to the transmission which constitutes the digital phonorecord delivery, and (ii) digital phonorecord deliveries in general.[34]

To date, establishing rates for incidental DPDS has been deferred. However, a wide variety of issues for online music delivery are implicated as the Copyright Office considers how best to address the issue. Indeed, the question "what is an incidental DPD?" arguably transcends mere copyright law and enters the realm of the metaphysical. As the Copyright Office's Notice of Inquiry observes:

> [T]here is considerable interest in the streaming of recorded music. Streaming necessarily involves a making of a number of copies of the musical work—or portions of the work—along the transmission path to accomplish the delivery of the work. RIAA [Recording Industry of America] and MP3.com relate that copies are made by the computer servers that deliver the musical work (variously referred to as "server," "root," "encoded," or "cache" copies), and additional copies are made by receiving computer to better facilitate the actual performance of the work (often

[29] 65 Fed. Reg. 77330 (Monday, Dec. 11, 2000). The notice is also available on the Copyright Office's web site, www.copyright.gov.
[30] 17 U.S.C. § 114(j)(4).
[31] 65 Fed. Reg. at 77331.
[32] *Id.* at 77332.
[33] 66 Fed. Reg. 14099 (2001).
[34] 17 U.S.C. § 115(c)(3)(D).

> referred to as "buffer" copies). Some of these copies are temporary; some may not necessarily be so. Are some or all the copies of a musical work made that are necessary to stream that work incidental DPDS? If temporary copies can be categorized as incidental DPDS, what is the definition of "temporary"? Some "temporary" copies may exist for a very short period of time; other s may exist for weeks. If the concept of a "transient" copy more relevant than the concept of a "temporary" copy? If fragmented copy can be an incidental DPD, does it make a difference in the analysis whether the copy is temporary or is permanent?...[35]

Many parties will be affected by any resolution of the issue. RIAA, for example, seeks an interpretation of the DPD status of "On-Demand Streams"[36] and "Limited Downloads,"[37] asserting that they are incidental DPDS. Napster filed comments opposing RIAA's position, arguing that Congress must clarify the status of incidental DPDS, not the Copyright Office. DiMA argues that all temporary copies of a musical work that are made to stream constitute a "fair use" which should not be subject to any royalty. And, MP3.com, reiterating concerns expressed in testimony before Congress, argues that a distinction must be made between different types of streaming. In the context of its "locker" service, which permits subscribers to access music that they have previously purchased, MP3.com argues that its users have already compensated copyright rights holders when they purchased the original CD.

The DPD controversy leads to the broader question of *how* music royalties should be distributed over the Internet. Some argue that digital transmission on the Internet blurs the distinction between public performance and computer-driven reproduction. Online firms argue that royalties to compensate composer and publishers for streamed music should track traditional over-the-air broadcast and retail sales: Mechanical royalties are triggered when CDs or tapes are sold and performance royalties apply when music is broadcast or played publicly. Hence, they assert that when a consumer listens to music on the Internet (without saving it), it should constitute a performance as opposed to a reproduction; downloading a song for future use, they contend, is a reproduction.[38]

CONCLUSION

The public has expressed great interest in Napster and the litigation against it. But to the extent that Napster's business model is based on adjudicated copyright infringement, it is not likely to have a significant impact shaping the future direction copyright law may take to facilitate online music delivery. And, while many have called for legislation to streamline the licensing of sound recordings on the Internet, others believe it is unnecessary because

---

[35]66 Fed. Reg. at 14101-02.

[36]An "On-Demand Stream" is defined, in the filings of the RIAA, as an "on-demand, real-time transmission using streaming technology such as Real Audio, which permits users to listen to the music they want when they want and as it is transmitted to them." 66 Fed. Reg. at 14100.

[37]A "Limited Download" is defined, in the filings of the RIAA, as "an on-demand transmission of a time-limited or other use-limited (i.e. non-permanent) download to a local storage device (e.g., the hard drive of the user' s computer), using technology that causes the downloaded file to be available for listening only either during a limited time (e.g. a time certain or a time fled to ongoing subscription payments) or for a limited number of times." *Id.*

[38]Jon Healy, *Net Music Services in Royal Bind; Web: Online firms say publishers' demand for reproduction and performance royalties is holding up business*, LOS ANGELES TIMES May 21, 2001 at C1.

widespread demand and the market itself will shape a viable new business environment for online music.

The foregoing discussion illustrates several areas where Congress and the Copyright Office have had difficulty adapting traditional licensing practices to new laws, technologies, and business models. In some instances, issues may be resolved administratively or judicially as the new language of online music takes on discernable and concrete meaning. Or conversely, these licensing questions may be a starting point for legislative proposals to streamline music licensing on the Internet.

THE COPYRIGHT DOCTRINE OF FAIR USE AND THE INTERNET: CASE LAW

Douglas Reid Weimer

Domestic case law has been developing which examines the copyright doctrine of fair use within the context of copyrighted works placed on the Internet without the permission of the copyright owner. Various efforts are being undertaken by the courts, Congress, and the industry to divide enforcement responsibilities and protection rights among the various interested parties: copyright owners, the access providers, website operators, and Internet consumers.[1]

Generally speaking, American courts have considered the placement or publication of copyrighted materials on the Internet to be another form of expression or communication. Hence, the courts have applied a fair use legal analysis in Internet cases similar to that applied with respect to more traditional forms of communication. The report examines the statutory background and development of the fair use doctrine in copyright law and its application to works placed on the Internet.

BACKGROUND

The copyright owner possesses various exclusive ownership rights in the work.[2] However, the fair use doctrine permits, under certain circumstances, the unauthorized use of copyrighted works. The doctrine, which has its origins in common law, was first codified in the Copyright Act of 1976.[3] The statute provides four criteria for the determination of

---

[1]This chapter is limited to an examination of the domestic issues concerning the copyright doctrine of fair use within the context of the Internet. International copyright law and the Internet may present various currently unresolved concerns and legal issues.

[2]17 U.S.C. § 106. These ownership rights" include the *rights* to do and to authorize: 1) *reproduction* of the work; 2) preparation *of derivative works;* 3) *distribution* of copies of the work to the public by sale or other transfer; 4) with literary, musical, dramatic, and choreographic works and other works, *performance* of the work publicly; 5) with literary, musical, dramatic, and other works, the *display* of the copyrighted work publicly; and 6) in the case of sound recordings, public performance of digital audio transmissions.

[3]17 U.S.C. § 107.

whether the unauthorized use of a work is a "fair" use, or whether it is an infringing use.[4] These are: 1) the amount and character of the use; 2) the nature of the copyrighted work; 3) the amount copied in relation to the whole copyrighted work; and 4) the effect of the copying on the potential market for the copyrighted work.[5] Courts have examined the factual circumstances surrounding each case and have applied these criteria on a case-by-case basis.[6]

The Internet is a cooperative network of networks.[7] It links millions of users nationally and internationally, including individuals, schools, libraries, and corporations. There is no single individual or organization that owns, oversees, or controls the Internet. For many users, the costs of accessing the Internet are paid by their organizations, such as universities, national laboratories, corporations, and governments.[8] Other individuals pay subscription fees to Internet service providers, like America Online or CompuServe, which provide links to the Internet.[9] The World Wide Web is the Internet's most popular application. The growing number of Websites and bulletin boards[10] provides great distribution capabilities for all types of material. Since computers can reproduce virtually perfect copies of copyrighted works, including text, audio, and video, the Internet provides the potential for distributing and redistributing replicas of copyrighted material to large numbers of Internet users. The technological achievements of the Internet have greatly increased the possibilities for copyright infringement.[11]

Internet users who view information and download that information are copying. If the material that is being copied is copyrighted, the possibility of infringement may rest upon an application of the fair use doctrine to the circumstances surrounding the unauthorized use of the material.[12] By viewing materials on the Internet, there is a fixation of material on a computer's Random Access Memory (RAM). This fixation in the RAM may support an infringement claim based upon the copyright owner's exclusive right of reproduction.[13] However, if the copyright owner places his/her work on the Internet, it could be inferred that the owner would expect other Internet users to read and download the copyrighted work. Legal complications arise when persons other than the copyright owner publish the copyrighted works on the Internet.

---

[4]If a use is infringing, the copyright owner may bring an action for infringement against the unauthorized user of the copyrighted work. 17 U.S.C. § 411.

[5]17 U.S.C. § 107.

[6]*See,* CRS Rept. No. 95-888, *Copyright and Fair Use After Acuff-Rose and Texaco;* CRS Rept. No. 93-396, *Copyright Law: Recent Case law Developments in The "Single Receiving" Exemption;* CRS Rept. No. 93-515, Photocopying *of Scientific Journal Articles: American Geophysical Union v. Texaco, Inc.*

[7]*See* CRS Rept. No. 98-649, *Spinning the Web: The History and Infrastructure of the Internet.*

[8]*Id.* at 13-14.

[9]*Id.* at 14. The extensive usage of the Web has generated various legal issues other than the fair use of copyrighted works. Among these issues are: trademarks, privacy, fraud, security, copyright first sale doctrine, trade secrets, and First Amendment issues.

[10]An electronic bulletin board is a means of exchanging information with distant areas through a computer and modem. The electronic bulletin board is comprised of an electronic storage medium (computer memories or hard disks), which is attached to telephone lines through modem devices, which are controlled by a computer.

[11]Christopher Wolf, *'Net Users Could Face IP Liability,* NAT'L Law J. C34, C35 (May 20, 1996)(cited to afterward as "Wolf").

[12] Circumstances may exist where a user pays a subscription fee for the use of particular information on the Interact. The service provider may specifically address the issues of copying/downloading in the access agreements with the users. However, many Interact sites do not impose a user fee or contain copyright information concerning the material on the site.

[13]*See* Wolfe, *supra,* note 11.

Case Law and the Internet

American courts have been seeking equitable resolutions to copyright infringement actions over the unauthorized use of copyrighted works on the Internet. Court decisions applying the fair use principles to Internet use provide some legal guidance; however, case law precedent is still developing and certain issues remain unresolved. Still, the most recent cases have continued the traditional application of the fair use principles to Internet use of copyrighted materials.

An early case that dealt with the fair use principles and online service involved an electronic bulletin board with was open to the public.[14] The scheme involved the electronic exchange of copyrighted Sega video games through the bulletin board. The bulletin board operators asserted a fair use defense, which was based upon the argument that the operators themselves did not download or retain copies of any Sega video games. The applied the four fair use factors to this situation and rejected the defendants' fair use defense. The court determined that the *use* was for a commercial purpose—to download the copyrighted games, so as to avoid their purchase from the copyright owner. Considering the *nature* of the copyrighted work, the court observed that the work involved creativity, fiction, and fantasy. Since the entire work was copied, the third factor—the *amount* of the work used, favored the plaintiff's claim. In considering the fourth factor, the *effect of copying on the potential market,* the court concluded that the unauthorized copying of the copyrighted works would adversely impact the potential market, as few persons would purchase the copyrighted works if they were available through the bulletin board. Hence, the court concluded that all four factors favored the plaintiff and that the defendants' unauthorized use of the copyrighted works was an infringing use. Another subsequent decision that dealt with the fair use doctrine and Internet use involved the same parties and a similar factual situation.[15] The court applied the four fair use factors to the facts at hand.[16] After balancing all of the factors, the court reached the same conclusion as in the earlier decision, finding that the fair use doctrine did not apply.[17]

Several online cases have involved the unauthorized use of certain written works of L. Ron Hubbard, founder of Scientology. The simplified factual situation concerning these cases follows. In unrelated litigation, the Religious Technology Center (RTC) attempted to seal an affidavit concerning church ideology. Lerma—a former follower of Hubbard—obtained the affidavit and published it on the Internet through his Internet access provider—Digital Gateway Systems (DGS). The RTC brought and infringement against the former minister—Elrich—for posting on an Internet bulletin board certain materials containing Hubbard's published and unpublished works. The RTC also named as defendants the bulletin board operator—Klemesrud and the Internet access provider—Netcom. These cases are summarized below.

In *Religious Technology Center v. Lerma,*[18] the court dealt primarily with RTC's infringement action against the Post, certain reporters, and Lerma. This case did not deal chiefly with the Internet or online aspects of fair use. The action was based primarily upon

---

[14]*Sega Enterprises, Ltd. v. MAPHIA,* 857 F. Supp. 679 (N.D. Cal. 1994).
[15]*Sega Enterprises, Ltd. v. MAPHIA,* 948 F. Supp. 923 (N.D. Cal. 1996)
[16]*Id.* at 934-935.
[17]*Id.* at 936.
[18]908 F. Supp. 1353 (E.D. Va. 1995).

the unauthorized dissemination of information owned by the RTC and did not address the substantive copyright issues.[19]

In another case involving the RTC's infringement action, the same defendants moved for summary judgment and the district court concluded that the fair use doctrine was applicable to the Post and its reporters.[20] In reaching this conclusion, the court examined the four fair use factors and applied them in a traditional copyright analysis. The court concluded that the purpose and character of the use of the material was for newsgathering and this favored the defendants. In evaluating the nature of the work, the court deemed it to be informational rather than creative, and that a broader fair use approach was appropriate. The court determined that the amount of the work used in relation to its entirety was not significant. Finally, the court found that the unauthorized use of the copyrighted material by the post and by its reporters was a fair use.

In an unpublished opinion, the court subsequently examined the copyright infringement claim against Lerma.[21] Lerma first argued that the disputed works were not copyrightable. The court rejected this argument. He next raised the fair use defense for his unauthorized use of the copyrighted works. After examining each of the four fair use factors, the court concluded that Lerma's use could not be construed as a fair use. Finally, Lerma argued that the RTC misused its copyright and that Lerma's unauthorized use of the material was an infringing use. The RTC was awarded $2,500 in statutory damages.

In another series of cases, the RTC brought action against Erlich (the former minister), the bulletin board operator, and the Internet access provider. In two separate opinions, the district court of Northern District of California addressed various copyright issues, including fair use.[22] Erlich did not dispute that he copied the works. He advanced a fair use defense.[23] The court granted in part the plaintiff's motion for a preliminary injunction against Erlich and concluded that his use of the RTC's materials was unlikely to qualify as fair use. In evaluating Erlich's purpose and character of the use, the court determined that it was for criticism or comment and was thus for noncommercial use. Therefore, the fair use factor was held to be slightly in Erlich's favor.[24] In looking at the nature of the copyrighted work, the court considered that some of the works were published while others were unpublished. The court determined that the unauthorized use of the unpublished works favored the plaintiffs. In assessing the third factor, the court favored the plaintiffs. As for the potential market of the work, the court concluded that Erlich's use would not have an adverse effect on the market. The court engaged in an "equitable balancing" of the factors and found that Erlich could not assert a fair use defense for his copying.[25]

In *Religious Technology Center v. Netcom On-Line Commu.*,[26] another action involving the RTC and Erlich's access provider and the bulletin board, the court granted in part and denied in part the defendants' motion for summary judgment and judgment on the pleadings, and denied the plaintiffs' motion for a preliminary injunction. The district court applied the fair use analysis to the action of the Internet access provider, Netcom. The court determined

[19] *Id.* at 1355-1358.
[20] *Religious Technology Center v. Lerma,* 908 F. Supp. 1361 (E.D. Va. 1995).
[21] Religious Technology Center v. Arnaldo Pagliarina Lerma, 1996 U.S. Dist. LEXIS 15454 (E.D. Va. Oct. 4, 1996).
[22] The court examined other issues, such as trade secret and tort claims, which are not discussed in this chapter.
[23] *Id.* at 1242-1250.
[24] *Id.* at 1244.
[25] *Id.* at 1249-1250.
[26] 907 F. Supp. 1361 (N.D. Ca. 1995).

that the access provider was not liable for direct infringement; rather, the court examined it as a case of contributory infringement on the part of Netcom and determined the plaintiffs raised a genuine issue of fact concerning Netcom's contributory infringement.[27] Although Netcom was a commercial enterprise, the court found that its use of copyrighted work was of a different nature than the plaintiffs' use. In looking at the nature of the copyrighted works, the court determined that Netcom's use of the works was merely to facilitate their posting to the bulletin board—an entirely different use from the use of plaintiffs—and therefore favored Netcom. Regarding the amount of the copyrighted work copied, the court determined that Netcom copied no more of plaintiffs' work than was necessary to function; thus, this factor did not favor the plaintiffs. The court concluded that the postings on the Internet by Netcom raised a genuine factual issue as to whether the market for plaintiff's work was diminished. Because the court was not able to make a determination concerning the fourth fair use factor—the market harm—the court decided that the fair use defense was *not* available to Netcom on motion for summary judgment.[28] In conclusion, the court determined that there were issue of fact to be determined in the case and that a fair use defense was not available for Netcom on summary judgment.

In late 1997, the U.S. District Court for the Northern District of Illinois ruled that an Internet service provider was not liable for direct copyright infringement, despite the fact that materials were directly copied on a website that the service provider maintained for a subscriber.[29] However, the Internet subscriber was found to have infringed certain copyrighted "clip art" images by using them on the Internet. The court concluded that the subscriber's use of the clip art was primarily for commercial uses, for promoting his organization, and for generating revenue. Hence, the fair use defense was not available for the defendant and the unauthorized use of the "clip art" on the Internet was found to be an infringing use. In 1998, the same court—the U.S. District for the Northern District of Illinois—reach a finding of infringement in a similar case involving the use of "shareware," copyrighted software which is loaded to potential purchasers under certain conditions.[30] The court went through an extensive fair use analysis within the context of shareware.[31]

In another case concerning fair use and the Internet, still images taken from a copyrighted videotape of a celebrity couple exchanging in sexual activity were placed on the Internet without the couple's permission. Applying the fair use doctrine to a rather complex factual situation, the U.S. District Court for the Central District of California held that the unauthorized placement on the Internet of still images from a copyrighted videotape was not a fair use.[32] The court considered each fair use factor within the context of the factual situation.[33]

The U.S. District Court for the Eastern District of Texas examined a unique case where the plaintiff's copyrighted works—model legal codes—had been adopted as municipal laws

---

[27] *Id.* at 1373-1375.

[28] *Id.* at 1381. Apparently, the bulletin board provider did not assert a fair use defense; therefore, the court did not utilize the fair use analysis.

[29] *Marobie-FL v. National Assn of Fire Equip. Dist.*, 983 F. Supp. 1167 (N.D. Ill. 1997).

[30] *Storm Impact v. Software of the Month Club,* 13 F. Supp. 2d 782 (N.D. Ill. 1998).

[31] *Id.* at 787-790.

[32] *Michaels v. Internet Entertainment Group, Inc.*, 5 F. Supp. 2d 823 (D.C. Cal. 1998).

[33] *Id.* at 834-836. The final disposition of this case was reached at *Michaels v. Internet Entertainment Group*, 1998 U.S. Dist. LEXIS 20786 (1998).

by various communities.[34] The defendant then posted these copyrighted works on the Internet and was sued for infringement. The court applied the fair use analysis to the factual situation at hand and determined that the fair use defense was not applicable in this situation.[35] Hence, the posting of certain copyrighted model codes, even when they have been adopted as municipal laws or ordinances, did not lose their copyright protection, and could not be posted on the Internets without permission of the copyright owner.

In *Kelly v. Arriba Soft Corp.*,[36] the court examined the fair use doctrine within the context of a "visual search engine" on the Internet. The defendant's visual search engine allows a user to obtain a list of related Web content following a search inquiry. The visual search engine produces a list of reduced "thumbnail" pictures related to the inquiry.[37] The plaintiff argued that the use of the "thumbnail" copyrighted pictures obtained through the visual search was an infringement of his copyright interest. The court undertook an extensive fair use evaluation of the circumstances surrounding the visual search engine and the unauthorized use of the copyrighted photographs.[38] The court weighed all of the fair use factors together and determined that the defendant's use of the copyrighted photographs as part of their visual search engine was a fair use of the plaintiff's images.[39]

The posting of copyrighted news articles on the Internet has been the subject of recent litigation.[40] The defendant posted copyrighted articles from newspapers on an Internet "bulletin board" website so that visitors to the site could comment and criticize the articles. Applying the fair use factors to the instant case, the court determined that the defendant's posting of full-length, copyrighted articles on the Internet was not a fair use of the copyrighted material. The court noted that the website operator could have avoided infringement if summaries of the articles had been posted or if hyperlinks to the articles on the newspapers' own websites had been provided.

The practice of "streaming"—the visual transmission of copyrighted television programming—on the Internet was the subject of a recent action. The defendant was transmitting portions of the plaintiffs' copyrighted programming on the Internet. The plaintiff sought and received a temporary restraining order.[41] The U.S. District Court for the Western District of Pennsylvania did not examine the fair use doctrine or any other copyright defenses in its opinion.

In recent litigation, several motion picture studios brought an action to prevent the defendants from providing a computer program on their websites that allowed users to decrypt and copy the plaintiffs' copyrighted motion pictures from digital versatile disks.[42] Although the defendants argued that their activities were within the fair use exception, the court rejected this defense and granted the plaintiffs' motion for preliminary injunction.

---

[34] *Veeck v. Southern Bldg. Code Congress Intern.*, 49 F. Supp. 885 (E.D, Tex. 1999).
[35] *Id.* at 891.
[36] 77 F. Supp. 1116 (C.D. Cal. 1999).
[37] *Id.* at 1117.
[38] *Id.* at 1118-1121.
[39] *Id.* at 1121.
[40] *Los Angeles Times v. Free Republic*, (C.D. Cal., No. CV 98-7840-MMM-AJWX, 1/8/99).
[41] *Universal City Studios, Inc. v. Shawn C. Reimerdes*, 82 F. Supp. 2d211 (S.D.N.Y. 2000).
[42] *Universal City Studios, Inc. v. Shawn C. Reimerdes*, 82 F. Supp. 2d 211 (S.D.N.Y. 2000).

CONCLUSION

These cases have illustrated the judicial process—the "equitable balancing"—that courts undertake in their evaluation of fair use claims. It appears that the courts are using the same analysis and criteria for Internet litigation as they have with other intellectual property determinations. The courts have examined in detail the factual situation surrounding the litigation and they have applied each of the fair use criteria to the case-by-case circumstances. The courts then evaluate or weigh the statutory criteria and determine whether, on balance, the evidence favors a finding of fair use of the copyrighted material or not.

While these cases provide judicial precedent, the use of copyrighted materials on the Internet is not entirely resolved. Factual circumstances may change the judicial outcome in various situations. In addition, various areas of fair use litigation and the Internet may still be developing. Among these subject areas are: possible liability for Internet server and bulletin board providers; whether online use is legally distinguishable from the use of the printed form; unintended or unintentional use of copyrighted materials; use of materials by schools and libraries; and other issues.

ONLINE SERVICE PROVIDER COPYRIGHT LIABILITY: ANALYSIS AND DISCUSSION OF H.R. 2180 AND S. 1146

Dorothy Schrader

The Internet and other computer networks provide, in the judgment of most experts, unparalleled opportunities for worldwide communications and economic growth. It is also generally agreed that, in order to tap this potential fully, many difficult technical and policy issues must be confronted and resolved. One of these policy issues concerns the scope of protection for copyrighted works against unauthorized copying or other unlawful use. A subsidiary copyright policy issue concerns the liability of online service providers ("OSPs")[1] for the infringing acts of third party customers or users of OSP facilities or services.

The general issues relating to Internet uses of copyrighted material are implicated by two new international intellectual property treaties and the bills intended to implement the obligations of the treaties. The President in July 1997 submitted to the Senate, for its advice and consent to ratification, the World Intellectual Property Organization Copyright Treaty (WIPO) and the WIPO Performances and Phonograms Treaty. Based on the Administration's recommendations for implementing legislation, S. 1121 and H.R. 2281 were introduced at the end of July 1997. The bills would make the minimal changes in United States copyright law that the Administration believes are needed to make United States taw consistent with the obligations of the treaties.[2]

---

[1] This chapter has elected to use the phrase "online service provider" to refer to various activities of providing service or access to the Internet and other computer networks. Others use the terminology "Internet service providers" (ISP) or internet access providers" (IAP), or a combination of the two phrases. In this chapter, "OSP" is used as a shorthand designation for persons or companies who transmit, route, provide connections and access, or otherwise facilitate computer network transmissions without initiating or altering the content of the transmission. These service or access providers include telephone companies, providers of browsing, navigational, and search engine services, some libraries and educational institutions, online services, and other network facilitators

[2] For an overview of the WIPO treaties and the Administration's proposed implementing legislation, see D. Schrader, World Intellectual Property Organization Copyright Treaty: An Overview, CRS Report No. 97-444 A and World Intellectual Property Organization Performances and Phonograms Treaty: An Overview, CRS Report No. 97-523 A.

The Administration's WIPO treaties implementation bills address two substantive issues—protection against circumvention of anti-copying systems and protection against removal or alteration of copyright management information. They do not address any of the other copyright policy issues that arguably are implicated by the treaties such as OSP copyright liability for contributory or vicarious infringements by third parties, the scope of the exclusive rights granted by the treaties (especially those relating to reproduction, distribution, "transmission," and "public communication"), and the limitations on rights (such as fair use, ephemeral copying, and distance learning).

An alternative WIPO treaties implementation bill, S. 1146, does address several Internet copyright policy issues, including OSP liability. Also, H.R. 2180 deals with OSP liability separate from implementation of the WIPO treaties.

This chapter summarizes and analyzes the OSP liability provisions of S. 1146 and H.R. 2180 and notes arguments for and against these provisions.

BACKGROUND

NII Recommendations and Bills

The White House Information Infrastructure Task Force convened a Working Group on intellectual property issues ("IP Working Group"), which examined the Internet copyright policy issues and issued its final report and recommendations in September 1995.[3] In the course of its meetings and deliberations, the IP Working Group heard from rights holders, OSPs, libraries, educational institutions and others about OSP copyright liability. The IP Working Group rejected the proposals from the OSPs for amendments to the copyright law to clarify OSP liability.[4] The Working Group recommended no amendments that would address the issues of contributory or vicarious infringement liability in the context of the Internet or national information infrastructure ("NII").

Under existing copyright law, direct infringers are held to a standard of strict copyright liability, generally without regard for the intent of the actor.[5] OSPs apparently acknowledge that they are liable for their own direct infringements. Under judicially developed doctrines, someone who has the right and ability to control the infringer's actions and a financial interest in the use of the copyrighted work may be held vicariously liable.[6] Also, someone who, with knowledge of possible infringing activity, induces, causes, or materially contributes to an infringement, may be held liable as a contributory infringer.[7]

---

[3] DEPARTMENT OF COMMERCE, INTELLECTUAL PROPERTY AND THE NATIONAL INFORMATION INFRASTRUCTURE, REPORT OF THE WORKING GROUP ON INTELLECTUAL PROPERTY RIGHTS OF THE INFORMATION INFRASTRUCTURE TASK FORCE (September 1995) (hereafter: the "'IP Working Group Report").

[4] Basically, the OSPs argued for a higher standard of knowledge or a greater ability to control the infringing conduct to trigger their copyright liability than is arguably required by the existing copyright doctrines of vicarious or contributory infringement. IP Working Group Report at 122-124.

[5] Willful, intentional infringement, however, may subject the infringer to a higher statutory damage cap of $100,000 rather than the $20,000 statutory damages cap for ordinary infringement.

[6] Shapiro, Bernstein & Co. V. H.L. Green Co., 316 F.2d 304 (2d Cir. 1962).

[7] Gershwin Publishing Corp. V. Columbia Artists Management, Inc., 443 F.2d 1159 (2d Cir. 1971).

A manufacturer, however, generally has the freedom to market any device that is capable of substantial non-infringing uses, without incurring contributory infringement liability.[8]

Acting upon the recommendations of the Administration's IP Working Group Report, bills were introduced in the 104th Congress (S. 1284 and H.R. 2441) to make changes in the copyright law related to Internet uses of copyrighted works. These bills contained no provisions concerning the copyright liability of OSPs. Hearings were held on the bills, but no further action occurred.

Under the auspices of the House Subcommittee on Courts and Intellectual Property, a series of negotiating meetings was held in 1996 in an attempt to reach a compromise solution on OSP copyright liability. Participants included OSPs, telephone companies, library and educational interests, book and music publishers, and motion picture companies.

According to one participant, the negotiations broke down about the details of the copyright owners' proposal for a system of "notice and takedown," under which copyright owners would notify OSPs of copyright infringements on the Internet and • the OSP would then close down the infringing site. The parties could not agree on the obligatory nature of the "notice and takedown" system, the scope of the exemption for acting as a "mere conduit" in transferring information, and liability for hyperlinking and software access tools such as search engines and browser.[9]

Although these private sector negotiations did not resolve the OSP liability issue, the issue was thoroughly explored in these discussions, and many of the ideas discussed were later included in the OSP liability bills introduced in the 105th Congress.

New WIPO Treaties and Implementation Bills

At a diplomatic conference in December 1996, delegates representing more than 125 countries adopted two new intellectual property treaties, known as the WIPO Copyright and WIPO Performances and Phonograms Treaties. The Copyright Treaty covers copyright protection for computer programs and for databases as intellectual works, and use of copyrighted works in digital, electronic environments, including transmissions over the Internet. The Performances and Phonograms Treaty covers protection for performers and producers of sound recordings,[10] and tracks many of the rights extended to copyright subject matter under the Copyright Treaty.

Before the delegates agreed on the new treaties, they engaged in extensive discussions about, among other issues, the copyright liability of OSPs. In the end, the delegates followed international copyright practice in not spelling out in the text of the treaties that is liable.[11]

[8] Sony Corp. V. Universal City Studios, Inc., 464 U.S. 417 (1984) (the "Betamax" VCR case).

[9] Lutzker, Neither Aiding Nor Abetting, LEGAL TIMES, October 6, 1997, Special Report on Intellectual Property at 18, 20.

[10] United States law uses the phrase "sound recordings" to describe the intellectual content of audio works that is the object of copyright protection. "Phonograms" is the international term commonly used to refer to protection of "sound recordings." Although the United States protects sound recordings under the copyright law, the majority of foreign countries protect phonograms under legal theories other than copyright. Most commonly, phonograms are protected under so-called related or neighboring rights.

[11] International copyright treaties have not traditionally included text that defines who is liable for infringement. Copyright treaties have generally specified fights and, to a lesser extent limitations on rights, without spelling out who is liable for violations of the treaty rights.

The delegates formally adopted, however, an "agreed statement" to the effect that the mere provision of physical facilities to enable communications is not itself an act of communication—that is, merely providing telephone lines, modems, and other connections does not infringe the public communications right.[12]

In forwarding the two WIPO Treaties to the Senate for its advice and consent, the President has recommended implementing legislation that does not address the issue of OSP copyright liability. That is, S. 1121 and H.R. 2281 would make no change in the copyright law concerning the judicially created standards under which an OSP might be held liable for copyright infringement.

Title I of an alternative implementation bill, S. 1146, contains provisions regulating the copyright liability of OSPs. Hearings were held on the general issue of OSP liability before the Senate Judiciary Committee on September 4, 1997.

H.R. 2180 also deals with OSP liability. Some of its provisions are similar to S. 1146's liability provisions, but the two bills are not companion bills. Hearings were held on OSP liability and treaty implementation issues before the House Subcommittee on Courts and Intellectual Property on September 16-17, 1997.

SUMMARY OF THE OSP LIABILITY BILLS

Digital Copyright Clarification and Technology Education Act of 1997 (S. 1146)

S. 1146 is an alternative bill to implement the two WIPO treaties. In comparison to the Administration's implementation bills (S. 1121 and H.R. 2281), S. 1146 proposes different statutory text with respect to circumvention of anti-copying technologies and removal or alteration of copyright management information.[13] The bill consists of three titles, of which only Title I (OSP liability) is analyzed in this chapter.[14]

The bill would add a new section 512 to title 17 of the U.S. Code,[15] entitled "Liability relating to material on the Internet and on-line." OSPs, who merely transfer information on computer networks without having any control of the content, are generally absolved from either direct, vicarious, or contributory copyright infringement liability. Of course, OSPs are liable if they initiate or generate the infringing transmission.

---

[12] The "agreed statement" was adopted as an interpretation of Article 8 of the Copyright Treaty. The statement reads as follows:

"It is understood that the mere provision of physical facilities for enabling or making a communication does not in itself amount to communication within the meaning of this Treaty of the Berne Convention. It is further understood that nothing in Article 8 precludes a Contracting Party from applying Article 11bis(2)."

[13] Title III of H.R. 1146. For an analysis of these provisions of S. 1146, see CRS Report 94-444 A at 22-23. This chapter concerns the OSP liability issue alone.

[14] Title II of H.R. 1146 proposes several amendments to the Copyright Act to update the limitations on the rights of the copyright owner in the context of digital, electronic uses of copyrighted works, especially in the case of libraries and educational institutions. Title III deals with the same WIPO treaties implementation issues as the Administration bills (except that S. 1146 does not include technical amendments relating to treaty relationships and eligibility of foreigners to claim copyright in the U.S.).

[15] The Copyright Act is codified as title 17 U.S.C.

Notice and Takedown System

S. 1146 basically adopts the proposal referred to as "mandatory notice and takedown" when an OSP acts merely as a "conduit" for computer network communications.

For purposes of this "notice and takedown" procedure, an OSP qualifies for the possible exemption if it did not initiate the placement of the material on the network, did not determine the content &the material, and did not contract for placement of the specific material on the network. If these conditions are met, OSP liability depends upon notice of a possible infringement. OSPs have no liability without actual notice of an infringement and then only if they fail to act to takedown the allegedly infringing material. Copyright owners are expected to monitor and enforce their own rights under this bill, with cooperation from the OSPs through a notice system.

Upon receiving a notice of infringement that complies with statutory requirements,[16] an OSP is expected to remove, disable or block access for 10 days or until it receives a court order, to the extent blocking is technologically feasible and economically reasonable.

Employees or agents of a nonprofit educational institution, library or archives would enjoy a special exemption from the "notice and takedown" procedure. These persons are deemed not to have notice of infringement from the copyright owner if the person "reasonably believed (i) that the allegedly infringing use was a fair use... or (ii) was otherwise lawful."[17]

Conduit Exemption

If the statutory conditions are satisfied, the "conduit" exemption applies to network service transmissions, private communications ("E- mail"), real-time communications services ("chat rooms" and "list-serves"), and to site-linking tools and navigational aids including a search engine or browser.

The bill does not apply only to OSPs. Any person acting as a "mere conduit" in transmitting material through an electronic communications system or network is exempt from direct, vicarious, or contributory infringement copyright liability. A person acts as a "conduit" with respect to "network services and facilities" when such person "transmits, routes or provides connections" on behalf of a system user provided the services are for the purpose of managing, controlling or operating a communications system or network and the "conduit" person does not generate, or make any material alteration of, the content in the course of the transmission. [18]

[16] Among other requirements, the notice must describe the infringing material, give information about its location on the network, provide proof of copyright registration or an application for registration or a court order that the use is unlawful, contain a sworn statement that the notice of infringement is accurate, be signed physically or electronically by an authorized person, and be accompanied by any payment the Register of Copyrights determines is necessary to deter frivolous notices.

[17] Proposed addition to 17 U.S.C. at §512(b)(3)(B).

[18] Proposed addition to 17 U.S.C. in §512(a).

Limitation of Liability for Blocking Actions

An OSP who removes, disables, or blocks an allegedly infringing site upon statutory notice &infringement has no liability to the person whose site or material is blocked whether or not the material is infringing.

Redress for Wrongful Notifications

If someone materially misrepresents in a statutory notice that certain online material is infringing, relief may be obtained against that person by the actual copyright owner or the OSP. A federal or State court may award statutory damages of not less than $1000 and any actual damages, including costs and attorneys' fees.

Other Defenses Not Affected by Blocking or Non-blocking Actions

Whether or not an OSP removes, disables, or blocks allegedly infringing material shall not adversely bear upon any defense to copyright infringement. For example, the fair use defense of 17 U.S.C. §107 is not affected by any decision of an OSP to remove or not to remove alleged infringing material.

Regulatory Oversight

The Register of Copyrights would be authorized to issue regulations specifying additional information for inclusion in the statutory notice of infringement and shall issue a standard form for the notice in both electronic and hard copy formats. Failure to provide the additional information in the notice or to use the Copyright Office form, however, shall not invalidate the notice.

On-Line Copyright Liability Limitation Act (H.R. 2180)

Like Title I of S. 1146, the On-Line Copyright Liability Limitation Act H.R. 2180) would add a new section 512 to the Copyright Act, tire 17 U.S.C., to establish statutory standards for determining the copyright liability of online service and access providers (OSPs) and any other persons who engage in the exempt activities. The basic approach of the bills is similar and many provisions are common to both. These are not companion bills, however.

Major Differences between S. 1146 and H.R. 2180. A major distinction is that H.R. 2180 would exempt qualifying OSPs from copyright liability in cases of direct or vicarious infringement, but not in cases of contributory infringement. If the OSP is found liable as a contributory infringer, however, the only remedy for the copyright owner would be an injunction to stop the infringement.

Other major differences are:

> H.R. 2180 does not specifically include an exemption for private or real-time communications or for use of navigational tools such as search engines and browsers;

H.R. 2180 does not specify the content of the notice of infringement and does not specifically legislate a "notice and takedown" procedure;" and

H.R. 2180 does not fix a minimum statutory damages fine for material misrepresentations about infringing material online.

Summary of H.R. 2180

H.R. 2180 would establish a statutory standard to govern the copyright liability of OSPs. If the statutory conditions are met, this statutory standard replaces the judicially created doctrine of vicarious infringement, and limits the remedy for contributory infringement to injunctive relief. The exemption from copyright liability depends upon the OSPs' level of control, participation in any infringing activity, and knowledge of the infringement. If the exemption does not apply, the doctrines of existing law relating to direct, vicarious, or contributory infringement will attach to the infringing conduct.

Exemption from Direct or Vicarious Liability. An OSP would be exempt from direct or vicarious liability based solely on transmitting or providing access to copyrighted material online if the OSP did not—

initiate placement of the material online;

generate, select, or alter the content;

determine the recipients of the material;

receive a direct financial benefit attributable to the infringement;

sponsor, endorse, or advertise the material;

and the OSP did not—

know or have an awareness by notice or other information that the material is infringing, or know or have an awareness that it is prohibited by law from accessing the material.

There is no affirmative obligation, however, to seek information about a possible copyright infringement online.

Limitation on Contributory Infringement Remedy

Under H.R. 2180, a court could find an OSP liable as a contributory infringer even if the OSP only engaged in the conduct of transmitting or providing access to material on-line and did not initiate the infringement, determine the recipients, receive a direct financial benefit, or otherwise engage in conduct that would disqualify it from the direct or vicarious liability exemption. Presumably, the court would make additional findings that the OSP had knowledge, or an awareness, of the possible infringing material and induced, caused, or materially contributed to the infringement.

If the OSP is held liable for contributory infringement, H.R. 2180 would limit the remedy to an injunction. Further, injunctive relief would be available "only to the extent that all acts required by such relief are technically feasible and economically reasonable to carry out."

Limitation of Liability for Blocking Actions

A person who removes, disables, or blocks an allegedly infringing site in response to information by notice or otherwise has no liability to the party whose site or material is blocked, whether or not the material is infringing.

Since H.R. 2180 does not specify a statutory notice of infringement, this limitation on liability is available on a broader basis than the similar provision in S. 1146 (which depends upon taking the blocking action pursuant to a statutory notice). Also, the limitation in H.R. 2180 is not limited by time—unlike the limitation in S. 1146 (which applies for 10 days or until the OSP receives a court order concerning the alleged infringement).

Redress for Wrongful Notifications

If someone knowingly materially misrepresents that certain online material is infringing, any person who relies on the misrepresentation may recover their damages, including costs and attorneys' fees. Recovery depends upon proof of damages since there is no mandatory fine.

By contrast, S. 1146 does not require a "knowing" misrepresentation. Also, S. 1146 sets a minimum statutory damage remedy of $1000.

Other Defenses Not Affected by Blocking or Non-blocking Actions

Whether or not an OSP removes, disables, or blocks access to allegedly infringing material shall not adversely bear upon any defense to copyright infringement. For example, the fair use defense of 17 U.S.C. §107 is not affected by any decision of an OSP to remove or not to remove the alleged infringing material.

Although H.R. 2180 expresses this principle in different language than the comparable provision in S. 1146, both bills seem to achieve the same result.

ARGUMENTS FOR AND AGAINST THE OSP COPYRIGHT LIABILITY BILLS

Arguments in Favor

The basic principles of the OSP copyright liability bills are apparently supported by those companies and persons who might qualify for the exemptions from liability proposed by the bills.[19] These companies and persons include the telephone companies, online access and service providers, libraries and educational institutions, and some software companies (i.e., generally those who create linking, navigational, or browsing tools and protocols relating to interoperability of software). The viewpoints of these groups or interests are generally represented by the Ad Hoc Copyright Coalition and the Digital Future Coalition.[20]

Relationship to WIPO Treaties

A critical issue for the supporters of the OSP liability bills is that OSP liability must "be considered in conjunction with the legislation implementing the World Intellectual Property Organization treaties on digital copyright."[21] Supporters argue that OSP liability must be clarified because the WIPO treaties expand and elaborate on the rights of copyright owners in the digital environment. This expansion and elaboration increases the potential liability risk for OSPs and any other users of computer networks.[22]

Uniqueness of the Internet

Supporters of the OSP liability bills argue the "size, scope, and utility of the Internet differ so greatly from all previous media that analogies provide limited assistance when we ask how to accommodate the needs [OSPs] and copyright holders. What we need is a new set of norms."[23] Internet traffic consists of billions of discrete packets of digitized information or messages. The OSPs cannot prevent the infringements of third parties. Without clarifying legislation, it is argued, OSPs "risk being held liable for massive damages for copyright infringement perpetrated by individuals without the knowledge of the [OSP],"[24] given the nature of Internet operations and their worldwide scope.

Inadequacy of Existing Law

Existing law on OSP liability is unsettled and uncertain, according to supporters of the OSP liability bills. This uncertainty alone is "inimical to the growth of [the Internet]."[25] Even more troubling to supporters is the possible application & the contributory infringement doctrine to fix liability based on "constructive knowledge" of an infringement. "If all courts applied a standard that contributory infringement exists only when the defendant had actual knowledge &the occurrence of copyright infringement, then USTA would not be troubled. Unfortunately however, some courts construe the knowledge requirement not as actual

---

[19] For example, MCI Communications Corporation supports the basic principles of H.R. 2180, although it may seek further improvements in the text, according to MCI's technology counsel, Tim Casey. MCI Proposes Private Sector Solutions on Internet Issues, National Journal's Congress Daily, July 21, 1997.

[20] These "coalitions" have overlapping memberships.

[21] Statement of George Vradenburg III, Senior Vice President and General Counsel of America Online, Inc. on behalf of the Ad Hoe Copyright Coalition, Hearing on OSP Copyright Liability [S. 1146] Before the Senate Judiciary Committee, 105th Cong., 1st Sess., September 4, 1997 (unpublished) at 6. Hereafter: "Senate Hearing on S. 1146."

[22] Id. at 6.

[23] Statement of Roy Neel, President and CEO, United States Telephone Association, Senate Hearing on S. 1146, September 4, 1997 (unpublished) at 3.

[24] Id. at 3.

[25] Id. at 5.

knowledge, but as constructive knowledge—meaning that had the defendant engaged in further investigation, it might have uncovered the infringing nature of the subject material."[26]

Unlike dance hall proprietors (who are generally liable for infringements of music performed on premises controlled by them), it is argued that it is unrealistic to hold OSPs to a requirement of investigating and monitoring the millions of messages that are transmitted simultaneously over the Internet.

Exemption for Mere Conduit Activity Is a Matter of Fairness. Supporters of the OSP liability bills argue that "Congress must make clear that service providers which act simply as a conduit for transmitting information are immune for third-party infringement: No other option is practical."[27] Liability for copyright infringement should fall, according to supporters of the pending bills, "on those who create an infringing work or on those who reproduce or perform it with actual knowledge of the infringement and who are capable, as a legal and practical matter, to do something about it. The innocent or powerless transmitter should not be held liable for infringing acts of others... Fundamental fairness must limit the service provider's exposure."[28]

Shared Enforcement Responsibility Subject to Actual Notice to OSP

Copyright owners should take the lead in detecting copyright infringements and enforcing their rights in connection with uses of their works on the Internet, according to OSP liability bill supporters. Copyright owners and OSPs can then cooperate and work together to protect copyrights against unauthorized Internet uses.

Content owners must locate and identify infringing materials, and service providers must be willing to help remove them where it is legal and appropriate to do so. A balanced approach must also assure that any mechanisms designed to require or incent service providers to remove such materials from their systems be carefully designed to reflect important privacy, competitive and other interests of third parties, and to provide a speedy judicial resolution of infringement or fair use claims. System providers should be protected from any claims that removal of potentially infringing material was wrongful, and transmitters whose material is removed must have a speedy resolution of their claims of wrongful removal.[29]

Arguments against the OSP Liability Bills

Opposition to the pending OSP liability bills and, perhaps, to any legislation on this subject comes from the copyright or content owners whose material is transmitted via the Internet and other computer networks. The Creative Incentive Coalition, comprising motion picture, software, newspaper, and sound recording companies (and other related interests), represents many of these opponents.

[26] Id. at 5.
[27] Statement of George Vradenburg III, Senate Hearing on S. 1146, at 5.
[28] Id. at 4-5.
[29] Id. at 5-6.

Under the auspices of the House Subcommittee on Courts and Intellectual Property, the private sector interests affected by the OSP liability issue held a series of negotiating meetings in 1996, at which ideas and proposals for a compromise solution to this copyright policy issue were explored. Although less formal discussions may continue, the collapse of the organized talks without reaching a compromise may affect the positions of the parties on this year's OSP liability bills. That is, the negotiating position of both sides may harden somewhat. Copyright owners, for example, may be less willing to consider any liability exemption for OSPs.

According to one participant in the 1996 negotiations, the copyright owner witnesses at the Senate hearing on S. 1146 "now stressed their opposition to any exemption legislation. They indicated that any such limitation on liability would remove the most important incentive that OSPs have to cooperate in containing infringements—the threat of litigation."[30]

WIPO Treaties Ratification Should Precede Any OSP Liability Legislation

While it is not always clear whether copyright owners oppose OSP liability legislation on principle or oppose the details of specific proposals, the critical point for copyright owners is that ratification of the WIPO treaties should not be held hostage to resolution of the OSP liability issue. The Creative Incentive Coalition argues that ratification of the WIPO treaties this year is needed to vindicate the United States' "strong interest in protecting creative minds and the capital they represent. The longer we delay the more we make it clear we don't give a damn."[31]

Opponents of the OSP liability bills argue that the United States must ratify the WIPO treaties quickly to maintain U.S. leadership in intellectual property protection. The OSP issue, it is argued, is too complex and controversial to be resolved in the implementing legislation. If this issue is considered, it will open the door to other complex issues, which will delay ratification of the treaties. If ratification of the WIPO treaties is delayed or even linked to OSP liability legislation, opponents argue this will be perceived abroad as a relaxation of U. S. copyright liability standards. "If we were to change our law to further limit the liability of OSPs and ISPs, the weakening of that worldwide chain of copyright protection would be a clear and present danger to a very substantial segment of our economy."[32]

Existing Copyright Liability Law Is Adequate

Copyright owners argue that the judge-made doctrines of vicarious and contributory infringement are working well and present no special problems for OSPs and the economic vitality of the Internet. They assert that the known facts "include no hard evidence that existing copyright law is imposing unreasonable or debilitating liability on OSPs and ISPs."[33]

---

[30] Lutzger, Neither Aiding Nor Abetting, Legal Times, October 6, 1997, Special Section on Intellectual Property at 18, 22.

[31] Statement of Jack Valenti, Chairman of the Motion Picture Association of America, Coalition Calls for Ratification of Copyright Treaties in '97, National Journal's Congress Daily, September 15, 1997.

[32] Statement of Fritz Attaway, Senior Vice President, Government Relations and Washington General Counsel of the Motion Picture Association of America ("MPAA"), Senate Heating on S. 1146, September 4, 1997 (unpublished) at 11.

[33] Statement of Fritz Attaway, Washington General Counsel of the MPAA, Senate Heating on S. 1146, September 4, 1997 (unpublished) at 11.

According to copyright owners, the "good news is that current copyright law appears, for now, to be flexible enough to handle the new, ever-changing technology of the Interact."[34]

Copyright owners argue that there have only been a handful of cases where the copyright liability of OSPs was at issue and that the one decision that resulted in an opinion favored the OSP.[35] One copyright owner representative has stated that it is not aware of any major cases being filed in the last year nor "of any instance where AOL, Bell Atlantic; Sprint, MCI, among others, have been sued for copyright infringement."[36]

Internet Piracy Is the Crisis Issue—Not OSP Liability

Copyright owners argue that there is no evidence that "the absence of a firm rule on the copyright liability of network operators is in any way chilling the development of the Internet, investment in network-based operations, or new entrants into these markets. In fact, competition is thriving."[37] By contrast, copyright owners argue that "[t]here is hard, confirmable evidence that [the motion picture] industry alone is losing over $2 billion to pirates each and every year, and that piracy in the digital world will become even more costly."[38] The software industry asserts that it loses $12 billion each year to piracy.[39]

The rapid growth of the Internet, it is argued, "also means that the peril faced by [the recording] industry is of the same magnitude. Our sound recordings are easily copied to a computer hard drive... [and] can be 'uploaded' to the Internet with the push of a button.... And once the recordings are stored on servers on the Internet, they are available to be downloaded by millions of users."[40]

General Liability Immunity for OSPs Cannot Be Justified

Since, in the view of copyright owners, the current taw provides a sound balance between their rights and limitations on rights, it is argued that "the copyright law should not be changed to create general immunities for providers of network services."[41] To copyright owners, "any proposal to exempt Internet Access Providers from copyright liability is a solution in search of a problem. We don't have a problem now. But if we try to legislate a

[34] Statement of Cary Sherman, General Counsel of the Recording Industry Association of America ("RIAA"), Senate Hearing on S. 1146, September 4, 1997 (unpublished) at 5.

[35]Id. at 6. The reference to one decision presumably is to the Netcom case, in which the district court held the OSP was not vicariously liable. Religious Technology Center v. Netcom, 907 F. Supp. 1361 (N.D. Cal. 1995). The district court reserved a decision, pending further proceedings, on the issue of contributory infringement.

[36] Statement of Daniel Burton, Vice President, Novell, on behalf of the Business Software Alliance ("BSA") and the Software Publishers Association ("SPA"), Senate Hearing on S. 1146, September 4, 1997 (unpublished) at 5.

[37] Statement of Dan Burton, on behalf of BSA and SPA, Senate Hearing on S. 1146, September 4, 1997 (unpublished) at 5.

[38] Statement of Fritz Attaway, Washington General Counsel of the MPAA, Senate Hearing on S. 1146, September 4, 1997 (unpublished) at 11. This figure refers to total motion picture piracy -- not just to piracy on the Internet.

[39] Statement of Dan Burton, on behalf of BSA and SPA, Senate Hearing on S. 1146, September 4, 1997 (unpublished) at 4. This figure also is apparently a total for all software piracy- not only piracy on the Interact.

[40] Statement of Cary Sherman, on behalf of the RIAA, Senate Hearing on S. 1146, September 4, 1997 (unpublished) at 3.

[41] Statement of Dan Burton, on behalf of BSA and SPA, Senate Hearing on S. 1146, September 4, 1997 (unpublished) at 5.

solution, we must surely **will** have a problem in the future...We need cooperation, not immunity."[42]

While he was not willing to support general immunity for OSPs, at least one copyright owner representative described specific activities that probably should not lead to liability: "caching by end-users should not create liability, because, in effect, such copies are implicitly licensed...; [where] the service provider is passively enabling distribution of a work.., copyright liability should not result...; [and storage of e-mail] should not lead to liability, so long as the only service provided by the operator of the system is to store the work pending retrieval."[43] This same representative, however, also argues that a "notice and takedown" system "is simply an unworkable model.... [M]aking notice a precondition to suit is not a solution."[44]

Existing Law Encourages Cooperation between OSPs and Copyright Owners

In addition to arguing that existing copyright law should not be changed because it represents a sound balance between rights and limitations on rights, copyright owners argue that the potential liability of OSPs fosters collaborative efforts to detect end stop copyright infringement "An outright exemption from liability would discourage the IAPs from working with creators to avoid infringements."[45] Another copyright owner representative reported they have had "good experiences in obtaining the help and collaboration of network operators in removing and/or blocking access to infringing material. In part, we believe such collaboration is due to the incentives now provided by the copyright law for on-line services and other intermediaries to cooperate with software companies.... [T] he ephemeral character of many pirate software sites makes it extremely difficult to take action against pirates without help from service providers."[46]

CONCLUSION

Online service and access providers (OSPs) seek legislative clarification of their copyright liability for transmitting, routing, providing connections and access, and otherwise facilitating Internet and other computer network transmissions. Since Internet traffic consists of billions of discrete packets of digitized information or messages, OSPs argue that they cannot prevent infringements by third parties and should not be liable for third party infringements. Without clarifying legislation, OSPs argue that, in conducting routine Internet business, they are exposed to potentially massive damages for copyright infringement by third parties.

---

[42] Statement of Cary Sherman, on behalf of the RIAA, Senate Hearing on S. 1146, September 4, 1997 (unpublished) at 7.

[43] Statement of Dan Button, an behalf of BSA and SPA, Senate Hearing on S. 1146, September, 4, 1997 (unpublished) at 7-8.

[44] Id. at 8-9.

[45] Statement of Cary Sherman on behalf of the RIAA Senate I-leafing on S. 1146, September 4, 1997 (unpublished) at 7.

[46] Statement of Dan Burton on behalf of BSA and SPA, Senate Hearing on S. 1146, September 4, 1997 (unpublished) at 6.

Two pending bills, Title I of S. 1146 and H.R. 2180, would generally exempt from copyright liability those OSPs who act as "mere conduits" and do not generate, initiate, or modify the content of the transmissions. The principles of these bills are generally supported by the telephone companies, libraries and many educational institutions, and many Internet browser, navigational, and search engine companies,[47] as well as the online service and access providers.

These groups also argue that OSP liability legislation must be included in, or enacted in conjunction with, any bills implementing United States adherence to the WIPO Copyright and Performances and Phonograms Treaties. Since, according to these groups, the WIPO treaties expand and elaborate on rights of copyright owners in the digital environment, legislation is needed to balance the expansion of rights, which increases the potential liability risk for OSPs.

The specific OSP liability bills now pending are opposed by rights holders, including motion picture and sound recording producers, book and music publishers, and many software companies. Rights holders argue that existing copyright law is working well to define who is liable for infringing uses of copyrighted works on the Internet. They argue that there is no evidence that OSPs have been subject to unreasonable or debilitating liability under the existing doctrines of vicarious and contributory infringement.

The real crisis, according to rights holders, is rampant piracy on the Internet and elsewhere; therefore, the WIPO Treaties should be ratified and implemented without attempting to change existing law concerning OSP liability. Rights holders urge early action to approve the WIPO Treaties and enact the implementing legislation in order to maintain United States leadership in intellectual property internationally, and to encourage other countries to improve protection for copyrighted materials in digital, electronic environments. Since the United States is a global leader in producing the hardware and software needed to conduct Internet businesses, early approval of the treaties will benefit the U.S. economy, according to rights holders.

[47] Many of these groups at least sometimes engage in Internet transmission activities and might also qualify for the "conduit" exemption from liability.

DIGITAL MILLENNIUM COPYRIGHT ACT, P.L. 105-304: SUMMARY AND ANALYSIS

Dorothy Schrader

BACKGROUND

The Internet, other computer networks, and advances in electronic and digital technologies provide unparalleled opportunities for worldwide communications and economic growth, in the judgment of most experts. In order to tap fully the potential of these new technologies, it is also generally agreed that legislatures will need to confront and resolve many difficult technical and legal policy issues. The scope of copyright protection, and any limitations on the rights of copyright owners, for the use of copyrighted works in digital, electronic environment was addressed by the 105th Congress in enacting the Digital Millennium Copyright Act (DMCA), P.L. 105-304.[1]

The Digital Millennium Copyright Act is the outcome of several years of congressional consideration of copyright policy issues relating to domestic development of the national information infrastructure (once called the "information superhighway;" now referred to as the "Internet"), and to international development of two new intellectual property treaties.

A Working Group on Intellectual Property of the White House National Information Infrastructure (NII) Task Force convened a series of conferences exploring the copyright policy issues related to the NII. Their September 1995 report led to the introduction in the 104th Congress of S. 1284 and H.R. 2441, which would have implemented the Working Group's recommendations.[2] Hearings were held on the NII copyright policy issues, but the bills were not enacted.

At the international level, two new intellectual property treaties were created by a diplomatic conference of States in Geneva, Switzerland, on December 20, 1996, under the auspices of the World intellectual Property Organization (WIPO). These are the WIPO

[1] The Act of October 28, 1998, consists of 5 Titles, which generally took effect on the date of enactment, except for the technical amendments made by Title I concerning treaty relationships and miscellaneous provisions in Title IV.

Copyright Treaty and the WIPO Performances and Phonograms Treaty.[3] The WIPO Copyright Treaty covers copyright protection for computer programs, for databases (to the extent they are "intellectual creations"), and for digital, electronic uses of copyrighted works in general. The WIPO Performances and Phonograms Treaty covers protection for performers and producers of sound recordings (called "phonograms" internationally), and generally applies the same or equivalent protection to sound recordings as that applied to other copyright subject matter by the WIPO Copyright Treaty.[4]

The President forwarded the two WIPO treaties to the Senate for its advise and consent to ratification by the United States and requested the introduction of legislation to implement the two substantive provisions of the treaties which the Administration deemed would require legislation to satisfy the obligations of the treaties. S. 1121 and H.R. 2281, as originally introduced, embodied the Administration's recommended "minimalist approach" to implementing legislation.

The bills were premised on the assumption that existing United States copyright law was largely consistent with the treaty obligations. S. 1121 and H.R. 2281 would have created new legal protection against devices and activities that are primarily designed to circumvent anti-copying technologies and against fraudulent removal, alteration, or provision of copyright management information ("CMI"). Technical amendments were also included in the bills to update the Copyright Act's references to treaty relationships.

After the introduction of the Administration's implementation bills, alternative implementation bills were introduced (S. 1146 and H.R. 3048)[5] that addressed Internet copyright policy issues as well as WIPO Treaties implementation. Two other bills (H.R. 2180 and H.R. 3209) proposed amendments solely concerning the copyright liability of online service providers (OSPs).

The Senate Judiciary Committee held hearings on S. 1121 and S. 1146 on September 4, 1997. The House Subcommittee on Courts and Intellectual Property held hearings on H.R. 2281 and H.R. 2180 on September 16 and 17, 1997. The House Judiciary Committee on April 1, 1998, approved an amendment version of H.R. 2281, which included the core elements of a private sector agreement on online service provider liability.[6] The Senate

---

2 DEPARTMENT OF COMMERCE, INTELLECTUAL PROPERTY AND THE NATIONAL INFORMATION INFRASTRUCTURE, REPORT OF THE WORKING GROUP ON INTELLECTUAL PROPERTY RIGHTS OF THE INFORMATION INFRASTRUCTURE TASK FORCE (1995).

3 For an overview of these treaties, *see* D. Schrader, *World Intellectual Property Organization Copyright Treaty: An Overview,* CRS Report No. 97-444 A, and D. Schrader, *World Intellectual Property Organization Performances and Phonograms Treaty: An Overview,* CRS Report No. 97-523 A.

4 Two treaties, rather than one treaty, were developed because a majority of countries do not protect sound recordings as copyright subject matter. The United States protects sound recordings as copyright subject matter, but other countries (and especially the members of the European Union) protect sound recordings under so-called "related" or "neighboring rights," unfair competition, or other non-copyright legal theories. Also, the fact of a separate treaty for phonograms allows for the extension of protection to performers (most of whom are not considered "authors" within the meaning of the copyright law in those countries that protect sound recordings as copyright subject matter).

5 H.R. 3048 and S. 1146 contained the same proposals relating to fair use, library reproduction, distance learning, ephemeral recordings, operational copying by computers, and protection against removal or alteration of CMI. The provisions dealing with anti-circumvention of copying technologies were virtually identical except for a definition of "effective technological measure." H.R. 3048, moreover, contained other amendments relating to the first sale doctrine and "shrink-wrap" licenses not found in S. 1146 but did not contain any provisions on online service provider (OSP) liability, which were included in S. 1146.

6 H. Rept. 105-551 (Part I), 105th Cong., 2d Sess. (1998).

Judiciary Committee on May 11, 1998, approved a new bill, S. 2037, as a successor to S. 1121.[7]

S. 2037, which was entitled the "Digital Millennium Copyright Act of 1998," embodied the full private sector agreement on OSP copyright liability, made changes in the anti-circumvention and CMI provisions, and included amendments concerning several other Internet copyright policy issues.[8]

The Senate passed S. 2037 by unanimous vote on May 14, 1998.

H.R. 2281 (under the short title, the "WIPO Copyright Treaties Implementation Act") was subject to sequential referral to the House Commerce Committee. The Subcommittee on Telecommunications, Trade, and Consumer Protection held a hearing on June 5, 1998. The full Commerce Protection made several amendments to H.R.2281 and reported the bill on July 22, 1998, under the short title, the "Digital Millennium Copyright Act of 1998."[9] This version of H.R. 2281 generally included the amendments already embodied in S. 2037 as passed by the Senate. The Commerce Committee made additional amendments, especially concerning anti-circumvention, fair use, the first sale doctrine, and encryption research.

The House of Representatives passed H.R. 2281 on August 4, 1998, under the short title, the "Digital Millennium Copyright Act of 1998." The House-passed version combined the Senate amendments to S. 2037 with additional amendments by the House Judiciary and Commerce Committees. The Floor Manager's Amendment to H.R. 2281 also added two new forms of intellectual property protection (in separate titles) that were not earlier considered part of the WIPO Treaties implementation process. Title V incorporated the "Collections of Information Antipiracy Act," which had passed the House earlier as H.R. 2652. This Title would have created 15 years of federal misappropriation-style protection for databases that are not sufficiently creative to be eligible for copyright protection. Title VI of the House version of H.R. 2281 would have enacted the Vessel Hull Design Protection Act, which also passed the House as separate legislation in the form of H.R. 2696. This Title would have created 10 years of design protection for boat hulls larger than a rowboat and smaller than 201 feet in length.

Senate and House conferees agreed on a common bill (H.R. 2281), which passed the Senate on October 8, 1998, and passed the House on October 12, 1998. The Senate consented to United States ratification of the two WIPO Treaties on October 21, 1998. The President signed H.R. 2281, the Digital Millennium Copyright Act, into law on October 28, 1998 (P.L. 105-304).

---

[7] S. Rept. 105-190, 105th Cong., 2d Sess. (1998).

[8] The amendments embodied in S. 2037: 1) declared that nothing in the anti-circumvention provisions enlarges or diminishes the existing doctrines of vicarious or contributory infringement, or affects existing defenses such as fair use; 2) clarified that electronics manufacturers have no obligation to design consumer products to achieve protection against circumvention; 3) expanded the exemption of 17 U.S.C. 112 for ephemeral copying by broadcasters to apply in digital contexts and to override the new anti-circumvention measures under certain conditions; 4) expanded the exemption of 17 U.S.C. 198 for libraries and archives to preserve copies for their collections in digital formats; 5) protected personal privacy interests on the Internet; 6) provided exceptions from the anti-circumvention provisions for computer interoperability, for libraries and nonprofit educational institutions in malting purchasing decisions, and with respect to the right to control access by minors to the Internet; 7) excepted law enforcement and intelligence activities from the anti-circumvention and CMI provisions; and 8) directed the Copyright Office to report on distance learning and on the liability of nonprofit educational institutions and libraries when they act as OSPs for patrons.

[9] H. Rept. 105-551 (Part II), 105th Cong. 2d Sess. (1998).

The Digital Millennium Copyright Act consists of five Titles. Title I implements the two WIPO treaties. Title II establishes certain exemptions from copyright liability for online service and access providers. Title III exempts computer maintenance and repair companies from copyright liability for the reproduction of a computer program that occurs by mere activation of the computer. Title IV contains miscellaneous provisions relating to ephemeral recordings and transmissions of digital sound recordings; the assumption of contractual obligations in collective bargaining agreements between motion picture producers and artistic contributors; and the rank and authority of the Register of Copyrights and the rank of the Commissioner of Patents and Trademarks. Title V creates federal design protection for vessel hulls, which sunsets after 2 years.

WIPO Treaties Implementation—Title I

Title I of the Digital Millennium Copyright Act bears the short title "WIPO Copyright and Performances and Phonograms Treaties Implementation Act of 1998." This act amends title 17 of the U.S. Code by adding a new Chapter 12, which creates civil and criminal liability for circumvention of copyright protection technologies and for the knowing provision of false copyright management information ("CMI") or the intentional removal or alteration of CMI. The technological protection measures typically include encryption, scrambling, passwords, and electronic envelopes. Devices to bypass these measures are usually described as "black boxes." The Act also makes technical amendments to 17 U.S.C. 101,[10] 104,[11] 104A(h),[12] 411(a),[13] and 507(a).[14]

Protection against Circumvention of Anti-Copying Technology

The WIPO Treaties contain "substantively identical provisions on technological measures of protection (also commonly referred to as the 'black box' or 'anti-circumvention' provisions). These provisions require contracting parties to provide 'adequate legal protection and effective legal remedies against the circumvention of effective technological measures'"[15] used by authors and other copyright owners to restrict unlawful access to their copyrighted works.

[10] Section 101 defines terms and phrases used in the Copyright Act.

[11] Section 104 specifies the "points of attachment," *i.e.*, the conditions under which works by foreign nationals are eligible for copyright protection in the United States.

[12] Section 104A restored copyright in certain foreign works that fell into the public domain in the United States because of a failure to comply with copyright formalities.

[13] Section 411(a) makes registration with the United States Copyright Office a prerequisite to a suit for copyright infringement for works of United States origin but excepts certain works of foreign origin from mandatory registration.

[14] Section 507 is a statute of limitations provision.

[15] CONFERENCE REPORT ON THE DIGITAL MILLENNIUM COPYRIGHT ACT, 105- 796, 105th Cong., 2d Sess. 63-64 (1998) (hereafter: "DMCA Conference Report").

Basic Nature of Violations

New Section 1201, 17 U.S.C., implements the "anti-circumvention" obligations of the WIPO Treaties. Subparagraph (a)l(A) provides that "[n]o person shall circumvent a technological measure that effectively controls access to a work protected under this title [17].

This prohibition is, however, delayed for two years after the date of enactment, in order to allow time "for the development of a record as to how the implementation of these technologies is affecting availability of works in the market place for non- infringing uses,"[16] and for the conduct of a rulemaking proceeding by the Librarian of Congress. That proceeding can be repeated every 3 years. "It is anticipated that the main focus of the rulemaking proceeding will be on whether a substantial diminution of that availability is actually occurring in the market for particular classes of copyrighted works.... [T]he rule-making may also, to the extent required, assess whether an adverse impact is likely to occur over the time period relevant to each rule-making proceeding. However, the determination should be based upon anticipated, rather than actual, adverse impacts only in extraordinary circumstances in which the evidence of likelihood of future adverse impact... is highly specific, strong and persuasive."[17]

Section 1201 (a)(2) also prohibits the manufacture, importation, offering to the public or other trafficking in any technology, product, service, device, component or part thereof that is primarily designed or produced to circumvent an anti-copying system. The 2-year delay-affecting subparagraph (1) does not apply to violations of this subparagraph (2). The prohibition against manufacture or sale of devices applies if one of three conditions is met: (1) the device is primarily designed for circumvention; (2) the device has only a limited commercially significant purpose other than circumvention; or (3) the device is marketed by someone who is trafficking in circumvention devices.

Section 1201(b) creates another anti-circumvention violation that parallels the violation fixed by subparagraph (a)(2) of Section 1201. The "1201(b)" type of violation occurs when a person who has obtained authorized access to the copyrighted work circumvents the limits of the controls that the copyright owner has placed on lawful access to the work. Again, the prohibition on manufacture and sale, etc., of “black boxes" applies if one of three conditions is met—the device or service was primarily designed for circumvention, has only a limited commercially significant purpose other than circumvention, or is marketed by someone who traffics in circumvention technologies.

Exemptions from Violations

In the course of legislative debate on WIPO Treaties implementation, several new or clarifying exemptions were added. Section 1201(c) declares that the circumvention provisions do not: (1) affect fair use or any other existing limitations on copyright infringement or the existing rights and remedies of the Copyright Act; (2) enlarge or diminish the existing doctrines of vicarious or contributory copyright infringement; (3) obligate electronics-computer manufacturers to design consumer products to achieve protection against circumvention so long as the products or parts do not otherwise fall within the ban of Section

[16] *Section-By-Section Analysis of H. R. 2281 As Passed By the United States House of Representatives on August 4, 1998,* Committee on the Judiciary, House of Representatives, 105th Cong., 2d Sess. 6 (Comm. Print, Serial No. 6, 1998) (hereafter: "Sectional Analysis of H.R. 2281, August 4, 1998").

1201(a)(2) or (b)(1); or (4) enlarge or diminish free speech or press rights for activities using consumer electronics, telecommunications, or computer products.

Circumvention for purposes of achieving interoperability of computers and reverse engineering by persons with access to a lawful copy are generally permissible under Section 1201(f), unless the activities otherwise constitute copyright infringement.

Law enforcement and intelligence activities are generally exempt from violations of the circumvention provisions.[18] Nonprofit libraries, archives, and educational institutions are exempt for purposes of making decisions about acquiring a copy of the work.[19] Persons engaging in encryption research are generally exempt if they lawfully obtained the encrypted copy, made a good faith effort to obtain authorization before circumvention, and their acts are necessary to conduct encryption research and do not otherwise constitute copyright infringement or violate the Computer Fraud and Abuse Act of 1986.[20] Similarly, Section 1201(j) exempts circumvention for purposes of legitimate security testing of a computer or computer system or network provided the acts do not constitute copyright infringement or violate the Computer Fraud and Abuse Act of 1986.

In applying Section 1201(a) to a component or part, the court may take account of the fact that the part has the sole purpose of preventing access by minors to material on the Internet.[21] Also, it is not a violation of Section 1201 (a)(1)(A) to circumvent a technological measure that also has the purpose or capability of collecting or disseminating personally identifying information about the online activities of a natural person.[22]

Technological Measures for Analog VCR

As noted, the anti-circumvention provisions generally do not require the design of consumer electronics or computer products to achieve protection against circumvention. In a departure from that general principle, Section 1201(k) requires that "analog video cassette recorders must conform to the two forms of copy control technology that are in wide use in the market today—the automatic gain control copy control technology and the color stripe copy control technology."[23]

The House-Senate conferees explained that this provision was included "in order to deal with a very specific situation involving the protection of analog television programming and prerecorded movies and other audiovisual works in relation to recording capabilities of ordinary consumer analog video cassette recorders.... Before agreeing to include this requirement in the final legislation, the conferees assured themselves in relation to two critical issues—that these analog copy control technologies do not create 'playability' problems on normal consumer electronics products and that the intellectual property necessary for the operation of these technologies will be available on reasonable and non-discriminatory terms."[24]

---

[17] 17 Sectional Analysis of H.R. 2281, August 4, 1998, at 6 (Emphasis in original).
[18] Section 1201(e), 17 U.S.C.
[19] Section 1201(d), 17 U.S.C.
[20] Section 1201(g), 17 U.S.C.
[21] Section 1201(h), 17 U.S.C.
[22] Section 1201(i), 17 U.S.C.
[23] DMCA Conference Report, 105-796 at 67.
[24] *Id.* at 68.

Protection for the Integrity of Copyright Management Information

The two WIPO Treaties contain substantively identical obligations to protect the integrity of copyright management information ("CMI"), *i.e.*, information which identifies the work, the author, or the owner of rights or which specifies the terms and conditions of use. CMI also includes any identifying numbers or codes.

Basic Rights

The Digital Millennium Copyright Act implements the treaty obligations to protect CMI in the new Chapter 12 to title 17 U.S.C. The Act generally prohibits the knowing provision, distribution, or importation of false CMI and the intentional removal or alteration of CMI or the distribution or importation of CMI knowing that information has been altered or removed.

The purpose of the CMI provisions is to facilitate widespread use of CMI by copyright owners in order to make licensing of works (or obtaining permission to use works) easier and more beneficial both to the public and copyright owners. Pursuant to the WIPO Treaties, the provisions cannot, and are not, legislated as a formality (*i.e.*, as a condition of the exercise or enjoyment of the copyright), nor can the CMI requirements prohibit the free movement of goods.

The new fights to protect the integrity of CMI systems apply both to analog and digital formats. In this respect, the DMCA exceeds the minimum treaty obligations since the WIPO Treaties require protection only for electronic rights management information.

The prohibitions do not apply to "the ordinary and customary practices of broadcasters or the inadvertent omission of credits from broadcasts of audiovisual works, since such acts do not involve the provision of false CMI with the requisite knowledge and intent."[25]

Exemptions

The lawfully authorized activities of law enforcement and intelligence agencies are exempt from the CMI requirements.[26]

Broadcasters, cable systems, and those who provide programming to these entities are also generally exempt from liability under the CMI provisions, if they do not intend to induce, enable, facilitate or conceal a copyright infringement.[27] The conditions for applying the limitation on liability differ depending upon whether the transmission is an analog or a digital one.

In the case of an analog transmission, an eligible person will not be liable if it is not technically feasible to avoid the violation or if avoidance would create an undue financial hardship.

In the case of a digital transmission, the exemption is dependent upon the status of efforts to create voluntary standards for transmission of CMI. The Act contemplates that voluntary standards will be developed. Until a standard is set, an eligible person is not liable if the transmission would cause a perceptible visual or aural degradation of the digital signal, or if

[25] Sectional Analysis of H.R. 2281, August 4, 1998, at 19.
[26] Section 1202(d), 17 U.S.C.
[27] Section 1202(e), 17 U.S.C.

the transmission would conflict with an applicable government regulation or industry standard other than CMI standards. If a voluntary CMI standard has been set, the eligible person will not be liable if the CMI was not located in accordance with the industry standard.

Civil and Criminal Remedies

The Digital Millennium Copyright Act establishes nearly the same civil and criminal remedies for violations of either the anti-circumvention provisions of 17 U.S.C. 1201 or the CMI provisions of 17 U.S.C. 1202.

Civil Remedies

The civil remedies for violations of the anti-circumvention and CMI provisions are found in Section I203, 17 U.S.C. They include: injunctions, impoundment of infringing material or profits of the violator not counted as part of damages or statutory damages, at the option of the plaintiff. The statutory damages for violation of Section 1201 range from $200-$2500 per act of circumvention. For violation of the Section 1202 CMI provisions, the plaintiff may be awarded between $2500-$25,000 for each violation.

If there are repeated violations within a 3-year period, the court may award triple damages. The court also has the discretion to reduce or remit damages if the violator proves, and the court finds, the offender was not aware and had no reason to believe that the law was violated. Under the same circumstances, in the case of a nonprofit library, archive, or educational institution, the court must reduce or remit damages for innocent violations.

Criminal Penalties

Nonprofit libraries, archives, or educational institutions are exempt from any criminal liability for violation of Sections 1201 or 1202.

Other violators shall be fined no more than $500,000 or imprisoned up to 5 years, or both, for first offenses. For subsequent offenses, the maximum fines and prison time are doubled.

Title I Studies or Reports

Encryption research. New Section 1201(g) of Title 17 U.S.C., in addition to creating certain exemptions for encryption research from the anti-circumvention provisions, also directs the Register of Copyrights and the Assistant Secretary for Communications and Information of the Department of Commerce (hereafter: the "Assistant Secretary for Comm.-Info") to report back to the Congress on the effect of the legislation on encryption research.[28] The report, which is due 1 year after enactment, will also assess the adequacy and effectiveness of the anti-copying measures used by copyright owners.

Impact on electronic commerce. Section 104 of Title I directs the Register of Copyrights and the Assistant Secretary for Comm.-Info to report back to the Congress on the effects of

[28] 17 U.S.C. 1201(g)(5).

Title I on the development of electronic commerce and associated technologies. The report must also evaluate the DMCA's effect on the operations of the first sale doctrine of I7 U.S.C 109 and the computer program exemptions of 17 U.S.C. 117. This chapter is due within 2 years after enactment.

Effective Date

The amendments to title 17 U.S.C. made by Title I of the DMCA are generally effective on the date of enactment, October 28, 1998. The technical amendments relating to international treaty relationships will take effect when the United States becomes bound by the two new WIPO Treaties. The Senate on October 21, 1998 gave its consent to United States ratification of the Treaties. The instruments of ratification will be deposited with the Director General of WIPO in due course. The WIPO Treaties will not enter into force, however, until 30 States have deposited instruments of accession or ratification.[29]

ONLINE COPYRIGHT INFRINGEMENT LIABILITY LIMITATION—TITLE II

The potential liability of online service and access providers (OSPs) for infringing activities of their customers was originally one of the major controversies regarding WIPO Treaties implementation.[30] The original implementation bills recommended by the Administration did not address the issue, on the theory that, since the Treaties themselves do not address *who is liable* for any copyright infringements, the matter could be left to judicial interpretation.

That outcome was opposed by many groups including coalitions representing the OSPs, telecommunications entities, the electronics industry, and library and educational institutions. Without legislative guidance, these groups argued there would be unacceptable business uncertainty and protracted litigation to delineate who is liable for infringements by OSP customers. The issue of OSP liability was resolved by a negotiated agreement among the private sector interests most directly affected by use of copyrighted works on the Internet.[31] That agreement formed the basis for most of Title II of the DMCA.

Title II of the DMCA—the "Online Copyright Infringement Liability Limitation Act"—amends Chapter 5 of the Copyright Act by adding a new section 512 relating to limitations on

[29] Three countries (Belarus, Indonesia, and The Republic of Moldova) have ratified the Copyright Treaty. Two countries (Belarus and The Republic of Moldova) have ratified the Performances and Phonograms Treaty.

[30] This chapter uses "OSP" as shorthand for persons and entities who transmit, route, provide connections, or otherwise facilitate computer network service and access for customers without initiating or altering the content of the transmission. Although OSPs are the main beneficiaries of the liability provisions in Title II of the DMCA, entities other than OSPs can claim the exemption if they meet the statutory conditions.

[31] The negotiations that culminated in an agreement on OSP copyright liability on March 31, 1998 were conducted for several years under the auspices of the Senate Judiciary Committee and the Subcommittee on Courts and Intellectual Property of the House Judiciary Committee. The private sector negotiators included representatives of copyright owners and authors; the telecommunications industry, electronics industry, and computer equipment industry; and online service providers.

OSP liability for online infringements by their customers. The limitations on liability benefit persons or entities that act as online service providers.[32]

The Act gives a two-part definition of the term "service provider." With respect to digital network communications [17 U.S.C. 512(a)], a "service provider" is "an entity offering the transmission, routing, or providing of connections for digital online communications, between or among points specified by a user, of material of the user's choosing, without modification to the content of the material as sent or received."[33] The term service provider as used in subsections (b)-(j) and (1)-(m) of section 512 means "a provider of online services or network access, or the operator of facilities therefore," as well as entities that meet the first part of the definition of a "service provider."[34] The second part of the definition includes universities that act as service providers, and entities that provide Internet access, e-mail, chat room, and web page hosting services.

The Digital Millennium Copyright Act basically absolves the OSPs from copyright liability when they merely act as "conduits" of information transferred over their networks, without having any control over the content of the transmission. The DMCA creates "safe harbors" from either direct, vicarious, or contributory copyright infringement when the conditions of the exemption are met.

Upon receiving a notice of infringement that complies with statutory requirements,[35] an OSP is expected expeditiously to remove, disable, or block access, to the extent blocking is technologically feasible and economically reasonable. Upon receipt of a counter-notice from a provider of the blocked site, the OSP shall retain the block for 10-14 days but no longer, unless the copyright owner files suit for copyright infringement.

The exemptions from liability apply both to network service transmissions and to private and real-time communications services.

The Senate-House conferees reached an agreement on further limits on the liability of nonprofit educational institutions that act as service providers.

Digital Network Communications

An OSP is not liable for monetary relief and injunctive relief is carefully circumscribed when an OSP acts as a "mere conduit" in transmitting the copyrighted work(s). Some of the specific restrictions to qualify for this exemption are:

- the transmission was initiated by someone other than the OSP;
- the transmission is provided through automatic, technical processes without selection of content by the OSP;

[32] Title II of the DMCA took effect upon enactment, October 28, 1998.
[33] Section 512 (k)(1), title 17 U.S.C.
[34] *Ibid.*
[35] Among other requirements, the notice must be in writing describe the infringing material, give information about location of infringing material on the network, identify the copyrighted work(s), contain a sworn statement that the notice of infringement is accurate, and be signed physically or electronically by an authorized person.

- the OSP does not select the recipients of the copyrighted material, except as an automatic response to provide service;
- the OSP does not maintain a copy of the copyrighted material that is accessible to recipients for a longer period than is necessary for the communications; and
- the material is transmitted without change.

System Caching

The OSP is not liable for monetary relief and injunctive relief is carefully circumscribed when the copyrighted material is temporarily stored on the system or network as part of an automatic process without change for use in refreshing, reloading, or other updating in accordance with accepted industry standards for data communications.

Information Storage

An OSP is not liable for monetary relief and injunctive relief is carefully circumscribed when an OSP stores infringing material on its network at the direction of a system user, if the OSP does not have actual knowledge of the infringement, is not aware of facts or circumstances that make the infringement apparent, or, upon obtaining such knowledge or awareness, acts expeditiously to remove or disable access to the infringing material.

Information Location Tools

The standards applicable to storage of information apply generally to OSP liability for referring or linking users to an online location that may contain infringing material. That is, the OSP is not liable without actual knowledge or an awareness of facts that make the infringement apparent, or if the OSP acts expeditiously to remove or disable access upon obtaining knowledge or awareness of an infringement.

Limitations on Liability of Nonprofit Educational Institutions

In general, a university or other nonprofit educational institution is eligible for the same limitations on OSP liability as those described above for commercial OSPs. In recognition, however, of the special nature of the university environment, additional limitations on liability were added in Section 512(e). Special rules were developed for determining whether universities are liable for the acts of faculty members or graduate students.

Teaching/Research Function

Online infringing activities of faculty members or graduate students, which occur when they are teaching or engaging in research, will not be attributed to the university, if certain conditions are met. These conditions are:

(1) the infringing activities must not involve online access to instructional materials that are required or recommended for a course taught by the infringing instructor within the last 3 years;

(2) the institution must not have received more than 2 claims of copyright infringement concerning the particular instructor within the last 3 years; and

(3) the institution must provide to the users of its system or network materials that accurately describe and promote compliance with copyright law.

When these conditions are met, the instructor's knowledge or awareness of infringing activities will not be attributed to the university.

Non-Teaching/Non-Research Function

The special rules on liability do not apply when a faculty member or graduate student is performing a non-teaching/non-research function (for example, when the person is exercising administrative responsibilities or is carrying out operational responsibilities that relate to the institution's role as a service provider). In those cases, the knowledge, awareness, and actions of the employee can be attributed to the university. However, in those cases, the limitations on liability available to commercial service providers would be available to the university.

Nothing in subsection 512(e) creates any new liability for universities under the doctrines of respondent superior or contributory infringement, where liability did not exist before enactment of the DMCA. Also, "subsection (e) has no impact on the fair use (section 107) doctrine or the availability of fair use in a university setting; similarly, section 110 of the Copyright Act dealing with classroom performance and distance learning is not changed by subsection (e)."[36]

Injunctive Relief

Monetary relief is not available against a qualifying service provider and injunctive relief is circumscribed. Section 512 (j) limits the scope of injunctive relief that may be obtained against a qualifying service provider. Distinctions are drawn between service providers qualifying for the limitations under Section 512 (a) (digital communications networks) and those qualifying under Section 512 (b)-(d).

---

[36] DMCA Conference Report, 105-796 at 75-76.

Section 512 (b)-(d) Injunctive Relief

Only three forms of injunctive relief may be granted if a qualified service provider has cached, temporarily stored, or unknowingly facilitated the location of infringing material.

1) The court may provide for the removal or blocking of infringing material residing at a specific location on the provider's network. This is essentially an order to comply with the "removal-blocking" provisions of Section 512 (c) (1)(C).

2) The court may order the provider to terminate service to the subscriber who is engaging in the infringing activity.

3) In unusual cases, if the court considers it necessary, the court may grant other injunctive relief than that specified in Clauses (1) and (2), but must determine that this relief is the least burdensome to the service provider among comparably effective forms of relief.

Section 512(a) Injunctive Relief

In the case of transmission of infringing material via transitory digital network communications, injunctive relief is further narrowed. If a court determines that any injunctive relief is appropriate, it may grant one or both of two forms of relief.

1) The court may order termination of service to the subscriber.

2) Where the infringement relates to a foreign online location, the court may enter an order to take reasonable steps to block access to a specific, identified foreign online location.

Blocking orders are not available against a service provider qualifying under Section 512(a) in the case of infringing activity on a site within the United States or its territories.

In granting even this circumscribed injunctive relief, the court must first consider new criteria relating to the digital online environment.[37] The DMCA prohibits most forms of ex parte injunctive relief (including temporary and preliminary relief) against a service provider who qualifies for the Section 512 limitation on liability. An exception is made only for "orders ensuring the preservation of evidence or other orders having no material adverse effect on the operation of the service provider's communications network."[38]

Other Limitations on Liability

The Digital Millennium Copyright Act also creates penalties for knowing, material misrepresentations about infringing online activity; absolves OSPs of non-copyright liability if the OSP in good faith acts to disable or remove allegedly infringing material, subject to certain requirements for notifying the subscriber of receipt of a statutory notice of

---

[37] Section 512 (j)(2), Title 17 U.S.C.

[38] Section 512 (j)(3), Title 17 U.S.C.

infringement from the copyright owner; confirms that traditional copyright defenses (such as fair use) are unaffected by an OSPs blockage of, or failure to block, access to alleged infringing material; and provides that copyright owners who seek the identification of the direct infringer from the OSP must obtain a subpoena from a court.

COMPUTER MAINTENANCE OR REPAIR EXEMPTION—TITLE III

Title III of the DMCA enacts the "Computer Maintenance Competition Assurance Act," which amends Section 117 of title 17 U.S.C. Section 117 contains certain limitations on copyright liability relating to computer programs. Title III adds a new limitation relating to maintenance or repair of computers by independent service organizations. The Act overturns a decision of the Ninth Circuit holding that an independent computer service-repair company infringes the copyright in a computer program by causing reproduction of the program through activation of the computer, in the course of maintenance or repair work.[39]

Under the revised Section 117 limitation, neither the owner or lessee of a machine that makes a copy of a computer program upon activation of the machine does not infringe the computer program copyright nor does the person authorized to maintain or repair the machine. The copy of the computer program must be destroyed immediately after the maintenance or repair work is completed.

This Act "has the narrow and specific intent of relieving independent service providers, persons unaffiliated with either the owner or lessee of the machine, from liability under the Copyright Act when, solely by virtue of activating the machine in which a computer program resides, they inadvertently cause an unauthorized copy of that program to be made."[40] This amendment does not affect the liability of persons who make unauthorized adaptations, modifications or other changes to the computer program. The amendment makes no change with respect to the scope of the term "reproduction" as it is used in the Copyright Act.[41]

MISCELLANEOUS PROVISIONS—TITLE IV

Title IV of the Digital Millennium Copyright Act contains miscellaneous provisions relating to ephemeral recordings of digital broadcasts; exemptions for the preservation activities of libraries and archives in the digital environment: new compulsory licenses for malting ephemeral recordings and transmissions of digital sound recordings; the assumption of contractual obligations relating to motion picture collective bargaining agreements; and the rank and authority of the Register of Copyrights and the rank of the Commissioner of Patents and Trademarks. The amendment concerning motion picture contracts is made to title 28 rather than title 17. The miscellaneous provisions also mandate two studies of copyright issues—distance education (SEC. 403) and assumption of motion picture contracts (SEC. 406).

---

[39] *MAI Systems Corp. v. Advanced Computer Systems of Michigan, Inc.*, 991 F. 2d 511 (9th Cir. 1993).
[40] Sectional Analysis of H.R. 2281, August 4, 1998, at 41.
[41] DMCA Conference Report 105-796 at 76.

Ephemeral Recordings of Digital Broadcasts

"Ephemeral recordings" are copies of transmission programs made by a transmitting organization for delayed transmission and for archival purposes. Under 17 U.S.C. 112 of the copyright law in effect before enactment of the DMCA, commercial and noncommercial broadcasters were given the benefit of an exemption from the reproduction right to make at least one copy of a broadcast program for delayed transmission or archival purposes.[42] This exemption clearly applies to analog transmissions, but its application to digital transmissions (which are now occurring on an experimental basis) has been uncertain.

The DMCA amends 17 U.S.C. 112 and 114 to address two issues concerning the scope of the ephemeral recording exemption in digital contexts.[43] One amendment explicitly extends the Section 112 exemption to non-subscription broadcasts of sound recordings in digital formats.

Subscription music services, web casters, satellite digital audio radio services and similar entities who operate under statutory licenses for the performance of sound recordings pursuant to 17 U.S.C 114(f) are also entitled to make ephemeral recordings of the sound recordings they transmit. [44]

The second amendment concerns the relationship between the ephemeral recording exemption and the anti-circumvention provisions of new Section 1201 of the Copyright Act. "Concerns were expressed that if use of copy protection technologies became widespread, a transmitting organization might be prevented from engaging in its traditional activities of assembling transmission programs and making ephemeral recordings permitted by Section 112 for purposes of its own transmissions within its local service area and of archival preservation and security."[45]

The DMCA provides that if a broadcaster is prevented by the copyright owner' s anti-copying measures from making the permitted ephemeral recordings, the copyright owner must make available the necessary means to make the recording, provided it is technologically feasible and economically reasonable to do so. If the copyright owner fails to provide the necessary means in a timely manner in accordance with reasonable business requirements, the broadcaster is not liable for violation of the anti-copying measures.

New Digital Audio Transmission License and New Ephemeral Recording Statutory License

Background

The Digital Performance Right in Sound Recordings Act of 1995 ("1995 Digital Audio Act")[46] created a limited public performance right in sound recordings. Under existing copyright law, public performances of analog sound recordings are not within the control of the copyright owner, *i.e.*, analog sound recordings can be played over radio and television or

[42] Noncommercial broadcasters and governmental entities can make up to 30 copies of a broadcast program under certain conditions. I7 U.S.C. 112(b).

[43] SEC. 402 of Title IV of the DMCA.

[44] DMCA Conference Report 105-796 at 79.

[45] DMCA Conference Report 105-796 at 78.

[46] Pub L. 104-39, Act of November 1, 1995, which generally took effect on February 1, 1996.

performed in other public places without the need to obtain a license or permission from the sound recording copyright owner. (Of course, performance of any musical work embodied in the recording must be licensed.) Effective February 1996, however, digital sound recordings were granted limited rights of public performance.

Under the 1995 Digital Audio Act, public performance rights were granted in subscription transmissions and interactive transmissions. The 1995 Act exempts non-subscription digital broadcasts that are not interactive. Moreover, the 1995 Act distinguishes between interactive and non-interactive subscription performances.

Non-interactive subscription services may be eligible for a statutory license.

With respect to pay-per-listen, audio-on-demand, and similar interactive services, copyright owners are granted an exclusive right. Interactive services must negotiate with sound recording copyright owners to obtain the right to transmit the sound recordings. The 1995 Act does, however place some strict conditions on the exclusive right relating to interactive services.

Since the enactment of the 1995 Digital Audio Act," services commonly known as 'web casters' have begun offering the public multiple highly-themed genre channels of sound recordings [on the Internet] on a non-subscription basis."[47] The web casters and sound recording copyright owners have disagreed about application of the 1995 Act.[48]

SEC. 405 of Title IV of the DMCA responds to this issue by adding two more statutory licenses for digital audio transmissions of sound recordings and for malting multiple ephemeral recordings,[49] One new license applies to certain non-subscription and new subscription services that perform digital sound recordings. A second new license applies to multiple "ephemeral" reproductions of sound recordings (stored in computer system "servers") in order to facilitate performances. The original statutory license of the 1995 Act, in slightly modified form continues to apply to "old" subscription services in operation on July 31, 1998, provided the pre-existing service continues to use the same method of transmission.

New Digital Audio Transmission License

In essence, 17 U.S.C. 114 is revised to contain two separate statutory licenses relating to digital audio transmissions of sound recordings. The new digital audio transmission license applies to "web casters" on the Internet and other new transmission services not in existence before July 31, 1998. Pre-existing subscription services are "grand fathered" under the original (but slightly modified) license of the 1995 Digital Audio Act.

A major distinction between the "old" and the "new" digital audio license is that the rates under the new license must be fixed at marketplace value. "In establishing rates and terms for transmissions by eligible non-subscription services and new subscription services, the copyright arbitration royalty panel shall establish rates and terms that most clearly represent the rates and terms that would have been negotiated in the marketplace between a willing

[47] Sectional Analysis of H.R. 2281, August 4, 1998, at 50.

[48] DMCA Conference Report 105-796 at 80.

[49] The details of this second 17 U.S.C. 114 statutory license are beyond the scope of this summary of the Digital Millennium Copyright Act. Most of the amendments to section 114 take effect upon enactment, but an obligation in Clause (ix) of section 114(d)(2)(C) relating to identification of the sound recording during transmission does not take effect until 1 year after enactment.

buyer and a willing seller."[50] Rates for preexisting subscription services and preexisting satellite digital radio services are fixed under different criteria that basically permit comparison of rates for comparable services but do not require marketplace fees[51]

The amendments to 17 U.S.C. 1 I4, and the statutory licenses created by the amendments, "are all fully subject to the safeguards for copyright owners of sound recordings and musical works contained in sections 114(c), 114(d)(4) and 114(i), ...[and] the conferees do not intend to affect any of the rights in section 115 that were clarified and confirmed" in the 1995 Digital Audio Act.[52]

Ephemeral Recording License

Section 112, 17 U.S.C. is amended by adding a new paragraph (e), which creates a new statutory license for making multiple reproductions of sound recordings embodied in an "ephemeral recording." This new license is intended primarily for entities that transmit "sound recordings to business establishments pursuant to the limitation on exclusive rights set forth in section 114(d)(1)(C)(iv)."[53] The new "112(e)" license is also available to Section 114(f) licensees who want to make more than the one recording permitted by the 112(a) exemption. Web casters might wish to reproduce multiple recordings for use on different computer servers "or to make transmissions at different transmission rates or using different transmission software."[54]

As was true under the law before enactment of the DMCA, to avail itself of the ephemeral recording provisions, the transmitting organization must have voluntary licenses to perform any music embodied in the transmission.

Contractual Obligations Related to Transfers of Motion Picture Rights

SEC. 406 of Title IV of the DMCA amends Part VI of title 28 U.S.C., by adding a new Chapter 180 regulating the assumption of contractual obligations in collective bargaining agreements between motion picture producers and the craft guilds and unions representing contributors to motion pictures, when rights in the motion picture are transferred.

The guilds expressed concern "about their inability to obtain residual payments that are due to their members in situations where the producer of the motion picture fails to make these payments, for example, where the producer/company no longer exists or is bankrupt.... Although the collective bargaining agreements generally require the production company to obtain assumption agreements from distributors that would effectively create...privity, some production companies apparently do not always do so."[55]

SEC. 406 of the DMCA requires that transfers of motion picture rights negotiated after enactment, shall be deemed to incorporate the collective bargaining agreements, if the transferee knew or had reason to know about the collective bargaining agreements, or, if there

---

[50] Section 114(f)(2)(B), 17 U.S.C.
[51] Section 114(f)(1)(B), 17 U.S.C.
[52] DMCA Conference Report 105-796 at 89.
[53] DMCA Conference Report 105-796 at 89.
[54] *Id.* at 90.
[55] Sectional Analysis of H.R. 2281, August 4, 1998, at 62.

is an existing court order against the transferor and the transferor does not have the financial ability to satisfy the obligation within 90 days after the order is issued.

Transfers relating to the public performance fight alone are, however, excluded from the assumption of contractual obligations. Also excluded are transfers related to security interests. Banks and other financial institutions are not subject to the statutory assumption of obligations in collective bargaining agreements merely because they obtain a security interest in the motion picture.[56]

Report by Comptroller General

SEC. 406(h) directs the Comptroller General, in consultation with the Register of Copyrights, to study and report to the Congress within 2 years of enactment on the conditions in the motion picture industry that gave rise to the amendment concerning assumption of contractual obligations, and on the impact of the amendment on the industry.

Exemption for Libraries and Archives

SEC. 404 of the DMCA amends the library reproduction exemption of 17 U.S.C. 108 to allow libraries and archives to take advantage of digital technologies when engaging in certain permitted activities.

Under the law in effect before enactment of the DMCA, Section 108(b) permitted the reproduction and distribution of one copy or phonorecord of an unpublished work solely for preservation, security, or deposit for research use in another library or archives. With respect to published works, Section 108(c) permitted reproduction of an entire copy or phonorecord for the purpose of replacing a damaged, deteriorating, lost, or stolen copy if an unused replacement could not be obtained at a fair price.

The amendments in the DMCA permit the reproduction of 3 copies or phonorecords rather than the one copy of the former law and delete the limiting reference to reproduction only in "facsimile" form. Any reproduction in a digital format of an unpublished work must not be distributed in that format to the public outside the premises of the library or archive. Also, in the case of published works, storage in an obsolete format is added as another justification for reproduction, if a replacement copy is unavailable at a fair price. Any digital reproduction of a published work cannot be made available to the public in the digital format outside the premises of the library or archives in lawful possession of the copy from which the reproduction is made. References to the "premises" of the library or archive mean only physical premises, and do not include online websites, bulletin boards, or homepages.[57]

Another amendment eases the burden of reproducing a copyright notice as a condition of the Section 108 exemptions. A notice already appearing on the copy that is being reproduced should be maintained and not deleted. If the copy being reproduced lacks a copyright notice, the library or archive simply places a legend or notation on the copy that "this work may be protected by copyright."

---

[56] DMCA Conference Report 105-796 at 92.

[57] Sectional Analysis of H.R. 2281, August 4, 1998, at 49.

Distance Education Report

Section 110(2) of title 17 U.S.C. exempts qualifying instructional broadcasts from copyright liability for the public performance of copyrighted works embodied in the broadcast transmissions. Nonprofit libraries and educational institutions urged the Congress to adapt the instructional broadcasting exemption to the Internet environment when enacting the Digital Millennium Copyright Act. Congress deferred this issue for further consideration after receiving a report from the Register of Copyrights.

SEC. 403 of the DMCA directs the Register of Copyrights, after consultation with representatives of copyright owners and nonprofit libraries and educational institutions, to submit a report to Congress on distance education, no later than 6 months after enactment.

The report shall include recommendations "on how to promote distance education through digital technologies, including interactive digital networks, while maintaining an appropriate balance between the rights of copyright owners and the needs of users of copyrighted works."[58] Paragraph (b) of SEC. 403 lists 8 factors that the Register shall consider in formulating recommendations.

Rank and Authority of Register of Copyrights; Rank of the Commissioner of Patents and Trademarks

SEC. 401(a) of the DMCA amends Section 3(d) of title 35, Section 701(e) of title 17, and Section 5314 of title 5, to create parity in the compensation paid to the Commissioner of Patents and Trademarks and the Register of Copyrights. Both officials will be paid at the pay fixed for level III of the Executive Schedule under Section 5314 of title 5 of the U.S. Code.

SEC. 401(b) clarifies the duties and functions of the Register of Copyrights by adding a new paragraph to Section 701 of title 17 U. S.C. "The new subsection... sets forth in express statutory language the functions presently performed by the Register of Copyrights .... Existing subsection 701(a) addresses some of the [legislative and executive or administrative] ... functions. New subsection 701(b) is intended to codify the other traditional roles of the Copyright Office and to confirm the Register's existing areas of jurisdiction."[59]

The amendment confirms the following areas of authority and jurisdiction of the Register of Copyrights and the Copyright Office of the Library of Congress: 1) the longstanding role as advisor to Congress on copyright matters and all matters within the scope of title 17; 2) the longstanding role in advising other federal agencies (such as the State Department and U.S. Trade Representative) on the adequacy of foreign copyright laws and as a technical consultant in bilateral, regional, and multilateral negotiations with other countries on copyright-related issues; 3) the longstanding role as a key participant in international meetings of various kinds, including as part of U.S. delegations as authorized by the executive branch; and 4) the preparation and submission to the Congress of studies and reports on various copyright policy issues. These statutory functions and duties are illustrative and not exhaustive.[60]

---

[58] SEC. 403(a) of the DMCA.
[59] DMCA Conference Report 105-796 at 77.
[60] DMCA Conference Report 105-796 at 77-78.

VESSEL HULL DESIGN PROTECTION—TITLE V

Title V of the Digital Millennium Copyright Act creates a new form of intellectual property protection for the design of boat hulls. The "Vessel Hull Design Protection Act" adds a new Chapter 13 to title 17 U.S.C. that protects the design of the hull of boats larger than a rowboat and smaller than 201 feet in length against copying. Protection extends both to the artistic and the utilitarian features. The Vessel Hull Design Act is, however, subject to sunset 2 years after enactment.

Background

The boat design title enacts a design protection proposal that had been considered and rejected in the form of broad design legislation for at least 20 years. The boat hull design proposal responds to a decision of the Supreme Court in *Bonito Boats v. Thunder Craft Boats*,[61] in which the Court held that state law protection of boat hulls was an unconstitutional interference with the federal patent and copyright laws.

The boat hull design proposal first passed the House of Representatives as a separate bill, H.R. 2696, and was added as a separate title to H.R. 2281 as passed by the House on August 4, 1998. The House-Senate conferees compromised by allowing the boat design Act to remain in H.R. 2281 as enacted, but subjected the Act to termination after 2 years.

The Register of Copyrights and the Commissioner of Patents and Trademarks shall submit a joint report to the Congress not later than 1 year after enactment, evaluating the effect of the Vessel Hull Design Act.

Boat design protection is intended to fill a gap that some perceive exists between the current design patent and copyright laws. The same argument has been made for legislation to enact a design right for useful articles in general. When general design legislation was considered by earlier Congresses, objections from the insurance industry, consumers, retailers, and others concerned about possible anti-competitive effects, were sufficient to prevent enactment.

Basic Boat Design Right

New Chapter 13 of title 17 U.S.C. is headed "Protection of Original Designs," although the definition of "useful article" is intended to make clear the protection is limited to designs of boat hulls. Section 1301 creates new legal protection for the original design of a useful article, which makes the design "attractive or distinctive in appearance." A design is "original" if it is the result of the designer's own creative endeavor, and represents a "distinguishable variation" compared to other designs. The distinguishable variation must be more than trivial and not copied from another person.

The overall shape of a boat larger than a rowboat and smaller than 201 feet in length can be protected against copying of its artistic or utilitarian features. The fact that protection can extend to solely utilitarian design features is a departure from earlier design proposals, which would have excluded designs dictated solely by utilitarian function.

---

[61] 489 U.S. 141 (1989).

In order to obtain boat hull design protection, an application for design registration must be made to the Administrator (the Register of Copyrights) within 2 years after the design is made public.

The boat design right is enforced through civil remedies only. These remedies include an injunction; actual damages or up to $50,000 or $1 a copy, as the court considers just;[62] the infringer's profits; destruction of infringing articles; and attorney's fees to the prevailing party.

Exclusions from Protection

The biggest "exclusion" from protection is achieved by defining a useful article to mean only a "vessel hull, including a plug or mold...." Also excluded from protection by Section 1302 are designs that are: 1) not original; 2) staple or commonplace; 3) different from staple designs only in insignificant details or dements that are common variants; or 4) embodied in a useful article made public by the designer/owner more than 1 year before an application for registration is made to the Copyright Office.[63]

CONCLUSION

The Digital Millennium Copyright Act, P.L. 105-304, amends the Copyright Act, title 17 of the U.S. Code, to legislate new rights in copyrighted works—and limitations on those fights—when those works are used on the Internet and in other digital, electronic environments. The Act is the outcome of at least 5 years of intensive congressional consideration of Internet copyright policy issues. Initially, these policy issues were considered in the context of the development of a national "information superhighway" or a national information infrastructure.

The focus shifted somewhat to international copyright policy issues and the worldwide Internet with the creation of two new intellectual property treaties in December 1996 under the auspices of the World Intellectual Property Organization (WIPO). The WIPO Copyright Treaty covers copyright protection for computer programs, those databases that qualify as intellectual works, digital communications over the Internet, and use of copyrighted works in digital, electronic environments. The WIPO Performances and Phonograms Treaty extends protection to performers and producers of sound recordings that essentially is equivalent to the protection afforded copyright subject matter by the WIPO Copyright Treaty.

Initially, the Clinton Administration and copyright owners proposed implementation of the WIPO Treaties through a "minimalist" approach. They advocated copyright law amendments to protect against circumvention of anti- copying technologies and protection assuring the integrity of copyright management information (CMI) systems. Other Internet copyright policy issues, under this approach, would have been addressed in separate

---

[62] Damages of $1 a copy would seem to have significance primarily for designs of useful articles other than vessel hulls. This damages provision is another example of the way Title V of the DMCA may lay the foundation for protection of the design of useful articles in general.

[63] Section 1302 actually lists a fifth exclusion—for designs "dictated solely by utilitarian function." Another clause of the Vessel Hull Design Act, however, specifies that this exclusion does not apply in the case of vessel hull designs.

legislation at some future time or left for resolution by the courts in copyright infringement cases.

Based on the arguments of online service providers, other telecommunications entities, the electronics industry, libraries, and educational institutions, Congress confronted most of the Internet copyright policy issues, and made policy choices,-in enacting the Digital Millennium Copyright Act. The Act, which generally took effect October 28, 1998, in addition to implementing anti-circumvention and CMI protection, generally exempts online service providers from copyright liability; exempts computer repair service companies; broadens the ephemeral recording exemption to apply in digital contexts; creates new statutory licenses for multiple ephemeral recordings, and transmissions, of digital sound recordings; and broadens the application of the library reproduction exemption in digital contexts. The Act also creates new federal design protection for vessel hulls, which sunsets after 2 years.

The Senate gave its advice and consent to the ratification by the United States of the two WIPO Treaties on October 21, 1998. The Treaties will not come into force, however, until 30 States deposit their instruments of ratification or accession with the Director General of WIPO.

"DIGITAL ERA COPYRIGHT ENHANCEMENT ACT": ANALYSIS OF H.R. 3048

Dorothy Schrader

The "Digital Era Copyright Enhancement Act" (H.R. 3048), as described by its co-sponsors Mr. Boucher and Mr. Campbell, would amend the Copyright Act, title 17 of the U.S. Code, to "update and preserve balance in the Copyright Act for the 21st Century; to advance educational opportunities through distance learning; [and] to implement the World Intellectual Property Organization Treaty and Performance and Phonograms Treaty."[1]

H.R. 3048 contains proposed amendments to the Copyright Act relating to fair use, library reproduction, the first sale doctrine, distance learning, ephemeral recordings, operational copying by computers, and "shrink-wrap" licenses. A new chapter 12 would be added to tile 17 U.S. Code enacting new legal protection against circumvention of anti-copying technologies and against fraudulent removal or alteration of copyright management information, to satisfy the obligations of two articles in each of the two new WIPO treaties.

BACKGROUND

The Internet, other computer networks, and advances in digital technologies provide unparalleled opportunities for worldwide communications and economic growth, in the judgment of most experts. It is also generally agreed that, in order to tap this potential fully, many difficult technical and policy issues must be confronted and resolved. One of these policy issues concerns the scope of protection for copyrighted works against unauthorized copying or other unlawful use.

The general issues relating to Internet uses of copyrighted material are implicated both by national legislative proposals and by two new international treaties in the field of intellectual property.

---

[1] Legislative purposes clause of the bill as introduced on November 13, 1997.

At the national level, bills were introduced in the 104th Congress (S. 1284 and H.R. 2441) to make changes in the copyright law related to the Internet uses of copyrighted works.[2] Hearings were held on the bills, and private sector groups held negotiating sessions under the auspices of the congressional oversight committees. No legislation was passed.

At the international level, two new intellectual property treaties were created by a diplomatic conference in Geneva, Switzerland, on December 20, 1996. The World Intellectual Property Organization ("WIPO") Copyright Treaty covers copyright protection for computer programs and databases (to the extent the latter are "intellectual" works), and clarifies or creates rights relating to use of copyrighted works over the Internet and in digital, electronic contexts.[3] The second treaty, the WIPO Performance and Phonograms Treaty, covers protection for performers and producers of sound recording (called "phonograms" internationally),[4] and tracks many rights extended to copyright subject matter be the WIPO Copyright Treaty.

The WIPO treaties have been sent to the Senate for its advice and consent, and the President has recommended implementing legislation that adopts a "minimalist" approach to treaty implementation. S. 1122 and H.R. 2281, as originally introduced in the First Session of the 105th Congress, embodied the Administration's proposals for WIPO treaties implementation.

The original Administration bills were premised on the assumption that existing United States law is largely consistent with the obligations of the treaties. Consequently, S. 1122 and H.R. 2281 as introduced proposed amendment of the U.S. copyright law concerning only two new substantive issues, as well as certain technical amendments. The Copyright Act would have been amended to provide new legal protection I) against circumvention of anti-copying technologies or alteration of copyright management information ("CMI").

The only other amendments originally proposed by S. 1121 and H.R. 2281 are technical in nature and relate primarily to consequential adjustments to those definitions and sections of the Copyright Act that affect treaty relationships and the eligibility of foreign authors to claim U.S. copyright.

Subsequent to the introduction of the Administration's implementation bills, two other WIPO implementation bills were introduced. S. 1146 and H.R. 3048 contain many common provisions, but they are not companion bills.[5] They differ from the original Administration bills substantially, both with respect to the issues addressed and in the legislative solutions for

---

[2] The bills in the 104th Congress tracked the recommendations of a Working Group on Intellectual Property, which was part of the White House Information Infrastructure Task Force. The Report of the Working Group was published in September 1995. Department of Commerce, Intellectual Property and the National Information Infrastructure, Report of the Working Group on Intellectual Property Rights of the Information Infrastructure Task Force.

[3] *For an analysis of this Treaty, see, D. Schrader, World Intellectual Property Organization Copyright Treaty: An Overview,* CRS Report No. 97-444A.

[4] For an analysis of this treaty, *see* D. Schrader, *World Intellectual Property Organization Performances and Phonograms Treaty: An Overview,* CRS Report No. 97-523 A.

[5] H.R. 3048 and S. 1146 contain the same proposals relating to fair use, library reproduction, distance learning, ephemeral recordings, operational reproduction by computers, and protection against removal or alteration of CMI. The provisions of these bills on protection against circumvention of anti-copying technologies are also virtually identical, except that the definition of "effective technological measure" differs slightly. H.R 3048 contains amendments relating to the first sale doctrine and "shrink-wrap" licenses not found in S. 1146. H.R. 3048 does not contain any provisions on online service provider liability whereas Title I of S. 1146 addresses this issue. Finally, H.R. 3209 deals only with the online service provider liability issue. A revised version of H.R. 3209 was added to H.R. 2281 at a House Judiciary Committee mark-up on April 1, 1998.

the common issues covered by all four bills. Unlike the original Administration bills (s. 1121 and H.R. 2281), S. 1146 and H.R. 3048 propose amendments of the Copyright Act concerning many of the Internet or National Information Infrastructure ("NII") copyright issues such as fair use, library reproduction, ephemeral copying, distance learning, and operational copying by computers. A separate bill, H.R. 3209, addresses only the online service provider copyright liability issue.

In the most recent developments, the House Judiciary Committee, On April 1, 1998, approved H.R. 2281 as amended,[6] and the Senate Judiciary Committee, on May 6, 1998, approved a new bill, S. 2037, which is the successor to S. 1121.[7] The Senate passed S. 2037, with a few essentially technical amendments, on May 14, 1998, by a vote of 99-0.

On March 31, 1998, representatives of copyright owners and online service providers had reached an agreement concerning the issue of OSP copyright liability. Based on the agreement, the House Judiciary Committee essentially combined H.R. 2281 with a revised version of H.R. 3209 and reported the bill as H.R. 2281. As revise, H.R. 2281 only partly reflects the private sector agreement on OSP liability. Additional elements of the agreement will reportedly be added to H.R. 2281 by means of a House Floor amendment.[8] At the same mark-up session, the House Judiciary Committee rejected a series of amendments to H.R. 2281 along the lines of the proposals in H.R. 3048.

The new Senate bill, S. 2037, contains the amendments made to H.R. 2281 plus the full private sector agreement on OSP copyright; liability and other amendments addressing additional copyright policy issues, including changes in the circumvention of anti-copying measures provisions, new provisions on library reproduction of copyrighted works, new provisions on ephemeral recordings, and other matter.

DISCUSSION OF H.R. 3048

The Digital Era Copyright Enhancement Act, H.R. 3048, proposes several amendments to the Copyright Act that would update the limitations on the rights of copyright owners in the context of digital, electronic uses of copyrighted works. The bill would make other changes in United States law to implement the obligations the United States would assume if the country ratifies the WIPO Copyright and Performance-Phonograms Treaties.

Fair Use

The bill would amend section 107 of the Copyright Act, title 17 U.S. Code, the specify that "fair use" applies to digital as well as analog transmissions. The courts would be instructed not to give independent weight to the means of performing displaying, or distributing a work, when evaluating the fair use statutory criteria.

---

[6] The written report of the Committee on the Judiciary to accompany H.R. 2281 has not been filed by May 18, 1998, the date of this CRS Report.

[7] S. REP. NO. 105-190, 105th Cong., 2d Sess. (Filed May 11, 1998).

[8] "Industry Groups Reach Accord on Online Copyright Liability Legislation," 55 BNA Patent, Trademark & Copyright Jour. 557-558 (April 9, 1998).

Library Uses

The existing library exemption of 17 U.S.C. §108 would be expanded under H.R. 3048 by permitting library reproduction of three copies or phonorecords (rather than the one copy of existing law); by deleting the references of existing law to reproduction only in "facsimile form;" and by adding, as a new justification for library reproduction, the factor that the work is stored in a obsolete format.[9]

First Sale Doctrine

H.R. 3048 would amend section 109 of the Copyright Act (which contains limitations on the public distribution right of copyright owners known as the "first sale doctrine"). The owner of a copy of a phonorecords in a digital format would be given an exemption to perform, display, or distribute the work by a transmission of a single recipient, if that person erases or destroys his or her copy or phonorecords as substantially the same time. To the extent necessary for such performance, display, or distribution, reproduction of the work would also be exempt.[10]

Distance Learning

The existing instructional broadcasting exemption of 17 U.S.C. §110(2) would be expanded by H.R. 3048 to exempt "distance learning"—that is, performances, displays, or distributions of works by analog or digital transmission to remote sites for reception of systematic instructional material by students officially enrolled in the course and by government employees as part of their official duties, would be exempt from copyright liability.[11]

Ephemeral Recordings

Section 112(b) of the Copyright Act, which now deals with performances and displays by means of "ephemeral" (i.e., temporary) recordings of works by nonprofit organizations and governmental bodies, would be expanded by H.R. 3048 to cover distribution of a work (in addition to public performance and display).[12]

---

[9] Similar library reproduction amendments are included in S. 2037 as passed by the Senate, except that S. 2037 adds the condition that copies or phonorecords reproduced in digital formats can be used only on the premises of the library in lawful possession of a copy and S. 2037 defines when a format is obsolete.

[10] S. 2037 does not contain any amendments concerning the first sale doctrine.

[11] S. 2037 would defer any specific amendments of the Copyright Act concerning distance learning pending submission of a report by the Register of Copyrights. The bill mandates a report by the Register within six months of enactment.

[12] S. 2037 contains a different amendment concerning ephemeral recordings than the proposal in H.R. 3048. An amendment of I7 U.S.C. §112 would extend the existing ephemeral recording exemption to non-subscription broadcasts of sound recordings in digital formats. Another amendment (which relates to the anti-circumvention provisions of the bill) requires copyright owners to make available to broadcasters the

Operational Reproduction by Computers

The existing limitations of 17 U.S.C. §117 apply to the rights of a copyright owner of a computer program. H.R. 3048 would create new limitations in an amended section 117 on the rights of any copyright owner, in the case of automatic, operational copying by computers. Under this amendment, it would not be infringement to make a copy of any work in a digital format if the copying: I) is incidental to the operation of a device in the course of a lawful use of the work, and ii) does not conflict with the normal exploitation of the work and does not reasonably prejudice the legitimate interests of the author.[13]

This exemption for copying that is "incidental" to operation of a device is intended to exempt the automatic reproduction of works, which occur when messages or communications are transmitted via a computer network. The condition that the copying must not "conflict with the normal exploitation" etc. tracks exactly the general limitation permitted by Article 10 of the WIPO Copyright Treaty and Article 16(2) of the WIPO Performances and Phonograms Treaty.

Preemption of "Shrink-Wrap" Licenses

H.R. 3048 would amend section 301 of the Copyright Act to preempt state common or statutory laws to the extent they would otherwise allow enforcement of certain non-negotiable licenses (so-called "shrink-wrap" licenses).

The term "shrink-wrap" license refers to the fact that unilateral licensing terms are commonly expressed on the outside wrapping of a computer software package, which is removed in order to use the software. The license provides that by removing the wrapping from the package, the purchaser of the software becomes bound by the licensing agreement. The enforceability of such licenses is not settled, but they are commonly employed by the software industry.

Under H.R. 3048, federal copyright law would preempt state laws in the case of licenses covering uncopyrightable material, or licenses which abrogate or restrict the Copyright Act's limitations on rights of copyright owners, as found in sections 107-114, 117, or 118 of the Act.[14]

---

necessary means to make ephemeral recordings, if the copyright owner's anti-copying measures would otherwise prevent the making of the recording.

[13] Although S. 2037 does not contain a broad exemption for operational reproduction by computers, it contains several provisions that create narrower exemptions for "automatic copying" of works in connection with computer uses. S. 2037 exempts computer repair or maintenance companies for the automatic reproduction of a computer program that occurs when the computer is activated. The OSP liability provisions or S. 2037 generally eliminate any monetary liability for the copying by an OSP that occurs when the OSP acts as a mere conduit in a transmission, copies material as part of system caching, or stores material at the direction of a system user.

[14] S. 2037 contains no provision dealing with shrink-wrap licensing.

Circumvention of Technological Measures

Article 11 of the WIPO Copyright Treaty and Article 18 of the WIPO Performances and Phonograms Treaty establish a new kind of legal protection for copyright owners, performers, and producers of phonograms. Treaty adherents shall provide adequate and effective legal protection and effective legal remedies against the circumvention of effective technological measures (that is, protection against infringing conduct in the nature of acts that defeat anti-copying technologies).

Each of the pending implementation bills addresses this obligation, but H.R. 3048 and S. 1146 differ fundamentally from the approach of the Administration bills, S. 1121 and H.R. 2281, as originally introduced. In general, the electronic industry favored the approach of H.R. 3048 (and S. 1146) and opposed the Administration's original bills. Rights holders generally have favored the Administration's original bills.

The electronic industry contended that the original Administration bills exceeded the minimum Treaty obligations concerning protection for technological measures whereas H.R. 3048 does not. H.R. 3048 creates remedies against acts of circumvention for infringing purposes; specifically provides that this "conduct" does not include the manufacture, importation, or distribution of a device or computer programs; and establishes only civil remedies.[15]

Rights holders, on the other hand, generally supported the original Administration bills. They argued that criminal penalties are necessary to enforce rights against circumvention of anti-copying technologies; that a meaningful law must protect against devices whose primary effect is to defeat anti-copying technologies; and that components parts must be specifically covered to guard against evasion of the law.

H.R. 2281, as reported by the House Judiciary Committee, adds a knowledge requirement to the anti-circumvention provisions in order to establish liability against someone who only markets the technology defeating device; exempts nonprofit libraries, archives, and educational institutions from liability under the anti-circumvention provisions they obtain access to the copyrighted work solely to make good faith determination about purchasing the work; allows a court to reduce or remit civil damages when the violator did not know and had no reason to believe that his or her activities constituted violations of the anti-circumvention provisions; requires a court to remit civil damages against a nonprofit library, archives, or educational institution if the nonprofit entity was not aware and had no reason to believe that its acts constituted a violation; and exempts the same nonprofit entities from any criminal liability for violation of the anti-circumvention provisions. Also, the bill exempts lawfully authorized investigative, protective, or intelligence activity of federal and state law enforcement or intelligence entities.

S. 2037, which replaced the Administration's bill (S. 1121) in the Senate, passed the Senate on May 14, 1998. This bill includes the changes adopted by the House Judiciary Committee in H.R. 2281 to the circumvention of anti-copying technology provisions, and lakes additional changes which, in their totality, apparently satisfy the concerns of the

---

[15] By contrast, the Administration's bills as introduced arguably prohibited sale of a device or component part thereof that is marketed or primarily used to circumvent anti-copying technologies; applied to manufacturers, importers, and distributors of such devices; and created criminal as well as civil remedies. H.R. 2281 as reported by the House Judiciary Committee and S. 2037 as passed by the Senate contain changes in the anti-circumvention provisions.

electronics-computer manufacturing industries on this issue.[16] S. 2037 allows circumvention for purposes of interoperability of computers; expressly declares that nothing in the anti-circumvention provisions enlarges or diminishes the doctrines of vicarious and contributory infringement; declares that electronics-computer manufacturers have no obligation to design consumer electronics, telecommunications, or computing products to achieve protection against circumvention; provides that with respect to a component of a product, the court may consider the necessity of the component's incorporation in the product for the sole purpose of preventing access by minors to certain Internet material (if the component does not itself violate the anti-circumvention right); but essentially requires that rights holders must cooperate with broadcasters and other transmitters to provide broadcasters/transmitters with the means to make ephemeral recordings.

Copyright Management Information

Under Article 12 of the WIPO Copyright Treaty and Article 19 of the WIPO Performance and Phonograms Treaty, member countries must provide "adequate and effective legal remedies against any person knowingly performing "prohibited acts relating to the removal or alteration of electronic rights management information. The remedies could be civil or criminal or both.

H.R. 3048 would implement this treaty obligation by creating civil remedies against knowing and intentional acts to mislead or induce infringement by removal or alteration of copyright management information ("CMI"). The civil remedies also apply against public distribution or importation of copies or phonorecords containing identifying information required by Copyright Office regulations.

The remedies of H.R. 3048 do no apply, however, to mere manufacture, importation, or distribution of a device. Finally, protection applies only to CMI information in electronic or digital form.[17]

H.R. 2281, as reported by the House Judiciary Committee, and S. 2037 as passed by the Senate contain several amendments to the copyright management information provisions. CMI is defined to include information about performers, writers, and directors of audiovisual works, except in the case of radio and television performances, in addition to information about authors. There are several changes in the liability provisions. In the case of innocent violations, where the court finds that the violator was not aware and had no reason to believe that his or her acts were a violation of the CMI provisions, the court may reduce or remit civil damages. Where the violator is a nonprofit library, archives, or educational institution that was not aware and had no reason to believe its acts were a violation, the court shall remit any civil damages. The same nonprofit entities are exempt from criminal penalties. The lawfully

---

[16] The Home Recording Rights Coalition ("HRRC") (which is a trade association representing manufacturers, distributors, and retailers of electronics products and some consumers) issued a press release, on May 1, 1998, praising the changes in S. 2037. The press release states that the amendment to the anti-circumvention provisions "significantly clarifies that this legislation would not chill the design of new generations of recordings and computer products." HRRC Press Release of May 1, 1998, entitled "HRRC Praises Senators Hatch, Leahy and Ashcroft for Clarification of WIPO Bill." (www.hrrc.org/).

[17] By contrast, the Administration's bills create criminal as well as civil remedies and extend protection to CMI in analog as well as electronic form.

authorized activities of federal and state law enforcement and intelligence entities are exempt from any liability for violations of the CMI provisions.

In addition to the above changes, S. 2037 also places limits on the liability of transmitting organizations such as broadcast and cable and their program suppliers for CMI violations. With respect to analog transmissions, there is no CMI violation if compliance is not technically feasible or would create an undue financial hardship and if there is no intention to induce, enable, facilitate or conceal an infringement. With respect to digital transmissions, liability depends upon setting of a digital transmission standard by consensus of representatives of transmitting organizations and copyright owners. Until the standard is established, the transmitting organization is generally not liable for CMI violations if the entity has no intention to induce, enable, facilitate or conceal an infringement and if transmission of the CMI would result in signal degradation or conflict with government regulations or an industry-wide standard adopted before enactment.

COPYRIGHT TERM EXTENSION AND MUSIC LICENSING: ANALYSIS OF SONNY BONO COPYRIGHT TERM EXTENSION ACT AND THE FAIRNESS IN MUSIC LICENSING ACT P.L. 105-298

Dorothy Schrader

Duration of copyright is one of the major parameters for establishing the amount of protection accorded to authors and other owners of copyright. It is also the principal dividing line between the property rights of such owners and the public domain -- that is, the domain of unprotected works, which are available to the public for unrestricted, uncompensated use. Under the United States Constitution, Art. I, See. 8, Cl. 8, Congress is authorized to grant copyright protection only for "limited Times."

P.L. 105-298 extends copyrights by 20 years and broadens the business exemption for performing music by playing a radio or television at the place of business.

Title I of the new law, the Sonny Bono Copyright Term Extension Act, amends the Copyright Act[1] by extending the copyright terms for all categories of copyrightable works by an additional 20 years. The added 20-year period applies retroactively to all works in which copyright subsists.

Title 17 of the new law, the Fairness in Music Licensing Act, makes two reforms relating to the licensing of music for public performance. One amendment of 17 U.S.C. 110 expands the exemptions available to businesses that perform music publicly by turning on radio and television sets in their places of business. The second amendment makes statutory provision for regional judicial review of the reasonableness of the rates charged by the music performing rights societies ("PRS") that license the public performance of non-dramatic music on behalf of music copyright owners.

This chapter reviews the background of this legislation and summarizes the main provisions of the Sonny Bono Copyright Term Extension Act (hereafter: "Sonny Bono Act") and the Fairness in Music Licensing Act (hereafter: "Music Licensing Act").

---

[1] The Copyright Act of 1976, as amended, is codified at title 17 of the U.S. Code, sections 101 *et seq*. The basic Act was enacted on October 19, 1976 by Public Law 94-553, with an effective date of January 1, 1978.

SONNY BONO COPYRIGHT TERM EXTENSION ACT – TITLE I

Background

Under the copyright law in effect before enactment of S. 505, copyright generally endured for a fixed term of 75 years from publication, or for the life of the author plus 50 years after the author's death. Specifically, for post-1977 works (i.e., works that secured copyright on or after January 1, 1978), the term for personal works (i.e., works created by known authors who are not employees of another person or entity) was the life of the author plus 50 years after death. For impersonal works copyrighted on or after January 1, 1978, the term was the shorter of 75 years from publication or 100 years from creation. For pre-1978 copyrighted works, the term was a fixed period of 75 years, computed from the date copyright was secured either by publication with notice of copyright or by registration as an unpublished work with the Copyright Office.

If a personal work is created jointly by two or more authors, the post-1977 term is measured by the life of the last surviving author.

These former terms of copyright had been established by the last general revision of the copyright law, the Copyright Act of 1976, which was effective January 1, 1978. Before that date, the copyright term under the Copyright Act of 1909 was a fixed period of years, consisting of a 28 year original term which could be renewed for an additional 28 years. For various reasons, including fairness and the wish to avoid possible impairment of contracts, Congress changed the basis for computing the copyright term under the 1976 Act only for post-1977 works. Congress adopted the "life-plus-50" basis for works copyrighted on or after January 1, 1978, and retained the fixed period of copyright for pre-1978 works. However, to balance the two methods of computing copyright terms, Congress added a 19-year period to the maximum 56-year period that otherwise would have applied to pre-1978 works; the resulting term was a total of 75 years.

Proponents of extending the copyright term an additional 20 years by legislation in the 105th Congress made two principal arguments: 1) they argued that economic fairness to the heirs of authors justified the 20 year increase because longevity has increased since the "life-plus-50" standard was first adopted by the Berne Copyright Convention[2] in 1908; and 2) they argued that the United States must match the recent 20-year extension of the copyright term adopted by the European Union[3] in order to avoid application of the rule of the shorter term[4] for musical works and other personal works and to enhance the bargaining position of the U.S. Government and U.S. copyright industries in international trade negotiations affecting intellectual property rights.

---

[2] The Berne Copyright Convention is the major international treaty relating to protection of copyright subject matter. The United States became a member on March 1, 1989.

[3] The European Union adopted a Directive on Copyright Duration, effective July 1, 1995, which generally set a copyright term of life-plus-70 for personal works, 70 years for works copyrighted by legal persons, and 50 years for related rights protection for the rights of producers of motion pictures and sound recordings.

[4] The "rule of the shorter term" is an exception to the general principle of the Berne Convention that works of foreign authors shall be given the same protection as works of nationals of the country where protection is claimed (i.e., "national treatment"). Article 7 of the Berne Convention permits reciprocity concerning the duration of copyright. The country where protection is claimed is entitled to compare the copyright term of its law with that of the country of origin of the work and apply the shorter term.

Several bills were introduced in the 105th Congress to extend the copyright terms by an additional 20 years.[5] The House Judiciary Committee favorably reported H.R. 2589 on March 18, 1998.[6] The House passed the bill on March 25, 1998 with several amendments, including the core provisions of the music-licensing bill, H.R. 789. The Senate passed S. 505 on October 7, 1998, Title II of which included a compromise version of the music licensing provisions. The House also passed S. 505 on October 7, 1998. The President signed S. 505 into law on October 27, 1998.

Summary of Sonny Bono Act

The Sonny Bono Act increased the term of existing and future copyrights by 20 years. Other sections of the Act: 1) grant a new, limited termination right[7] with respect to the 20-year period; 2) expand the classes of persons eligible to terminate licensing contracts; 3) grant libraries and nonprofit educational institutions a narrow exemption to use copyrighted works during the 20-year period, if the works are not commercially exploited in that period and copies are not available at a reasonable price; and 4) express a "sense of Congress" view encouraging private sector negotiations to reach voluntary agreements about establishment of an audiovisual works fund to allocate royalties received during the 20-year period from the exploitation of motion pictures.

Copyright Term Provisions

The Sonny Bono Act establishes the following terms of copyright protection:

- For post-1977 personal works, life of the author plus 70 years;
- For post-1977 impersonal works (works made for hire, anonymous or pseudonymous works), the shorter of 95 years from publication or 120 years from creation;
- For pre-1978 works, 95 years from the date copyright was secured either by publication with notice of copyright or, in the case of unpublished works, by registration.

All of the extended terms apply retroactively to any work in which copyright now exists, and to the works that have been retrieved from the public domain by the 1994 law implementing the Uruguay Round of the General Agreement on Tariffs and Trade (GATT).[8]

---

[5] H.R. 695, H.R. 1621, H.R. 2589, and S. 505.

[6] H.R. REP. 105-452, 105th Cong. 2d Sess. (1998).

[7] A "termination right" is an inalienable right granted by the Copyright Act to authors and their heirs to revoke an earlier contract assigning or licensing rights to another party, after a certain period of years and under certain statutory conditions.

[8] The Uruguay Round Agreements Act, Pub. L. 103465 (December 8, 1994). For eligible works, copyright restoration occurred automatically one year after the effective date of the entry into force of the World Trade Organization. Therefore, these copyrights were restored effective January 1, 1996. While the eligibility rules

Another special provision extends the term of works created but not copyrighted before 1978 (i.e., unpublished, unregistered works) by 20 years (by increasing their expiration date from 2027 to 2047), provided the work is published by December 31, 2002.[9] Preemption of common law/state law copyright in pre-February 15, 1972 sound recordings is also delayed another 20 years, from February 15, 2047 to February 15, 2067.[10]

Termination Provisions of Title I

Termination provisions affect transfer and ownership of the rights granted to authors under the Copyright Act. They are a means for regulating who benefits from a statutory increase in the length of the copyright term. The exercise of termination rights essentially effects a reversion of the copyright (or other partial rights) back to the original author-owner (or the heirs of the author) notwithstanding a contractual assignment of the property to another.

The 1976 Copyright Act created two termination provisions. One termination clause applies to "old law works" (i.e., works copyrighted before 1978), which is found at section 304(c) of the Act. This provision applies to grants (i.e., licensing agreements) executed before January 1, 1978 by the author or any statutory renewal claimant. The holder of the termination fight can terminate the pre-1978 grant with respect to the 19-year period added to the copyright term for "old law works" by the 1976 Act.

The second termination clause of the 1976 Act applies to "new law works" (i.e., works copyrighted on or after January 1, 1978). Under section 203 of the 1976 Act, grants of rights by the author relating to new law works can be terminated 35 years after their execution.

The Sonny Bono Act creates a third termination right relating to the 20-year added period for pre-1978 works and modifies who is eligible to terminate rights in both "old law" and "new law" works under the original termination provisions of the 1976 Act.

With respect to the new termination right in the 20-year added period, the Sonny Bono Act amends 17 U.S.C. 304 by adding a new paragraph (d). The new "304(d)" termination right applies to the author (in theory)[11] or other owner of a termination right in a pre-1978 grant, whose fight to terminate under section 304(c) has already expired without being exercised. The basic structure of the original "304(c)" termination fight is retained, but the

---

are complicated, in general copyright is restored for "foreign-origin," that is, non-United States-origin, Berne Convention works.

[9] The general revision of the copyright law effective January 1, 1978, preempted common law and state statutory copyrights in unpublished works. Congress granted these works a minimum federal term of 25 years, which could be increased to 50 years under the 1976 Act by publication on or before December 31, 2002. That maximum term is now increased to 70 years, if the work is published before 2003. The purpose of this provision has been to provide minimum federal protection for pre-1978 common law works in order to assure the constitutionality of federal preemption, and to encourage early publication of unpublished works

[10] Sound recordings were granted a 75-year delay in federal preemption under the 1976 Copyright Act because, unlike other categories of copyright subject matter, sound recordings did not enjoy dual common law and federal protection before February 15, 1972, the date federal copyright protection was first extended to sound recordings. Also, state common law and statutory protection for sound recordings was of recent vintage, whereas unpublished books and music, for example, might have been protected for decades or 200 years by state law, prior to federal preemption under the 1976 Act.

[11] In order for an author to be able to exercise the new termination right in the 20-year added period, the author must live more than 75 years after the copyright was secured in the work. Songwriter Irving Berlin lived more than 75 years after some of his copyrights were secured, but these instances are exceedingly rare. As a rule, the author's heirs will exercise the new "304(d)" right.

time limit for exercising the fight is changed, and the new "304(d)" termination right applies to the 20-year period added by the Sonny Bono Act to the term of copyright. Termination can be effected at any time during a 5-year period beginning at the end of the 75-year copyright term. The new "304(d)" termination right applies only to grants executed before January 1, 1978. It was not necessary to legislate a comparable right with respect to grants executed on or after January 1, 1978, since "new law" grants are first eligible for notices of termination in 2003.[12] Holders of "new law" termination rights will receive the 20-year added period when they exercise their right of termination.

As is true of the original termination rights of the 1976 Act, the "section 304(d)" termination right does not apply to works made for hire.[13]

If the section 304(c) termination right of the 1976 Act has already been exercised, the holder of the exercised termination fight owns the copyright in the 20-year added period, unless the copyright has already been re-assigned post-termination. Such re-assignments are not terminable. In that case, the assignee owns the copyright during the 20-year period added to the copyright terms by the Sonny Bono Act.

The second change made by the Sonny Bono Act in the termination provisions applies both to old and new law works. Sections 203(a)(2) and 304(c)(2) of title 17 U.S.C. are amended to change the persons eligible to exercise termination rights.

Under the original termination provisions of the 1976 Act, the author's executor under a will, administrator, personal representative, or trustee had no termination right. The next of kin had a termination fight in transfers, which they may have granted with respect to "old law" works; the next of kin had no termination rights in "new law" works.

The Sonny Bono Act grants a termination right to the author's executor to terminate the author's interest, if the author, spouse, children, and grandchildren are deceased. Also, in the absence of a will, if there is no surviving author, spouse, child, or grandchild, the administrator, personal representative, or trustee of the author's estate owns the author's termination interest in the case of both old and new law transfers by the author.

Reproduction by Libraries and Archives

Libraries, archives, and educational groups expressed concerns about diminution of the public domain as a consequence of adding 20 years to the copyright terms. In partial response to these concerns, the Sonny Bono Act amends 17 U.S.C. 108 to limit the fights of copyright owners against libraries, archives, and nonprofit educational institutions during the 20-year added period. These entities will be allowed to reproduce, distribute, display, or perform in facsimile or digital form, copies of works during the 20-year period for preservation, scholarship, or research purposes, if the works are not being commercially exploited and copies or phonorecords cannot be obtained at a reasonable price.

This exemption does not apply after notice by the copyright owner (in accordance with Copyright Office regulations) that the conditions for use are not satisfied or to subsequent users other than the exempt entities.

[12] New law grants cannot be terminated until 35 years after their execution. The notice of termination (which also specifies the exact termination date) must be served no earlier than 10 years before the termination date.

[13] Works made for hire are defined in 17 U.S.C. 101 as works created by employees within the scope of their duties and, subject to a written agreement, certain specially ordered or commissioned works.

Division of Motion Picture Royalties

Most theatrical motion pictures produced in the United States are works made for hire. The contributors to motion pictures such as the screenwriters, directors, and performers ordinarily do not own the copyright nor do they have any termination rights with respect to the term of copyright. By industry custom and practice, the rights of motion picture contributors in the United States are usually acquired through collective bargaining agreements between the production companies and the guilds or unions representing the contributing artists.

During the consideration of the copyright term extension bills, motion picture contributors expressed concerns about their right to receive royalties during the 20-year added period. The Sonny Bono Act makes no change in any law concerning the division of motion picture royalties,[14] but SEC. 105 of the Act does contain a "sense of Congress" statement on this point. The statement is intended to encourage voluntary agreements between motion picture producers and the various motion picture contributors leading to the establishment of an audiovisual fund or other mechanism for the division of royalties accrued during the 20-year added period.

Agreement on the division of motion picture royalties becomes especially important with respect to the royalties that accrue from exploitation of American motion pictures in Europe.

Article 2(2) of the European Union Directive on Copyright Duration sets the term for "cinematographic or audiovisual works" at the life of the author(s) plus 70 years after the death of the last of four contributors to survive -- the principal director, the author of the screenplay, the author of the dialogue, and the composer of any music specifically created for the motion picture. Another provision, Article 2(1), mandates that at least the principal director shall be considered the author of the motion picture. Article 3 (3) of the EU Directive provides that the "related rights" of the motion picture producer expire 50 years after fixation or publication (if published) whichever is earlier.

Since most theatrical motion pictures produced in the U.S. are works made for hire and the director is not considered an author, it is not entirely clear what European Union term applies to U.S. motion pictures or who is entitled to collect licensing fees in Europe during the 20-year added period. United States motion picture producers and the United States Trade Representative take the position that contracts assigning rights to the producers (including collective bargaining agreements) should be recognized in Europe.

The "sense of Congress" provision in the Sonny Bono Act is intended to facilitate private negotiations concerning division of motion picture royalties between producers and artistic contributors to motion pictures.

Effective Date

The Sonny Bono Copyright Term Extension Act took effect upon enactment, which was October 27, 1998.

[14] An earlier version of the Sonny Bono Act, H.R. 2589 as passed by the House in March 1998, contained an additional motion picture rights clause. SEC. 106 of H.R. 2589 would have amended title 28 U.S.C. by adding a new chapter 180 dealing with the assumption of contractual obligations (e.g., "residual" fights) when transferring motion picture fights. This provision was later added to another bill, H.R. 2281 (the Digital Millennium Copyright Act), and was enacted as part of that legislation.

FAIRNESS IN MUSIC LICENSING ACT – TITLE II

Background

Under the Copyright Act of 1976, the owner of copyright in a musical work is granted the exclusive right to perform the work publicly [17 U.S.C. 106(4)], subject to specified limitations or exemptions.

A musical work is "publicly performed" if it is rendered or played directly or by means of any device or process either i) at a place open to the public or any place where a substantial number of persons outside of the normal circle of family and social acquaintances is gathered, or ii) by transmission to a place open to the public or to the unassembled public which is capable of receiving the performance (for example, by radio, television, cable, or satellite).

Performances at "semi-public" places are generally considered public performances. These places include clubs, lodges, factories, summer camps, and schools; daycare, seniors, and other recreational centers; and possibly the common areas of hospitals, nursing homes, and other care facilities.

Performances of music at public places such as restaurants, bars, taverns, nightclubs, conventions, and stores are public performances, whether the music is performed live, or by recordings or transmissions, and whether the music is used as background, incidental, or theme music. Of course, performances of music in concert halls, opera houses, theaters, stadiums, outdoor arenas, and similar places open to the public, are public performances.

Although the above examples constitute public performances, the need to obtain a music performing license and pay copyright fees hinges upon the availability or absence of an exemption, limitation, or exception to the music copyright owner's public performance right. If the performance is neither exempt nor subject to compulsory licensing, the music user must obtain permission or a license to perform the music by negotiating the terms and conditions with the music copyright owner or an authorized agent. With few exceptions music performing licenses for performance of non-dramatic music are obtained from the performing tights societies ("PRS"), who act as agents for the music copyright owners.

By custom and practice, music publishers and composers-lyricists generally share the royalties obtained under the music performing right equally-- that is, 50-50, after the PRS deducts its administrative costs. Currently, there are two major PRS who control virtually all licensing of the performing right in non-dramatic music. These are the American Society of Composers, Authors, and Publishers (ASCAP) and Broadcast Music Inc. (BMI). Both PRS operate under antitrust consent decrees that establish restrictions and conditions on their music licensing activities.

The principal exemptions or limitations to the music performing fight are set forth in section 110 of the Copyright Act, or in the compulsory licensing sections.[15]

The existing music performing right was enacted as part of the 1976 general revision of the copyright law, the 1976 Copyright Act. Under its predecessor, the 1909 Copyright Act,

[15] The Copyright Act had 5 active compulsory licenses as of October 15, 1998: section 111 (cable retransmissions of broadcasts); section 114(f) (subscription digital audio transmissions of sound recordings); section 115 (mechanical reproduction of music); section 118 (public broadcasting license); and section 119 (satellite television license). All of these compulsory licenses affect public performance of music except the section 114(f) subscription transmission license (which applies to sound recordings) and the section 115 recording license (which affects only the reproduction right).

nonprofit performances of non-dramatic music were exempt from copyright liability. The statute did not define "nonprofit performances," however. The term was given meaning by the courts. Although the line drawn between "for- profit" and "non-for-profit" performances was never dear, in general, the nonprofit exemption was applied fairly broadly. For example, musical performances by public broadcasting and by religious broadcasters were arguably exempt.

In the 1976 Copyright Act, Congress dropped the broad exemption for nonprofit musical performances and replaced it with a broad performance right, to which Congress applied specific, more narrowly drawn exemptions. The 1976 Act also legislated a broad definition of the term "public," which resulted in application of the music licensing rights in "semi-public" contexts that formerly were arguably private performances.

The general effect of these changes from the 1909 Act was to create a need to obtain a music performing fight license on a broader basis than under the law in effect before 1978. Expanded enforcement efforts by the PRS have generated opposition and counter-legislative proposals from groups impacted by the broader music performing right.

In the 105th Congress, music licensing reform proposals were introduced under the title of "Fairness in Music Licensing Act." Essentially identical bills (H.R. 789 and S. 28) were introduced in the House and Senate. The bills proposed several reforms including: 1) expansion of certain exemptions to the public performance fight for businesses that perform music by turning on radios or televisions within their business establishments; 2) a new statutory requirement of arbitration of the fees charged by the PRS; 3) statutory conditions for radio per program licenses; 4) elimination of the vicarious and contributory infringement liability of landlords of the premises where music is performed; and 5) mandated access to PRS repertories and licensing information.

The supporters of music licensing reforms linked their legislative efforts with proposals to extend the copyright term an additional 20 years. Music licensing reform supporters argued that the additional 20-year period should be balanced by some concessions to music users. They pointed out that music copyright owners are among the principal beneficiaries of copyright term extension. Music and other copyright owners denied that there should be any link between term extension and music licensing proposals. Copyright owners opposed the music licensing reform proposals as unfair, unnecessary, and possibly contrary to the international treaty obligations of the United States.

Over the objections of copyright owners, H.R. 2589 was amended during floor debate in the House of Representatives to include three of the core provisions from the music licensing bill as Title II of H.R. 2589.[16] The House passed H.R. 2589 in this form on March 25, 1998.

Following pre-conference discussions with the Senate, the Senate on October 7,1998 passed a version of S. 505 that included two of the music licensing reform proposals in modified form. The House agreed and passed the same version of S. 505 on the same day. Title 11 of the bill is the "Fairness in Music Licensing Act of 1998." The President signed S. 505 into law on October 27, 1998. As enacted, Tire II broadens the business exemptions for public performance of music and creates a mechanism for regional judicial review (by means

---

[16] The three provisions were: expansion of the business exemptions; binding arbitration of the rates charged by the PRS; and elimination of the vicarious and contributory infringement liability of landlords.

of a "circuit rider" provision) of the reasonableness of the licensing fees charged by the PRS.[17]

Summary of Music Licensing Act

Business Exemptions

Under section 110(5) of the 1976 Copyright Act, performances of any work by public reception of broadcasts or other primary transmissions were exempt if – reception occurred by means of receiving equipment commonly used in private homes, there was no direct charge to see or hear the transmission, and the transmission was not further distributed. The key issues were whether the receiving equipment met the "home-style" standard and the number of receivers employed.

The Music Licensing Act broadens the business exemption of 17 U.S.C. 110(5) Distinctions are drawn between "food service/drinking establishments" and other business establishments such as stores based on the size of the business premises. A further distinction is made based on the nature and number of the receiving sets used to perform the music.

If the business qualifies for the exemption based on the size of the premises or the receiving equipment, the further conditions on availability of the exemption are that there must be no direct charge to see or hear the transmission, and the transmission itself must be licensed by the copyright owner of the musical work.

Store Exemption

The Music Licensing Act defines an "establishment" as a store, shop, or similar place of business open to the general public for the primary purpose of selling goods or services in which the majority of the nonresidential area is used for that purpose and in which non-dramatic musical works are performed. The exemption is available to business establishments other than "food service/drinking establishments" if-

i) the area of the business where the music is intended to be received covers less than 2000 square feet (excluding the customer parking area); or

ii) the area where the music is intended to be received covers 2000 square feet or more (excluding the customer parking area) and (A) any audio only performance occurs via not more than 6 loudspeakers, of which no more than 4 are in any one room, or (B) an audiovisual performance occurs via no more than 4 audiovisual devices, of which no more than 1 device is located in any one room and no such device has a diagonal screen size greater than 55 inches, and the audio portion is communicated by no more than 6 loudspeakers, of which no more than 4 speakers are located in one room.

---

[17] The final bill dropped the proposed elimination of vicarious and contributory infringement liability of landlords. Therefore, no change has been made in these judicially created doctrines with respect to music licensing. With respect to the liability of Internet service providers, however, legislation was passed in the form of H.R. 2281, the Digital Millennium Copyright Act, which impacts the vicarious and contributory infringement doctrines in general.

Food Service/Drinking Establishment Exemption

The Music Licensing Act defines a "food service or drinking establishment" as a restaurant, inn, bar, tavern, or any other similar place of business in which the public or patrons assemble for the primary purpose of being served food or drink, the majority of the nonresidential area is used for that purpose, and non-dramatic musical works are performed. The exemption is available to food service/drinking establishments if –

i) the area where the music is intended to be received covers less than 3750 square feet (excluding the customer parking area); or

ii) the area where the music is intended to be received covers 3750 square feet or more (excluding the customer parking area) and the receiving equipment meets the same conditions described in Clause (ii) above for stores.

Additional Damages

If a court finds that a defendant establishment, which claims the section 110(5) exemption, lacked reasonable grounds to believe its use of the work was exempt, the plaintiff shall be entitled, in addition to any award of damages, an additional award of two times the amount of the licensing fee that should have been paid during the preceding 3 years.

Retail Record and Audiovisual Stores Promotions

The Music Licensing Act also amends the section. 110(7) exemption of the Copyright Act which relates to the public performance of music in stores as part of promotional efforts to vend music, records, and playback equipment. Under the 1976 Copyright Act, this exemption applied to phonorecords. The Music Licensing Act extends the section 110(7) exemption to "audiovisual or other devices utilized in... performance" of music.

Regional Review of Music Licensing Rate Disputes

In accordance with the existing antitrust decrees governing the two major performing rights societies ("PRS")[18] — ASCAP and BMI, disputes about the rates the PRS charge music users to pay for performing right music licenses under the 1976 Copyright Act could be challenged and reviewed only by the designated Rate Court in the federal district court for the Southern District of New York.[19] One of the major objectives of supporters of music licensing reform proposals was to obtain local review of the music licensing rates.

The original proposals in H.R. 789 and S. 28 would have required binding local arbitration of rate disputes at the option of persons or entities defined as "general music users."[20] A modified version of the arbitration proposal remained in H.R. 2589 as passed by

[18] ASCAP is governed by a 1950 consent decree. The decree designated the district court for the Southern District of New York as the "Rate Court" for review of ASCAP rates. BMI is governed by a 1966 consent decree, which was modified only in 1994 to establish the district court for the Southern District of New York as the forum to review BMI music licensing rates.

[19] The performing fight societies can be sued in any federal district court for alleged antitrust violations, however.

[20] The original proposals distinguished between pre-litigation rate arbitration and court- annexed arbitration. The rates charged broadcasters and other transmitting organizations would not have been subject to pre-litigation arbitration, but these entities could have invoked court-annexed arbitration, if sued for copyright infringement.

the House of Representatives in March 1998. S. 505 as enacted dropped the proposal for rate review by binding local arbitration and substituted judicial rate review under a regional, "circuit-rider" procedure.

The Music Licensing Act provides that, notwithstanding existing and future consent decrees, "an individual proprietor who owns or operates fewer than 7 non-publicly traded establishments" in which music is performed and who disputes the reasonableness of the PRS rates, can obtain rate review on a regional basis. The individual proprietor files for rate review either with the designated Rate Court or in the district court at the seat of the regional Court of Appeals (other than the Court of Appeals for the Federal Circuit) in which the proprietor's establishment is located.

The rate review proceeding is presided over by the district court judge assigned to the Rate Court, who either "rides" the circuits to hear the cases or appoints a special master or magistrate judge to hear the cases in the appropriate region. Any decision of the special master or magistrate judge shall be reviewed by the Rate Court judge. The whole rate review proceeding shall be completed within 6 months after its commencement.

The final determination is binding only as to the individual proprietor who commenced the rate review. The PRS are relieved of any obligation of nondiscrimination among similarly situated music users, in complying with the regional rate decision.

The industry rate already set by the Rate Court shall be presumed to have been reasonable at the time it was set, but this presumption "shall in no way affect a determination of whether the rate is being correctly applied to the individual proprietor."[21] "Industry rate" is defined as the PRS fee set by negotiations, or by the Rate Court, for a significant segment of the music user industry to which the individual proprietor belongs.

An individual proprietor can bring only one rate review proceeding under the new section 512 of title I7 U.S.C.

Effective Date

The Fairness in Music Licensing Act takes effective 90 days after enactment, i.e., 90 days after October 27, 1998.

CONCLUSION

Enactment at the end of the 105th Congress of the Sonny Bono Copyright Term Extension Act extends the term of existing and future copyrights an additional 20 years. This legislation is expected to result in equivalent duration of protection for American copyrights in the European Union, or will at a minimum give United States negotiators arguments for longer terms of protection within the European Union and other foreign countries.

Within the United States, authors and other owners of the extended copyrights will profit from the increased term of copyright protection at least in the case of the relatively few works that have commercial value over a 95-year period. In those instances where the works are not commercially exploited during the 20-year added period, libraries and nonprofit educational

---

In H.R. 2589 as passed by the House in March 1998, broadcasters and other transmitting organization were completely excluded from the binding arbitration proposal in that bill.

[21] 17 U.S.C. 512(4).

institutions are granted an exemption to use the works, provided copies are not available at a reasonable price.

The passage of a modified version of the Fairness in Music Licensing Act responds to some of the concerns of music users about the fairness of traditional licensing practices of the performing right societies. The Act broadens the business exemption of 17 U.S.C. 110(5) for playing radios or televisions, and creates a new procedure for regional review of the licensing fees in the case of an individual proprietor of less than 7 non-publicly trade businesses. The proposals dropped from the Music Licensing Act in the final compromise (e.g., vicarious liability of landlords for performance of music on their premises and radio per program licensing fees) may or may not be the subject of new legislative proposals in the next few years.

INDEX

D

E

F

G

H

I

J

K

L

M

N